Opportunities for All

A FRAMEWORK FOR POLICY ACTION
ON INCLUSIVE GROWTH

OECD
BETTER POLICIES FOR BETTER LIVES

This work is published under the responsibility of the Secretary-General of the OECD. The opinions expressed and arguments employed herein do not necessarily reflect the official views of OECD member countries.

This document, as well as any data and any map included herein, are without prejudice to the status of or sovereignty over any territory, to the delimitation of international frontiers and boundaries and to the name of any territory, city or area.

Please cite this publication as:
OECD (2018), *Opportunities for All: A Framework for Policy Action on Inclusive Growth*, OECD Publishing, Paris.
http://dx.doi.org/10.1787/9789264301665-en

ISBN 978-92-64-30165-8 (print)
ISBN 978-92-64-30166-5 (PDF)

The statistical data for Israel are supplied by and under the responsibility of the relevant Israeli authorities. The use of such data by the OECD is without prejudice to the status of the Golan Heights, East Jerusalem and Israeli settlements in the West Bank under the terms of international law.

Photo credits: Cover © Fabio Parmeggiani

Corrigenda to OECD publications may be found on line at: *www.oecd.org/about/publishing/corrigenda.htm*.

Foreword

The OECD is at the forefront of developing a "people-centred growth model" in which well-being is the yardstick of success, not GDP per capita. In this model, everybody can contribute to growth, independent of their background or origins, and receive a fair share of the benefits. These are the central propositions of the OECD Inclusive Growth Initiative, launched in 2012 to provide answers on how to reduce the increased inequalities of income and opportunities that many OECD countries have experienced during the last decades.

At the core of this narrative is the fact that although promoting the growth and efficiency of markets is a precondition to increasing living standards, this by itself will not solve the problems of inequality and lack of inclusiveness, nor reduce the backlash against globalisation and technological innovation that disparities are fuelling. Based on past experiences, growth does not trickle down, particularly to those with the lowest incomes, if distributional impacts and equity considerations are not incorporated *ex-ante* in the design of policies. This requires a "whole of the government" approach to make sure that financial, fiscal or monetary decisions, among others, do not undermine social cohesion or social progress. They should work in synergy, and when dealing with trade-offs, well-being should be prioritised.

During the last ten years, the OECD has gathered a significant body of evidence on the increased inequalities of income and opportunities in many countries. The top 20% of the income distribution earns 9 times more on average than the bottom 20%. The distribution of wealth is even more unequal, with the top 20% keeping half, while the bottom 40% holds only 3%. Inequalities of income and opportunity compound disadvantages. A child whose parents did not graduate from secondary school has only a 15% chance of doing so itself, compared to 65% for more well-off children. Low-income people may experience lower life expectancy, and in some regions the gap with those at the top of the distribution can be as large as 7 years. OECD analysis of social and intergenerational mobility, and of ageing, shows the cumulative nature of these inequalities, and the fact that people's future may already be determined by the neighbourhood in which they were born. Gender inequalities aggravate this outcome.

At the same time, the incomes and wealth of those in the upper part of the income distribution continue to grow, and this winner-takes-all dynamics has also accelerated a growing productivity gap between leading and lagging firms. Many factors that drive these inequalities and weigh on productivity potential are cross-border in nature, so they affect economies in an interconnected way. At the same time, large inequalities may go hand in hand with environmentally unsustainable patterns of production and consumption, and inefficient use of natural resources.

This analysis confirms that while social policies are important and we should enhance their effectiveness, they are not the whole answer. As the *2016 Productivity Inclusiveness Nexus* report shows, high inequality is also an economic challenge that can reduce growth potential by preventing us from developing and benefitting from the talents of everyone, and enabling everyone to contribute fully to growth and thereby benefit from better jobs, better wages and better career prospects. The digital revolution in the world of work may worsen inequalities, so a major policy response is needed to address the fundamental causes of inequalities.

We need to act now. The OECD Framework for Policy Action on Inclusive Growth, unveiled in this report, provides a new blueprint to ensure that we grow *inclusively*. With this Framework, we go one step further with a substantive analysis of what could have been done better to strengthen the foundations for sustainable growth, if we had known better how inequalities can weigh on growth. Moving beyond GDP metrics and statistical averages, this report puts *people* at its centre, focuses on well-being *outcomes,* and emphasises the *distribution* of outcomes across the population.

The Framework is designed to help countries achieve growth on a sustainable basis with rising living standards while respecting environmental boundaries, by providing equal opportunities to all. It is a practical summary of OECD policy options to invest in people and places, support business dynamics, make labour markets more inclusive, and rebuild trust to strengthen social cohesion. Supported by a dashboard of 24 indicators, the Framework provides guidance to complement national development strategies on a number of Sustainable Development Goals that are relevant from an inclusive growth perspective.

The Framework does not adopt a “one size fits all” approach. Inequalities unfold in different ways across countries, and specific context and social preferences need to be taken into account. But some policies hold the promise of improving the life of everyone, for instance high-quality education from early childhood through to school age and beyond, with a focus on granting access to educational opportunities to children from disadvantaged families. Comprehensive and forward-looking skills and training policies are also central to preparing for the future of work and to bridge divides between workers. Other forms of investment in people’s capabilities, for instance in health, or in broader enabling factors, such as housing, infrastructures and connectivity, are also needed to shift towards a sustainable model of prosperity and well-being. Finally, actions in support of broad-based and grassroots innovation and entrepreneurship can strongly sustain a process of inclusive growth. Governments cannot win the fight for equality and well-being alone. The business sector, civil society and all citizens have a role to play. The OECD is there to orchestrate the conversation in support of better policies for better lives.

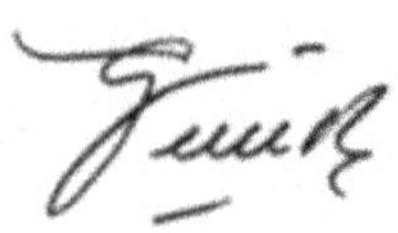

Gabriela Ramos

OECD Chief of Staff, Sherpa to the G20 and Leader of the Inclusive Growth Initiative

Acknowledgments

Under the leadership and supervision of Gabriela Ramos, Chief of Staff, Sherpa to the G20 and Leader of the Inclusive Growth initiative, Romina Boarini, the Coordinator of the Inclusive Growth Initiative and Senior Advisor to the Secretary-General, and Ziga Zarnic, Manager of the OECD Inclusive Growth Project, prepared this draft report with analytical and drafting inputs by the Inclusive Growth Unit (Mohamed Hammouch, Neil Martin, Sam Mealy) and support of the OECD Inclusive Growth Focal Group and the OECD Council and Executive Committee Secretariat under the supervision of Lucy Elliott (Sarah Finke, Laura Völker and Blandine Barreau). The administrative and communication assistance by Ana Fueyo and Alexandra Campbell as well as the editorial and data assistance by Valerie Delahouliere, Olivier Bucher, Agnes Loeb, Fernando Abrahao Monte and Thomas Coppel are greatly appreciated. The OECD Public Affairs and Communications Directorate (France Charlet, Kate Lancaster, Sandrine Levain, Jean de la Rochebrochard, Vincent Finat-Duclos, Laura Belli) is also greatly acknowledged for valuable support to the production and dissemination of the report. We are grateful to Patrick Love (NAEC Unit) for his editorial support as well as his substantive contributions to the report.

This report is an output of the OECD Inclusive Growth Initiative and has benefitted from consultations with Committee on Financial Markets (CFM), Committee on Fiscal Affairs (CFA), Committee on Industry, Innovation and Entrepreneurship (CIIE), Committee on Statistics and Statistical Policy (CSSP), Economic Policy Committee (EPC/WP1), Employment, Labour and Social Affairs Committee (ELSAC), Environmental Policy Committee (EPOC), Executive Committee (ExCo) and Public Governance Committee (PGC). Under the leadership of OECD Directors and their Deputies (Marcos Bonturi, Anthony Cox, Martine Durand, Montserrat Gomendio, Lamia Kamal-Chaoui, Greg Medcraft, Mathilde Mesnard, Mark Pearson, Grace Perez-Navarro, Mario Pezzini, Dirk Pilat, Pascal Saint-Amans, Stefano Scarpetta, Andreas Schleicher, Paul Schreyer, Naoko Ueda, Andrew Wyckoff) the report has benefited from contributions by:

- the Economics Department (under the supervision of Alain de Serres and Orsetta Causa who coordinated contributions by Cyrille Schwellnus, Christina Timiliotis, Cristina Vitale);
- the Directorate for Science, Technology and Innovation (under the supervision of Dirk Pilat and Chiara Criuscuolo who coordinated contributions by Nick Johnstone, Matej Bajgar, Giuseppe Berlingieri, Sara Calligaris, Flavio Calvino, Isabelle Desnoyers-James, Luca Marcolin, Jonathan Timmi, Rudy Verlhac);
- the Directorate for Labour, Employment and Social Affairs (under the supervision of Mark Pearson and Angelica Salvi del Pero who coordinated contributions by Alex Hijzen, Stijn Broecke, Oliver Denk, Michael Forster, Sebastian Königs, Chris James, Sandrine Cazes, Willem Adema, Eva Degler, Olivier Thevenon, Emily Hewlett, Michele Cecchini, Ana Llena Nozal, Hervé Boulhol, Peter Wyckoff);

- the Centre for Tax Policy and Administration (under the supervision of David Bradbury: Pierce O'Reilly, Bert Brys);
- the Statistics Directorate (under the supervision of Nadim Ahmad and Marco Mira D'Ercole: Carlotta Balestra, Lara Fleischer, Elena Tosetto, Richard Tonkin, Carrie Exton, Guillaume Cohen);
- the Directorate for Education and Skills (under the supervision of Dirk Van Damme: Ricardo Espinoza, Caitlyn Guthrie);
- the Centre for Entrepreneurships, SMEs, Local Development and Tourism (Jonathan Potter, under the supervision of Joaquim Oliveira Martins and in cooperation with Marissa Plouin and Paolo Veneri, who co-ordinated contributions by Marco Bianchini, David Bartolini, Kris Boschmans, Claire Charbit, Lucia Cusmano, Enrique Garcilazo, Eric Gonnard, David Halabisky, Sandrine Kergroach, Soo-Jin Kim, Lukas Kleine-Rueschkamp, Alexander Lembcke, Diogo Machado, Tadashi Matsumoto, Varinia Michalun, Debra Mountford, Abel Schumann, Isidora Zapata);
- the Directorate for Public Governance and Territorial Development (Sara Fyson led and co-ordinated contributions by Christiane Arndt-Bascle, Emma Cantera, Frederic Boehm, Stephane Jacobzone, Santiago Gonzalez. Chloe Lelievre, Lisa von Trapp, Sean Dougherty, Barbara Ubaldi, Celine Kauffmann, Adam Ostry);
- the Environment Directorate (Shaun Reidy, Edward Perry);
- the Development Centre (Alexander Kolev); and
- the Directorate for Financial and Enterprise Affairs (Sebastian Schich, Adele Atkinson, Kiril Kosev, Miles Larbey, Gert Wehinger).

Contents

Figures

Tables

Boxes

Part I. The Framework and Dashboard for Policy Action on Inclusive Growth

The upswing in the global economic outlook creates opportunities to ensure that growth is beneficial to all. Indeed, despite recent progress in some countries, more efforts are needed to transform economic growth into improved living standards for all. There is scope to strengthen business dynamism and align wage growth with productivity growth. There is also a clear economic imperative to tackle increased inequalities in income and opportunities in many OECD and partner countries. Indeed, bringing together an agenda for higher productivity with policies for inclusivity will enhance outcomes that matter for people. Moreover, inaction comes with risks. Inequalities are undermining people's confidence in open trade and markets, and could further weigh on long-term growth and macroeconomic stability.

Globalisation, digitalisation, demographics and climate change are transforming the way economies work, providing new opportunities for growth, but also raising the risk of deeper inequalities if the gains from growth are not evenly shared among people, firms and regions. The focus on stronger productivity growth is necessary, but not sufficient to sustain economic growth over the long-term unless equity issues are also addressed and embedded in the design of policy. The opportunities for growth at a global level could be better leveraged through domestic and international policies that can promote broad-based growth that is beneficial to all. There are trade-offs between some of these policies, but there are also standards and policies that can create win-win situations, such as investing in skills of children from low-income families, reskilling and upskilling displaced workers or promoting diffusion of technologies and innovation across all firms. The main message of the OECD Inclusive Growth Initiative is to put the emphasis on the policies that can improve the perspectives of the bottom 40% of the income distribution.

At the 2017 Ministerial Council Meeting, the OECD Secretariat was asked to develop a policy action plan for inclusive growth and to document inequalities of income and opportunities through a comprehensive evidence-based analysis [C/MIN(2017)9/FINAL]. The Framework for Policy Action on Inclusive Growth aims to help governments to sustain and ensure a more equitable distribution of the benefits from economic growth, which is supported by a dashboard of indicators. It consolidates OECD key policy recommendations around three broad principles:

1. Invest in people and places that have been left behind through (i) targeted quality childcare, early education and life-long acquisition of skills; (ii) effective access to quality healthcare, justice, housing, infrastructures; and (iii) optimal natural resource management for sustainable growth.

2. Support business dynamism and inclusive labour markets through (i) broad-based innovation and technology diffusion; (ii) strong competition and vibrant entrepreneurship; (ii) access to good quality jobs, especially for women and under-represented groups; and (iv) enhanced resilience and adaptation to the future of work.

3. Build efficient and responsive governments through (i) aligned policy packages across the whole of government; (ii) integration of distributional aspects upfront in the design of policy; and (iii) assessing policies for their impact on inclusiveness and growth.

Chapter 1. Main trends

The global upswing provides an opportunity to set the foundations for sustainable growth that benefits all

The global economy is recovering and moving back to cruising speed. The upswing in the global economic outlook creates significant opportunities to consolidate the global economic recovery ten years after the crisis, while providing the basis to address inequalities. The recovery has yet to translate fully into income gains for all groups as market insecurity and the low-income rate remain high in several OECD countries compared with their levels before the 2008 crisis (OECD, 2018f). The poverty risk has also increased in most OECD countries over the period between the mid-2000s-2015 (OECD, 2017b). Considering that the decade before the crisis has seen high levels of growth, but also increased inequalities in some countries, it is important to ensure that the return of economic dynamism benefits all.

Some countries have made progress in addressing inequalities, but more efforts are needed. Inequalities deepened by the financial crisis in several OECD countries have left large segments of the population with reduced opportunities to improve their economic conditions and well-being for them and their children. The global upswing provides the opportunity to make economies more resilient, and seize on the potential created by technological developments and greater global interconnectedness to strengthen governments' capacity to promote equal well-being opportunities. However, concerted action is required.

Opportunities for low-income groups are worsening

Affluent households have seen their living standards and wealth increase faster than those of the poorest and the middle class. Contrary to those at the top, households at the bottom of the income distribution have experienced stagnant wages and low income growth. In terms of real disposable household income, the poorest 20% earned one fifth of the income of the richest 20% in OECD countries in 2014. Real wages of the richest 1% increased by 45% between 1995 and 2011 – three times higher than the growth in real median wages in the OECD countries. The richest 5% held on average more than one third of the total wealth; and the richest 1% nearly one fifth.

OECD work on inequalities and growth shows that the accumulation of disadvantages for certain income groups can have detrimental effects on the prosperity and well-being of all. Large degrees of inequality weigh on the potential for future economic and productivity growth. While stronger growth can benefit all members of society, some groups may fall well short of their potential if they start off from a position of disadvantage. Social background continues to determine the life chances of people in many OECD countries. Overall, a child whose father earned twice the average income will go on to earn 40% more than a child whose father earned the average income. In many countries, policies have not been able to break the influence of socio-economic status on children's education outcomes: performance between students in the top quarter and students in the bottom quarter of ESCS reached on average 88 PISA points more in OECD countries, more than a year of schooling in educational terms (OECD, 2015f). Children at the bottom quarter of the PISA index of economic, social and cultural status have an 18% chance of pursuing a career in science – against a 32% chance for children from the top quarter. These effects are exacerbated for children of migrants, with a large performance gap compared to non-immigrant students (OECD, 2015f).

Social mobility is hampered by limited access to quality healthcare services, education and transportation services that are poorer for low-income groups and those living in lagging regions. Lack of access to affordable quality housing is another source of vulnerability for low-income groups. Many households in OECD countries are overburdened by housing costs: the median housing cost burden for mortgage payers is about 18% of disposable income and 23% for tenants. The cost burden is much higher for low-income households and, on average, represents more than one-third of disposable income. Housing conditions, the neighbourhood and environment in which they grow up in are essential factors that contribute to children's well-being and their future ability to thrive.

There is scope to improve business dynamism

The global economy is undergoing significant changes in the rate and composition of productivity growth, business dynamism and employment gains since the financial crisis in the context of digitalisation, globalisation, demographic and climate change. There is a potential for large economic gains. The reallocation of activity between firms, sectors and countries can help to ensure that these gains are shared in a way that supports long-term economic growth that is beneficial to all.

A dynamic business environment is a crucial condition for realising this potential. Young firms that represent 17% of employment have been the primary source of job creation (42% of total job creation) over the period 2001-2011 across a sample of 18 OECD and non-OECD countries (Criscuolo, Gal and Menon, 2014). However, business dynamism has slowed in many OECD countries. The firm population is ageing. Firms manage to survive without adopting improved practices to increase productivity growth. The uptake of new technologies is uneven and particularly low for small and medium enterprises (SMEs).

In addition, the gap between high-productivity firms and lagging firms has increased at the global level, but also within many countries and within industries. The OECD *Productivity-Inclusiveness Nexus* (OECD, 2017i) suggests that there might be a 'sorting' effect which increasingly separates frontier firms, able to access the best technologies and skills, from those that are less productive and fail to compete on the same grounds. The Next Production Revolution and the transition to the digital economy are exacerbating these trends. Only a quarter of businesses use cloud computing services, while on average 27% of the adults have reported no experience in using computers in 2012 across OECD countries (OECD, 2013).

The 'Great Divergence' in productivity has contributed to a divergence of wages between firms. However, wage inequality is also accounted for by growing wage inequality within firms, amid a declining wage premium for low-skilled workers in large firms and a growing wage premium for corporate executives and professionals. The latter may partly explain the decoupling observed between real median wage growth and aggregate labour productivity growth in the last two decades. This decoupling suggests that productivity gains are not always delivering wage gains for all workers (OECD, 2018f).

Digitalisation has not yet materialised into a broad-based productivity growth

The potential benefits of the digital transformation are many. In order to realise those benefits digitalisation should be broad-based, it should open access to market opportunities and support fast technology diffusion. This is not always the case as the digital economy features network effects and large economies of scale, potentially creating winner-takes-most dynamics in some industries. Concentration has increased in both manufacturing and services sectors in many OECD countries. New technologies have enabled "superstar firms" to expand their share in the economy. Some of these firms are achieving large market shares with a relatively small workforce, meaning they are able to attain "scale without mass" particularly in services. OECD research confirms that global frontier firms in the information and communications technology (ICT) services sector have significantly widened the gap in terms of multi-factor productivity not only with regard to non-frontier firms, but even within the group of global frontier firms – where differences between the very top firms (top 2%) and other frontier firms have grown.

These trends may be reinforced by the growing importance of concentration in ownership and access to data; for example, major providers of precision technologies (e.g. in the agriculture or transport sectors) generate large volumes of data that are considered an important data source for other companies (e.g. for biotech companies that optimise genetically modified crops or crop insurance companies in the agriculture sector) (OECD, 2017o).

Globalisation and technological change have contributed to job creation, but also to a considerable restructuring of labour markets. Most OECD countries have experienced an increase in the share of employment in high-skilled (and to some extent in low-skilled) jobs and a decrease in the share of employment in middle-skilled jobs. Digital technologies have facilitated non-standard forms of work. These trends provide opportunities for greater flexibility and can help overcome barriers to labour market participation. On the other hand, there is high variation in job quality among non-standard forms of work, in terms of job insecurity, pay, job strain and access to social protection and training.

High levels of inequality have negatively affected confidence in markets, and could further weigh on long-term growth and macroeconomic stability

To realise the gains of global interconnectedness, it is important to rebuild shared confidence in open trade and markets. Support for open trade and markets, for instance, has been negatively impacted by increasing regional inequality within countries. Territorial variation in job opportunities is important, but not the only factor. Confidence may vary from region to region depending on the industrial structure, distance to markets, resources to support innovation, availability of skills in the regional labour market, and access to public services for households; among others. Capital city regions and remote rural regions with natural resources are facing different challenges in terms of productivity growth and inclusion.

High levels of inequality may increase the risk that narrow interest groups could influence the policy-making process and "capture" its benefits, especially if not counter-balanced by well-designed regulation on lobbying and campaign finance. By undermining trust in government and institutions, high levels of inequality may reduce the political space for reform and may feed a backlash against globalisation and openness, as observed in some OECD countries over recent years with the rise of populist movements (OECD, 2017t; OECD, 2017u).

High inequality can result in lower economic growth as it undermines the ability of the bottom 40% to invest in education, affecting their opportunities and productivity, as well as those of their children. In the absence of broad-based insurance mechanisms that can help vulnerable segments of the labour market cope with the risk of unemployment, unequal societies may be less resilient and could suffer higher welfare costs from economic shocks. The rise in inequality during 1985-2005 in 19 OECD countries is estimated to have knocked 4.7 percentage points off cumulative growth between 1990 and 2010 (OECD, 2015e). Socio-economic background influences the access and use of suitable health services alongside permitting to benefit from better quality employment (OECD, 2017n). This translates in lower tax revenues and higher social protection expenditures. At the same time, the large increases in public debt observed since the early 1990s reduce the fiscal space available to implement inclusive growth policies.

Chapter 2. New policy approaches

The focus on stronger productivity growth is necessary, but may not be sufficient to sustain economic growth that benefits all

The financial crisis revealed the significant limits of existing economic growth models, including the assumption that growing the pie is enough to generate improvements in well-being for all. A focus on pro-growth policies that target efficiency in isolation has led some governments to follow policy options that have brought about unintended social consequences. The debt-to-assets ratio of the bottom wealth quintile reached on average 123% in 2014 across OECD countries. Similarly, the average gap between the bottom and top quintile leverages amounted to 117 percentage points' gap in 2014 across OECD countries. Mortgages and consumer loans contracts have often not been sufficiently secured or compiled with other assets through securitisation, particularly for the low-income groups (André, 2016).

It is important to reflect on the outcomes of the policy choices of the past, if we want to understand how we can move towards more inclusive growth. There is scope to better align structural and macroeconomic policies to sustain growth, for instance by ensuring that fiscal policy works counter-cyclically and that fiscal space is used for productive investments that improve opportunities of the worst-off (OECD, 2017p). Also, more could have been done to achieve these objectives by creating policy frameworks that open up markets and encourage private and public investment in people, cities, infrastructure and skills; and by helping those who may lose out from economic change to better adapt to new economic conditions, and to break the cycle of disadvantage.

The focus is on policies that promote win-win situations in terms of productivity growth and equity, because such policies can improve the perspectives of the bottom 40% of the income distribution. Well-designed packages of structural (e.g. labour and product market policies) and macroeconomic and financial market policies, as well as international coordination, could have eased the implementation of reforms and maximised their impact on growth, while promoting quality job creation and equity (OECD, 2018i). The main issue does not necessarily concern the way in which individual structural policies have been pursued to steer inclusive growth. The complexity of the inclusive growth agenda raises important challenges in terms of governance, as policy fragmentation needs to be reduced and institutional mechanisms integrated in order to design coherent policy packages and deliver them more effectively (OECD, 2016f).

An improved economic outlook provides an opportune moment to implement more ambitious structural reforms. Any short-term costs from reforms may be lower and shorter-lived when demand and job creation are stronger, especially if accompanied by complementary labour market reforms and income support that help displaced workers transition to new jobs and acquire new skills. Other actions needed to enhance inclusiveness, such as improving the participation of under-represented groups in the labour market, are also more likely to have durable benefits if implemented at a time of job-rich growth. Recent progress has, however, been modest in enacting reforms to reduce gender gaps, strengthen job creation and help workers find new jobs (OECD, 2018h).

Further efforts are also needed to exploit synergies and explore ways to mitigate trade-offs when implementing policies for inclusive growth. Some *Going for Growth* (OECD, 2018i) policy priorities cannot be unambiguously classified as pro-inclusive growth or not. Such is the case for reforms aimed at stimulating innovation and technological progress, including measures to reduce barriers to competition, firm entry and entrepreneurship. Progress along these lines is fundamental to spur productivity growth but may put further pressure on the relative demand for skilled workers through skill-biased technical change, and hence contribute to rising wage inequality among workers. At the same time, insofar as such reforms also contribute to job creation, they are likely to counteract reform-driven increases in wage dispersion, with an overall ambiguous effect on disposable income inequality. In a long-term perspective, competition and innovation policies may also contribute to enhance equity, for instance if they lead to a reduction in firms' rents and undermine the market dominance of incumbents, while promoting social mobility (OECD, 2018i). Recent evidence suggests that intergenerational income mobility increases with the degree of entrepreneurship and innovativeness in the economy (Aghion et al., 2015; 2016).

Not every policy reform is a win-win for inclusive growth, though. Trade-offs may, for example, arise in the case of some tax and benefit reforms, such as shifting from direct to indirect taxes or reducing marginal income tax rates (OECD, 2018i). This is the case when robust empirical evidence on their income inequality impact is lacking or relatively limited, or when the impact is highly dependent on reform design. One example is product market reforms, which have been found to increase both employment and wage dispersion so that the overall effect on household disposable income inequality is ambiguous (OECD, 2018i). Reducing barriers to competition is one key policy lever to boost growth with gains materialising relatively quickly. The equity effects of product market reforms are likely to depend on reform design as well as on time horizon (OECD, 2018i).

Growth and inclusiveness cannot be achieved by governments alone

Poor access to finance and talent can undermine business potential for growth. In addition, businesses can gain from being diverse and inclusive at the level of their board and workforces (OECD, 2017n), as well as by adjusting their corporate governance models throughout the supply chain (e.g. to support training and professional development of suppliers; see OECD work on due diligence and responsible business conduct, e.g. OECD, 2018d, 2016f and 2015a). Responsible business conduct is a lever that businesses can use to promote inclusive growth; for example, by raising compliance with laws on respect for human rights, environmental protection, labour relations and financial accountability. In this context, the OECD is also developing a platform that can help align government policies and business initiatives to seize opportunities from inclusive growth (Box 2.1).

Social dialogue and collective bargaining systems are coming under pressure to adapt, but they represent an avenue to improve quality jobs, making growth more inclusive. Digitalisation, globalisation and the rise in non-standard forms of employment – along with population ageing and the decline of the manufacturing sector – are testing their ability to foster the creation of quality jobs, reduce labour market inequality and promote productivity and resilience in labour markets. Union density and collective bargaining coverage have declined in most OECD countries (OECD, 2018f), a trend sometimes accelerated by the offshoring of production to countries where social dialogue and collective bargaining are weak or non-existent. This has been linked to labour's declining share of national income relative to capital.

Concerns are growing about the effectiveness of collective bargaining in the context of greater individualisation of the employment relationship and deep uncertainties surrounding the future of work. At the same time, new and complementary forms of social dialogue, collective organisation and bargaining are emerging to try to meet the challenges posed by new forms of work (OECD, 2018f).

Box 2.1. The role of business in inclusive growth

Rising inequality has limited the ability of some to access finance, invest in education and skills, which in turn can undermine the development of human capital and productivity growth. It can also make it difficult for employers to find people with the skills and knowledge they need.

The business case for inclusive growth is strong. On a macro level, more equal societies benefit business through a larger middle class and growing consumer purchasing power; enhanced government capacity to invest in education, health and infrastructure; and improved economic and political stability. Rising inequality has limited the ability of the bottom 40% to invest in their education and skills, undermining the development of human capital and potential productivity gains, also making it more difficult for employers to find people with the skills and knowledge they need and that are demanded by today's rapidly digitalising markets. Inequality of opportunity hurts business.

Increased diversity and inclusion, as well as female representation in C-suites and boards, have been linked to higher business performance and shareholder returns (Hunt et al., 2015). Aligning executive performance evaluation and compensation with long-term business goals, through longer equity vesting periods (Edmans et al., 2016), and with sustainability goals (Eccles et al. 2014) also leads to greater long-term profitability. Similarly, the promotion of responsible tax payment practices correlates with improved returns for some classes of shareholders (Babkin et al., 2017).

The OECD is launching the Business for Inclusive Growth Initiative with the intent to deliver: (i) a framework paper outlining the business case for inclusive growth and how governments and firms can advance public policies and business actions that promote inclusive growth in tandem; (ii) new indicators for business and investment impacts on inclusive growth and well-being; (iii) a platform through which businesses can share best practices and non-prescriptive guidelines for measuring the impact of business on well-being, sustainability and inclusive growth; and (iv) high-level policy discussions and the development of a policy network on inclusive growth including public and private stakeholders. These activities will complement and strengthen existing OECD work in this area, including responsible business conduct (RBC), quality FDI, the work on business and sustainable development, and OECD standards, such as the Guidelines for MNEs, and the work on Base Erosion and Profit Shifting (BEPS).

Sources: Babkin et al. (2017), Are Corporate Inversions Good for Shareholders? Journal of Financial Economics; Hunt et al. (2015), Why Diversity Matters, McKinsey & Company; Eccles et al. (2014), The Impact of Corporate Sustainability on Organizational Processes and Performance, Management Science, 60(11); Edmans et al. (2016), Equity Vesting and Investment, Review of Financial Studies.

Digital technologies and big data create opportunities for governments and businesses to connect with people. In this respect, there is a leeway to look into existing governance tools, such as Regulatory Impact Assessment (RIA), to develop similar exercises to ensure that policy evaluation and impact assessment are carried out through an inclusive growth lens. In general, connecting policies to people calls for a more integrated approach to decision-making that builds on integrity and transparency in public policy-making. This also means re-assessing public and corporate governance models in the context of mega-trends and seizing the opportunities that new technologies offer.

Big data and smart technologies have a strong potential to inform this type of governance tools. For example, the ability of blockchains to secure the transfer and traceability of value and data can facilitate innovative business models and new marketplaces driven by speed, dis-intermediation and lower costs, particularly in the field of financial services, government services and supply chain management.

The opportunities to grow at a global level can be leveraged by coherent domestic and international policies

Levelling the playing field through multilateral cooperation (including the WTO Trade Facilitation Agreement and cross-border competition in services) is necessary to realise the gains from trade, but may not always be sufficient to achieve inclusive growth. At the international level, the emergence of global value chains has highlighted the need for greater coherence between trade and investment policy frameworks, enhanced international tax cooperation, as well as for common labour and environmental standards.

While they bring undeniable benefits (e.g. in terms of access to GVCs, product variety and lower prices), globalisation and digitalisation also challenge governments' ability to tax mobile assets and put downward pressure on labour, environmental and governance standards. The ability to sustain growth in the global economy will also hinge on success in reducing environmental damages and risks, as well as in curbing the reliance on natural resources. Green growth considerations can be part of the design of policies for the long-term, with appropriate combinations of reforms to address potential short-term trade-offs. It is also part of the sustainable growth agenda of the OECD (OECD, 2015d; OECD, 2017j).

Coherent climate, investment, innovation, skills and fiscal policies must work together to create new markets, provide work opportunities and ease the adjustment costs for workers and businesses (OECD, 2017j). Acting on climate change to achieve the goals of the Paris Agreement can also bring about reduced exposure of people to air pollution. Exposure to air pollution is not uniform across income groups and varies across countries; generally air pollution is higher in poorer communities. Poverty may also contribute to the depletion of and a lack of investment in environmental resources. At the same time, large inequalities may go hand in hand with unsustainable patterns of consumption and use of natural resources by the richest individuals.

Chapter 3. The framework for policy action on inclusive growth

Key dynamics for policy action on inclusive growth

At the 2017 OECD Ministerial Council Meeting, Ministers of OECD Member countries stated that growth should be strong, sustainable, balanced and inclusive. Ministers asked the OECD to work through its committees and relevant bodies on the development of a Framework for Policy Action on Inclusive Growth for the 2018 Ministerial Council Meeting, and to document inequalities of income and opportunities through a comprehensive evidence-based analysis [C/MIN(2017)9/FINAL].

The OECD Framework for Policy Action on Inclusive Growth aims to help governments sustain and better share the benefits from economic growth. Supported by a dashboard of indicators to monitor trends on growth and inclusiveness, the Framework identifies possible policy responses that can improve outcomes in terms of inclusive growth. It builds on a range of OECD strategies and projects, including the Jobs Strategy, Skills Strategy, Innovation Strategy, Going for Growth Strategy, Going Digital project and Green Growth Strategy, among others, and is extensively supported by the analysis set out in Part II of the present report.

The framework is not prescriptive and does not propose a "one-size-fits-all" approach. The value of specific policy options will be context-driven and may change with countries' circumstances and priorities. The framework is meant to help countries assess their policy settings against their ability to promote equality of opportunities and deploy the OECD *Productivity-Inclusiveness Nexus* (OECD, 2017i). It can help governments consider *ex-ante* equity issues in their policy design. Policies for growth and inclusiveness may need to be constructed through an appropriate governance system that takes into account the level of complementarity between policy instruments at a granular level, as opposed to an aggregate level that may mask those complementarities.

The Framework highlights three key dynamics that policies can help to catalyse. Figure 3.1 illustrates the main building blocks of policy action to ***sustain and more equitably share the gains of economic growth*** by:

1. ***Investing in people and places that have been left behind*** through (i) targeted quality childcare, early education and life-long acquisition of skills; (ii) effective access to quality healthcare services, education, justice, housing and infrastructures; and (iii) optimal natural resource management for sustainable growth.
2. ***Supporting business dynamism and inclusive labour markets*** through (i) broad-based innovation, fast and deep technology diffusion; (ii) strong competition and vibrant entrepreneurship; (ii) access to good quality jobs, especially for women and under-represented groups; and (iv) resilience and adaptation to the future of work.
3. ***Building efficient and responsive governments*** through (i) aligned policy packages across the whole of government; (ii) integration of equity aspects upfront in the design of policy; and (iii) inclusive policy-making, integrity, accountability and international coordination.

Figure 3.1 The Framework for Policy Action on Inclusive Growth

With the aim to achieve growth that benefits all, and that allows for people, regions and business to fulfil their potential, the framework would look like:

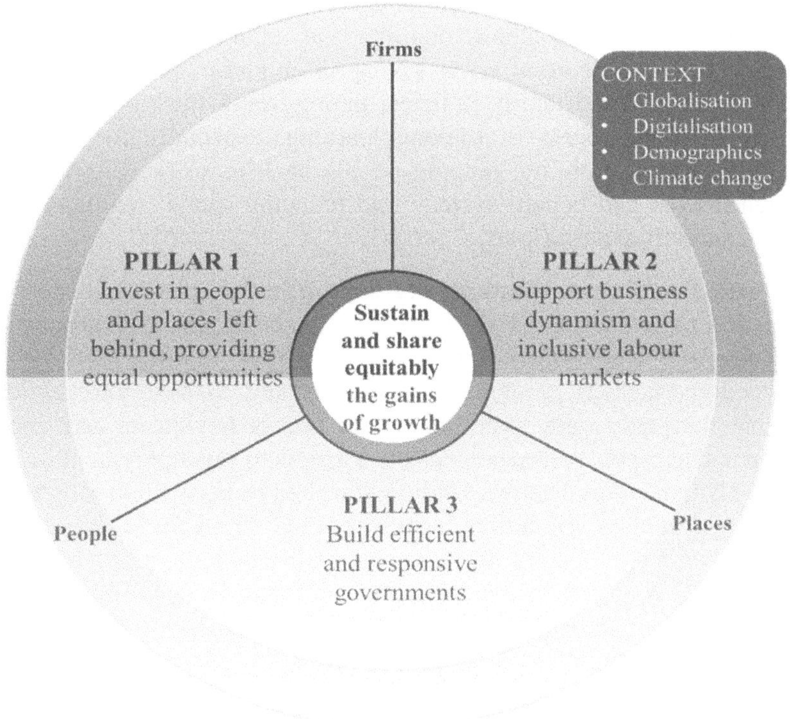

Source: OECD Secretariat.

Investing in people and places left behind, providing equal opportunities

By locking in opportunity, privilege and exclusion, inequalities may undermine intergenerational mobility. Disadvantages in places of origin, early education, health and the labour market often compound each other throughout the life cycle. The key dynamics for governments and the private sector to sustain are:

- ***Promoting life-long learning and acquisition of skills.*** High-quality initial education and training systems could be implemented from early childhood through to schooling age and beyond. Priority could be given to enhancing access to good-quality early education and childcare, especially for disadvantaged families. Vocational and tertiary education policies could focus on fostering youth skills and competencies, including through well-designed apprenticeship programs. More attention could be given to ensuring effective access and swift completion of tertiary education by the worst-off. To be effective, government, business and workers would need to agree on new ways to promote and finance skills development throughout workers' careers. Life-long learning policies could focus on continuous reskilling and adaptation to rapid technological change. This could be complemented with well-designed social welfare programs that encourage work, while protecting individuals and families from unanticipated risks. Social protection systems may need to adapt to the individualisation and diversification of work in the future. But all too often, skills policies stop there, and may not help workers, companies and economies to adapt to changes in production processes.

- ***Increasing social mobility.*** Increasing social mobility implies levelling the playing field for individuals, starting in childhood and continuing throughout the lifecycle by lowering barriers to labour mobility and reducing discrimination. This may require action in a range of areas: giving all children equal opportunities through health, education and family policies; giving youth the right start in the labour market; ensuring access to lifelong learning, especially for the least skilled; promoting career mobility; helping people back to work when needed; support through the tax and benefit system; and reducing spatial segregation, improving housing support and transport.
- ***Improving health and enhancing access to affordable housing.*** More efforts may be needed to weaken the link between socio-economic background and health, education and employment outcomes. This may require focusing on ex-ante interventions such as prevention campaigns and ex-post interventions such as ensuring that vulnerable individuals can access healthcare and receive health insurance that meets their needs, or have access to unemployment insurance. This may imply expanding health spending allocated to prevention targeted at key risk factors (e.g. health, pollution, accidents, and crime) and population groups, especially children. It could furthermore require housing and land use policies to improve access to affordable housing and broader economic development in distressed regions through the promotion of network infrastructure.
- ***Promoting regional catch-up.*** In the context of growing regional disparities, policies could focus on productivity-enhancing reforms so that lagging regions can attract and maintain investment. An integrated and predictable approach to investment policy-making may be needed to leverage and effectively manage physical capital, knowledge-based capital and natural capital through efficient allocation between regions. Investment in sustainable transport systems, affordable housing, clean energy networks and modern ICT networks would be key to support regional catch-up.
- ***Investing in communities' well-being and social capital.*** High-quality local administration, in line with the national inclusive growth agenda, is needed to encourage action by local communities and create common purpose within communities. This may include, for instance, fostering better connections between people and increasing their sense of civic engagement; as well as equal access to key public services and amenities such as health, education, nutrition, utility services (e.g. water, energy and transport) and access to nature and green areas.

Supporting business dynamism and inclusive labour markets

Governments and businesses need to look at the issue of how to trigger a growth process from a broader perspective. The OECD *Productivity-Inclusiveness Nexus* (OECD, 2017i) shows that a good place to start would be by creating the necessary pre-conditions for workers, entrepreneurs and firms to be productive and innovative in the workplace and in markets, as well as putting strong incentives in place to maintain momentum. This may require workers' real wages to keep up with rising productivity; and that corporate governance models be reassessed in light of new approaches including incorporation types and employee ownership, new business models and vibrant social dialogue; as well as the integration of a long-term perspective in the design of incentives and compensation for shareholders and executives.

A common challenge for governments and businesses consists in ensuring that the radical transformation of labour markets brought about by the emergence of the digital economy does not leave workers behind. People may need to be equipped with a wide range of skills to make the best out of digitalisation and be provided with the means to acquire relevant skills throughout their lives. The role of social partners and other stakeholders could be strengthened to ensure the creation of quality jobs and non-discrimination in the workplace, as well as to facilitate a smooth transition towards the future of work. Labour market policies and social protection systems, such as health insurance and unemployment benefits, may need to be adapted to new forms of work. Better coordination of product and labour market policies (including at the international level) can contribute to boost business dynamism and improve productivity growth, while also reducing labour market duality and easing the implementation of structural reforms. Standards may need to be enforced and further developed to promote inclusiveness at a global level. More specifically, the key dynamics for policies to catalyse are:

- ***Boosting productivity growth and business dynamism, while ensuring adaptation and diffusion of technologies across the board – in particular for small and young firms.*** This could be achieved through structural and regulatory policies that: improve the business environment and foster entrepreneurship; facilitate the reallocation of workers and capital; strengthen competition and limit wasteful granting of subsidies to firms; promote organisational change and the diffusion of technologies; strengthen trade and investment on a multilateral and non-discriminatory basis; and incentivise businesses and governments to invest in new business and governance models. Policies that spur business dynamism, innovation and the adoption of new technology need to be sensitive to firms' size and capacities, and avoid unduly strengthening the position of incumbents. International cooperation of tax policy and implementation of the OECD/G20 BEPS package is needed to level the playing field, while also promoting responsible business conduct.
- ***Achieving inclusive labour markets.*** This may require that appropriate labour market policies and employment protection be put in place to stimulate labour mobility and opportunities for placement and retention of quality jobs for all. Employment protection legislation would need to be properly designed in order to yield predictable contract termination costs and avoid creating different levels of job security across labour contracts, while protecting workers against possible abuses. Tax policies could be adapted to ensure more inclusive growth and deliver sustainable revenues; for example, by taking account of their impact on skills development and use, on savings behaviours and on business dynamism.
- ***Optimising natural resource management for sustainable growth.*** This can include policies to step up investment in low-emission technologies, smart and clean infrastructure, and the conservation and sustainable use of biodiversity and water resources; phase out environmentally harmful subsidies to consumers and producers; broaden the carbon pricing base; and engaging in structural reforms to support the reallocation of resources.

Building efficient and responsive governments

Citizens and society at large could have a stronger role to play in developing policies for economic growth. This will only happen once they feel their voice is being taken into account and their contributions are being translated into concrete improvements. Effective administrative justice can help to ensure public accountability, transparency, participation and openness. It constitutes an interface between public administration and society to protect the public interest and individuals' rights, while improving democratic accountability. Governments, and also businesses, need to be responsive to citizens, reliable in supplying services, fair in the application of laws and contract rules, and maintain a high standard of integrity. Involving under-served or excluded populations in decision-making could help to build trust between citizens, businesses and governments. Accessing government and corporate information and secure exchanges of data could be made easier through open governance initiatives.

- ***Embedding inclusiveness in policy-making.*** Coordinated action may be needed to strengthen institutional frameworks for mainstreaming and budgeting of gender and diversity, including through open government. Beyond anti-corruption measures, the policy-making process needs to be protected from undue influence to avoid the capture of public policy by narrow interest groups. Greater stakeholder engagement could contribute to strengthen policies, standards and projects in areas of broader public interest, following the Recommendation of the Council on Open Government [C(2017)140] (hereinafter the *OECD Recommendation on Open Government*).
- ***Using data and smart technologies to design citizen-centred policies.*** Providing citizens with the appropriate data, resources and information can allow them to make decisions about their own lives and professional development. Taking a citizen-driven approach can be a feature of innovative public sector governance approaches, to leverage on open and reusable data through digital means. It is important to evaluate the transaction costs and accountability of citizen-state interactions in a context marked by increasingly personalised services and the use of social media.
- ***Screening policies for inclusiveness and accountability.*** This may require more efforts to improve budget transparency and ensure sound public financial management, ex-post evaluation of regulatory policies, government reliability and the reaction capacity to adverse shocks, as well as greater responsiveness and openness to citizen input. The needs, preferences and concerns of stakeholders, including under-represented populations, would need to be reflected in the decision-making process. Further action may also be needed to better understand and integrate citizens' behaviour, demands and needs in the design and implementation of public service strategies in light of the digital transformation and open government conduct, as well as to improve public e-procurement systems (OECD, 2017o).

Box 3.1. The OECD Inclusive Growth Initiative

The OECD mission is to help countries achieve "sustainable economic growth and employment and a rising standard of living". Through the 1960 Convention, Members acknowledged that prosperity and strong economies are essential for attaining the purposes of the United Nations, as well as the preservation of individual liberty and the increase of general well-being. In response to rising inequalities and in the wake of the 2007-09 economic crisis, OECD Member countries have consistently recognised in their Ministerial Council Meeting Statements that sustainable economic growth, while necessary, will not be a sufficient condition for increasing standards of living unless the distributional aspects of policies are also addressed.

In 2017, Ministers asserted that growth should be strong, sustainable, balanced and inclusive. Ministers called for the OECD Secretariat to develop a policy action plan for inclusive growth and to document inequalities of income and opportunities through a comprehensive evidence-based analysis, as well as the concentration of wealth and market power [C/MIN(2017)9/FINAL]. Ministers highlighted the need for whole-of-government policy responses to inclusive growth challenges and mandated the OECD to "work through its committees and relevant bodies on the development of a Framework for Policy Action on Inclusive Growth for the 2018 Ministerial Council Meeting".

The OECD launched the Inclusive Growth Initiative in 2012, as part of its New Approaches to Economic Challenges (NAEC) programme, to help governments address these challenges. The Inclusive Growth Framework for Policy Action builds on the data, evidence and policy insights generated by existing work-streams (see Annex 1), as well as on the most up-to-date results from OECD research going into the 2018 MCM (e.g. NAEC, OECD work on well-being, the new Jobs Strategy, and the first results of the Going Digital project). The framework aims to provide countries with broad guidance on how to design and implement integrated policy packages that can improve their performance by:

(i) Showing clear links between the different dimensions of inclusive growth and capturing how policy influences these dimensions through key channels;

(ii) Adopting a sufficiently flexible structure that can be adapted to country-specific challenges and circumstances; and

(iii) Advocating a whole-of-government approach to the implementation, monitoring and evaluation of inclusive growth.

Dashboard of inclusive growth indicators

The dashboard includes a set of core inclusive growth indicators (Table 1) guided by the Framework for Policy Action on Inclusive Growth (Figure 3.1) and the availability of internationally comparable data. These core indicators measure key dynamics of inclusive growth (outcomes or drivers), which are complemented by secondary indicators used in the annexed part (Chapters 1 to 4) to facilitate interpretation of related policy challenges (see Annex for description of indicators). The dashboard is evolutionary and could be complemented by additional indicators, to consider further issues such as the labour share of national income, union density together with union coverage, children obesity, overweight rates, and indicators of natural resource management and carbon productivity.

All indicators are based on the internationally comparable statistics compiled by the OECD on a regular basis. The dashboard builds on and connects existing OECD frameworks that were developed to assess the multiple facets of inclusive growth; as well as emerging research on the future of work, digitalisation and open government (Box 3.1). These indicators are a subset of the statistical evidence that underpins sectoral and in-depth OECD analytical work on growth and inclusiveness. The dashboard is consistent with the work on the *Productivity-Inclusiveness Nexus*, the new OECD *Jobs Strategy*, *Going for Growth*, *Inclusive Growth in Regions*, as well as the *SDG Measurement Framework* and *Green Growth Indicators*; some of which have become a standard feature in the OECD country reviews (e.g. *Economic Surveys*, *Investment Policy Reviews*, *Environmental Performance Reviews* and *Multi-dimensional Country Reviews*). The dashboard also reflects some of the main aspects of the EU Social Scoreboard; by using similar metrics to capture labour productivity, earnings dispersion, gender labour income gap, childcare, and digital access of firms.

The dashboard is organised around four categories:

- ***Growth and ensuring equitable sharing of benefits from growth:*** These indicators help to track whether the economy is growing and living standards are increasing for different groups of population, defined in terms of income, age and region of residence.
- ***Inclusive and well-functioning markets:*** This category looks at the structure and functioning of the economy and marketplaces as the main drivers of growth and inclusiveness. This category considers product and labour markets, both from the aspect of efficiency and equity. It provides an understanding of the main economic forces underpinning people's living standards. These indicators gauge the productivity-inclusiveness nexus at a more granular level, e.g. at gender, sectoral and geographical levels.
- ***Equal opportunities and foundations of future prosperity:*** This category looks at the distribution of selected non-economic well-being components, such as health, education, socio-emotional skills, environmental quality of life and childcare. These elements capture people's opportunities to improve well-being and to participate in the economy and society.
- ***Governance:*** This category reflects a whole-of-the-government approach to monitoring efficiency and responsiveness of the government.

No policy strategy can be sustained if data and appropriate indicators are not available to monitor progress and identify policy targeting and prioritisation. The OECD has made significant progress advancing the measurement of inequality in cooperation with other international organisations and statistical offices; however, important gaps remain (Part II, Chapter 1). Exploring new methods and sources of (big) data can help to better capture various dimensions of inequality, e.g. data informing on behavioural aspects of consumption inequality and environmental justice and spatial segregation indicators at the local level, digitalisation-related indicators, mental health indicators, and measures of resilience and environmental risks. Going forward, it will be important to strengthen OECD's efforts in this field.

Table 3.1. Inclusive Growth Indicators

Category	Core indicator	
1. Growth and ensuring equitable sharing of benefits from growth	1.1	GDP per capita growth (%)
	1.2	Median income growth and level (%; USD PPP)
	1.3	S80/20 share of income (ratio)
	1.4	Bottom 40% wealth share and top 10% wealth share (% of household net wealth)
	1.5	Life expectancy (number of years)
	1.6	Mortality from outdoor air pollution (deaths per million inhabitants)
	1.7	Relative poverty rate (%)
2. Inclusive and well-functioning markets	2.1	Annual labour productivity growth and level (%; USD PPP)
	2.2	Employment-to-population ratio (%)
	2.3	Earnings dispersion (inter-decile ratio)
	2.4	Female wage gap (%)
	2.5	Involuntary part-time employment (%)
	2.6	Digital access (businesses using cloud computing services) (%)
	2.7	Share of SME loans in total business loans (%)
3. Equal opportunities and foundations of future prosperity	3.1	Variation in science performance explained by students' socio-economic status (%)
	3.2	Correlation of earnings outcomes across generations (coefficient)
	3.3	Childcare enrolment rate (children aged 0-2) (%)
	3.4	Young people neither in employment nor in education & training (18-24) (%)
	3.5	Share of adults who score below Level 1 in both literacy and numeracy (%)
	3.6	Regional life expectancy gap (% difference)
	3.7	Resilient students (%)
4. Governance	4.1	Confidence in government (%)
	4.2	Voter turnout (%)
	4.3	Female political participation (%)

Note: Core indicators can be complemented by secondary indicators; which for category 1 could be "Top 10% wealth share (% of total household net wealth)", "Regional median income gap (% difference)" and "Life expectancy gap by educational attainment (number of years)"; and for category 2 "Skills mismatch (%)", "Unemployment gap, by education (% points)", "Average employment gap, disadvantaged people (% points)" and "Employment rate of prime age workers (%)".
Source: OECD Secretariat.

Figure 3.2 illustrates some of the main OECD trends revealed by the dashboard of inclusive growth indicators, while Figures 3.A.1-A.4 (in Annex 3.A) provide further details on trends for the latest years available. GPD per capita has increased and has outpaced median income, which has fallen below average income in two-thirds of OECD countries during 2010-2015 (Figure 3.A.1). Income and wealth inequalities are large and still increasing.[1] The S80/20 income ratio has not improved on average between 2010 and 2014, and differences among OECD countries have deepened (Figure 3.A.1). The bottom 40% wealth share has stalled at 3% for OECD countries over 2010-2015. The top 10% owned a half and the richest 1% one fifth of the total wealth in 2014. In the context of ageing societies, inequality could further increase for the future generations. While societies benefitted from longer life expectancy (81 years) in 2014 than 2010, health conditions remain unequally distributed among the population (Chapter 1). An often-neglected issue concerns how the broader environment (e.g. exposure to air pollution) affects health. Outdoor air pollution has contributed to 411 deaths per million inhabitants in 2014, up from 386 in 2010 in OECD countries. About 11% of the population were poor, with income below 50% of the median income in 2014.

Productivity and employment-level differentials are substantial in OECD countries (Figure 3.2; Figure 3.A.2), despite productivity growth between 2010 and 2015. The OECD average gender wage gap has slightly decreased though unexplained differentials in earnings across gender remain large in some OECD countries. While labour markets have become more inclusive, women, the young, the elderly and the middle-aged men continue to participate less in the economy. The share of involuntary part-time employment has been on the rise among OECD countries2. The top 10% richest employees earned three times more than the bottom 10% in 2014. Some 47 % of total business loans were allocated to SMEs in 2016, and this share has not changed much since 2010 (Figure 3.A.2).

Figure 3.2 Tracking progress by inclusive growth indicator

OECD unweighted average, annualised change over 2010-15 or the latest available year

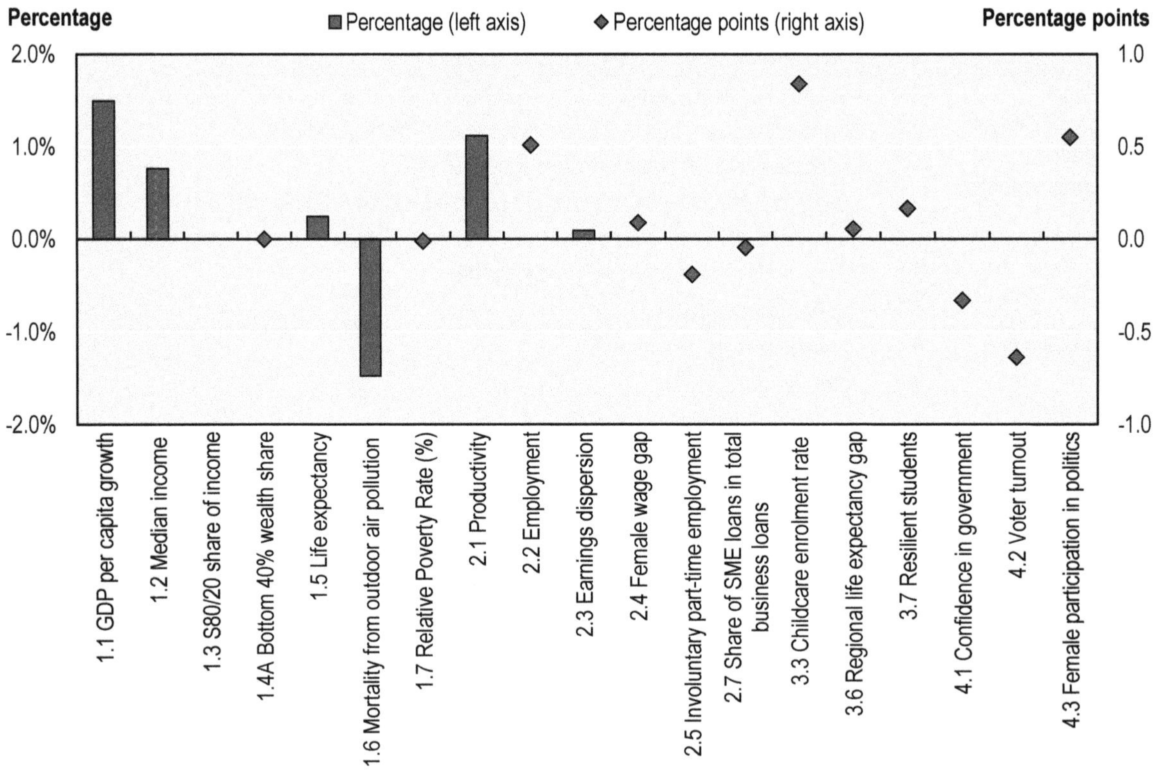

Note: Simple OECD averages are displayed. Indicators are adjusted as needed, so that better performance is depicted by high scores and lower performance by low scores for the following indicators: 1.3 S80/20 share of income; 1.6 Mortality from outdoor air pollution; 1.7 Relative poverty rate; 2.3 Earnings dispersion; 2.4 Female wage gap; 2.5 Involuntary part-time employment; 3.1 Variation in science performance explained by students' socio-economic status; 3.2 Correlation of earnings outcomes across generations; 3.4 Young people in NEET; 3.5 Share of adults who score below Level 1; 3.6 Regional life expectancy. The left axis refers to a 5-year annualised change measured in percentages between 2010 and 2015, or the latest year available. The right axis refers to a 5-year annualised change measured in percentage points between 2010 and 2015, or the latest year available. Annex B provides further details.
Source: OECD Secretariat. See Annex B for data sources.

StatLink http://dx.doi.org/10.1787/888933724423

Opportunities are not equally shared among people and places in OECD countries (Figure 3.2; Figure 3.A.3). Income inequality for those born in the 1980s is higher than among their parents at the same age, which in turn was higher than for their parents: the correlation of earnings between two generations was 38% in 2014. Life expectancy rates differ among regions, although regional life expectancy gap has declined since 2010. In OECD countries, the average childcare enrolment rate was 35% in 2014, up from 28% in 2004 and 31% in 2010. As much as 13% of variation in students' science performance was due to their socio-economic status in 2015. PISA outcomes show that investing in laggard schools, for instance through highly qualified teachers and principals, can help overcome the initial disadvantage of students, especially when this investment is made in early childcare and education. The 18-24 year-olds suffering from poor health are also 4 times more likely than their peers to be not in employment, education or training (NEET). Not having completed upper secondary education more than doubles the risk of becoming NEET later. Also, there were 29% of resilient students among disadvantaged students in 2015.

Electoral turnout has declined in OECD countries, especially among the young (Figure 3.2). Female participation in public decision-making remains crucial to support equal policy outcomes. Despite some improvement in recent years, there is no gender parity in most OECD countries. About 70% cast their ballots in the election and less than 50% had confidence in the government in 2016, down from 2007 (Figure 3.A.4).

Potential use of the framework for policy action on inclusive growth

The proposed Framework for Policy Action on Inclusive Growth is non-prescriptive and has not been used, as presented, in OECD country reviews. It has the potential to be applied in different ways. It can help countries consolidate the use of OECD data, analyses and policy recommendations from the OECD country surveillance (e.g. *OECD Economic Surveys*, *Territorial Development Reviews*, *Environmental Performance Reviews* and *Multidimensional Country Reviews*), policy research and horizontal projects (e.g. *Going Digital*, *Going for Growth*, *Employment Outlook* and *Future of Work*) and statistical work on measuring productivity, social progress and well-being (e.g. *Productivity Compendium*, *Measuring Progress towards SDGs* and *How's Life?*). Additionally, the Framework could help to identify knowledge gaps and advance OECD analysis in several areas, such as consolidating the inclusive growth and green growth streams of work, and expand the scope of work to developing and emerging economies. Finally, it could provide guidance to implement SDGs on a number of goals that are relevant from an inclusive growth perspective.

Countries are increasingly considering innovative approaches to integrate growth and inclusiveness considerations upfront in the design of policy. For example, in 2016 Japan extended the coverage of the employees' pension insurance scheme together with the company-based health insurance scheme to about 250,000 non regular workers (OECD, 2017f). Greece introduced a guaranteed minimum income scheme for the wider public, focusing on disadvantaged households, aiming to cover about 7% of the population (OECD, 2016e). The UK considered enhancing spending on public schools by nearly GBP 2.5 billion, through its Strategic School Improvement Fund, to support disadvantaged students and facilitate teacher mobility to disadvantaged schools (OECD, 2017g). Mexico enacted an electoral reform in 2014 stipulating gender parity in the nomination of candidates in federal and local congressional elections, in addition to introducing a gender perspective in its National Development Plan and implementing a specific national programme for Equal Opportunities and Non-Discrimination against Women (OECD, 2017h). Other countries are also putting in place a number of innovative programmes that are citizen-centred or built on participatory processes (Box 3.2).

Box 3.2. Examples of good practices: Innovative approaches in policy-making

Policy innovation labs and policy design labs aim to change the way governments design, implement, monitor and evaluate policies so to improve their efficacy and engagement with citizens. These labs vary in their approach, but share certain characteristics, such as (i) multi-stakeholder engagement with the public and private sector, academia, NGOs; (ii) cutting across traditional government siloes and levels of government; (iii) using multi-disciplinary methodologies such as complexity theory, behavioural economics and psychology, and agent-based modelling; (iv) putting emphasis on rapid experimentation and scaling impact, and (v) focusing on improving user experiences and outcomes by engaging citizens in the policy design and implementation process.

Prominent labs include Mindlab in Denmark, the Behavioural Insights Team and the What Works Network in the UK, and the Seoul Innovation Bureau in South Korea. Examples of innovative policy measures and approaches introduced by these labs are wide-ranging. They include Predictiv, a user-friendly digital platform for running randomised controlled trials to accelerate the policy experimentation process, launched by the Behavioural Insights Team in 2016. More than 30 trials have been conducted via the Predictiv platform to date and the results are already shaping government policy. For example, the UK Government Equalities Office and the Department for Work and Pensions are using the results of one trial to change government communications around Shared Parental Leave (OECD, 2018).

The Sharing City Agenda run by the Seoul Innovation Bureau, comprises a range of initiatives such as Tool Kit Centres that offer communities a shared space stocked with items such as tools and suitcases for residents to borrow, and Generation Sharing Household, a service that matches elderly people who have spare residential space with students in need of a place to live (ITeams, 2014). The Seoul Metropolitan Government (SMG) is trying to address these challenges with its Comprehensive Plan for 50+ Assistance (hereafter, Seoul's 50+ policy). Seoul's 50+ policy provides life training, emotional support, cultural experiences and also retraining for continued social opportunities for newly retired populations. The nucleus of the innovation is a comprehensive 50+ infrastructure planned across Seoul. This includes the establishment of the Seoul 50+ Foundation (the coordinating body), and several 50+ campuses and centres built on multi-sectoral collaboration. Nineteen 50+ centres are planned for city districts by 2020 and four centres are currently in operation. This infrastructure provides support and cultural spaces for the 50+ generation to interact among peers, drive changes and generate needs-based services for one other. It goes beyond traditional policy interventions, providing more comprehensive support and dealing with the practical and emotional side of life transitions (e.g. offering cooking classes for retired men or overall life-transitions courses for the newly joined). As of August 2017, 50+ programmes have registered over 15,000 people and other local municipalities are benchmarking 50+ campuses (OECD, 2018).

Asker Welfare Lab in Asker, Norway is a new concept for service delivery centred solely on the citizen, in which all relevant municipal services, together with external partners, invest together in a person's welfare. The lab takes an investment mind-set and treats citizens as co-investors. The aim is to raise the living standards of vulnerable individuals, thereby bettering the quality of life of each person and family in the programme. Most importantly, experts have to partner with the citizens whose lives they want to change, under the motto: "No decision about me shall be taken without me".

The Asker Welfare Lab is currently focused on three specific target groups: families with children experiencing "vulnerable living conditions", vulnerable youth between the age of 17-25, and families with children with disabilities. The Asker Welfare Lab model was tested during the pilot phase with 20-30 citizens/families. Living conditions and quality of life were measured before and after the encounter with the Investment Team, showing improvements. The municipal employees involved, who now have greater access to resources and can make investments at an earlier stage, feel that they can effect real change. Common planning also saves time that can be invested in more effective casework. The project has been recognised as a National Learning Project in Norway and was one of three projects to receive the annual National Innovation Award from the Ministry of Local Government and Modernisation. It has also been awarded a Best Practice Certificate from the European Public Sector Awards 2017 (OECD, 2018).

Sources: I-Teams (2014), Case Study: Seoul Innovation Bureau, http://theiteams.org/case-studies/seoul-innovation-bureau, accessed 15-2-2018; OECD (2018), Embracing Innovation in Government. Global Trends 2018, OECD Publishing, Paris, http://www.oecd.org/gov/innovative-government/embracing-innovation-in-government-2018.pdf. Online sources: http://mind-lab.dk/en, http://www.behaviouralinsights.co.uk/, https://www.gov.uk/guidance/what-works-network, http://english.seoul.go.kr/policy-information/key-policies/city-initiatives/4-social-innovation/.

To capitalise on these efforts, countries could consider using the Framework for Policy Action on Inclusive Growth in specific pilot studies and processes. Following expressed interest, pilot studies of this kind could be implemented to help governments assess the synergies and trade-offs of country-specific policies, or where different forms of engagement with stakeholders could be considered to steer cooperation on the inclusive growth agenda. The dashboard of inclusive growth indicators could be adjusted to specific country circumstances and provide a basis for action to improve efficiency and engagement of governments with citizens.

Reviewing the social contract in the context of a global economy

Stagnant median incomes, rising inequalities and reduced social mobility have led many to conclude that the social contract has ceased to function for them. The social contract is founded on the principle that life outcomes and opportunities would need to be shaped by individual choices and collective responsibility, rather than inherited circumstances. However, more analytical efforts are needed to provide granular evidence that would inform accordingly the policy design. Strong evidence can help to enhance public trust in government and to address new forms of exclusion by enabling all citizens to live productive and meaningful lives. Place-based and people-centred policies can be effectively combined to deliver targeted support for individuals throughout the life-cycle and build greater resilience in cities, regions and local communities. The notion of an "empowering state" provides a valuable opportunity for rethinking the role, mission and means of action of the state in a perspective that goes beyond the focus on income redistribution and correcting market failures.

Enhancing trust in governments in the globalised economy also means coordinating and synchronising policy measures with other countries in a joint effort to combine competitiveness and inclusivity. Concerted action across countries can increase the economic benefits generated by well-designed fiscal plans that are aimed at growth-enhancing investment in physical and human capital – for example, smart and clean cross-border infrastructures. Conversely, tax competition provides a topical example of an area in which domestic policy choices may lead to a "race to the bottom" resulting in lower tax rates. Lack of coordination with other countries on tax can lead to inefficient double taxation of international businesses or transactions. It can also result in double non-taxation, where no tax is paid on certain kinds of international business income. A lack of transparency on tax matters creates opportunities for some taxpayers to conceal income and assets offshore, which may exacerbate income and wealth inequalities.

The global governance architecture built around a number of international institutions plays a crucial role in supporting countries' efforts to relay high standards for protection of social, environmental and human rights. The development and promotion of common international standards and regulatory convergence can help the level playing field for trade and investment. The main instruments here include the *Policy Framework for Investment* (PFI) and the *G20 Guiding Principles for Global Investment Policymaking*; and the *OECD Guidelines for Multinational Enterprises*; and the *OECD Convention on Combating Bribery of Foreign Public Officials in International Business Transactions* (the *Anti-Bribery Convention* - ABC). The OECD is also working on other areas where multilateral cooperation can prove beneficial, including the control of illicit financial flows and cybersecurity. Cooperation with other international organisations has helped advance the global measurement agenda, for example through new datasets, such as the *OECD-WTO Trade in Value Added Database*, developed to better understand the opportunities and challenges of global value chains, on-going work to create similar frameworks to better understand the role of MNEs and FDI in these chains, including via a new database on the world's largest MNEs; new standards on such as the *System of Environmental Economic Accounting*; and new measures of inclusiveness and interconnectedness of financial flows and stocks.

The OECD has helped advance multilateral cooperation by establishing common rules, norms and standards – both through its own initiatives and through the G20, as with the *G20/OECD Principles of Corporate Governance*. The *OECD/G20 Base Erosion and Profit Shifting* (BEPS) and the *Multilateral Convention to Implement Tax Treaty Related Measures to Prevent BEPS* have contributed to improve confidence in the international tax system so that profits can be taxed where economic activities take place and value is created – potentially raising up to USD 240 billion in additional tax revenue per year. There has been increasing endorsement of the *OECD International VAT/GST Guidelines* (which were adopted in 2016 as an OECD Recommendation of the Council on the Application of Value Added Tax/Goods and Services Tax to the International Trade in Services and Intangibles [C(2016)120]), ensuring that the interaction of national VAT regimes facilitates rather than distorts cross-border trade and economic activity. The OECD has also pioneered the expansion of information exchange between tax administrations, notably with the introduction of the *Automatic Exchange of Financial Account Information* between tax administrations (AEOI) in 2017 and 2018 – which has helped countries raise over USD 100 billion in added revenue so far. Expanded information exchange reduces taxpayers' ability to evade taxes by not declaring income and assets held offshore, and increases the ability of countries to levy taxes more effectively on capital income.

Going forward, multilateral cooperation on growth and inclusiveness can take different forms, for example: (i) the collection and harmonisation of data, indicators and comparable analysis of the key dimensions of inclusive growth; (ii) peer learning and the sharing of best practices drawn from countries' experiences with inclusive growth strategies; and (iii) the development of policy guidelines for promoting inclusive growth based on a common framework. The collection of a solid evidence base is particularly important as it can provide the building blocks that are necessary for developing effective country reviews and policy recommendations. At the multilateral level, one initiative in this direction could consist in mapping out where and how issues of inclusion are addressed in international agreements and standards with the aim of identifying existing gaps. A stock-taking exercise of this kind could help to inform the debate among policy-makers on what can be done to make the multilateral system more inclusive.

End notes

1 Lower performance is depicted by low scores in Figure 3.2 as the indicator has been inverted.
2 Lower performance is depicted by low scores in Figure 3.2 as the indicator has been inverted.

References

Aghion, P. et al. (2016), Living the 'American Dream' in Finland: The Social Mobility of Inventors, mimeo.

Aghion, P. et al. (2015), Innovation and Top Income Inequality, NBER Working Paper, No. 21247.

Alex (2012), The Link between Job Satisfaction and Firm Value, with Implications for Corporate Social Responsibility, Academy of Management Perspectives, Vol. 13, No. 24, November 2012.

André, C. (2016), "Household debt in OECD countries: Stylised facts and policy issues", OECD Economics Department Working Papers, No. 1277, OECD Publishing, Paris,

Babkin et al. (2017), Are Corporate Inversions Good for Shareholders?, Journal of Financial Economics, Vol. 126, No. 2, July 2017.

Criscuolo, Gal and Menon (2014), "The Dynamics of Employment Growth: New Evidence from 18 Countries", OECD Science, Technology and Industry Policy Papers no. 14, OECD Publishing.

Eccles et al. (2014), The Impact of Corporate Sustainability on Organizational Processes and Performance, Management Science, Vol. 60, No. 11, December 2014.

Edmans et al. (2017), Equity Vesting and Investment, Review of Financial Studies, Vol. 30, No. 7.

European Commission (2017), Social Scoreboard 2017, Headline Indicators: Descriptions and Highlights, European Commission.

Hunt et al. (2015), Why Diversity Matters, McKinsey & Company, January 2015.

ILO (2017), Future of Work, Inception Report for the Global Commission of the Future of Work.

I-Teams (2014), Case Study: Seoul Innovation Bureau, http://theiteams.org/case-studies/seoul-innovation-bureau, accessed 15-2-2018.

OECD (1960), Convention on the OECD.

OECD (2011), 50th Anniversary Vision Statement, The 2011 Meeting of the OECD Council at Ministerial Level, C/MIN(2011)6.

OECD (2013), Skilled for Life? Key Findings from the Survey of Adult Skills, OECD Publishing, Paris.

OECD (2014), 2014 Ministerial Council Statement Resilient Economies and Inclusive Societies – Empowering People for Jobs and Growth, C/MIN(2014)15/FINAL.

OECD (2015a), G20/OECD Principles of Corporate Governance, OECD Publishing, Paris.

OECD (2015b), OECD Innovation Strategy 2015 – An Agenda for Policy Action, C(2015)45.

OECD (2015c), Policy Framework for Investment, 2015 Edition, OECD Publishing, Paris.

OECD (2015d), Towards Green Growth? Tracking Progress, OECD Publishing, Paris.

OECD (2015e), In It Together: Why Less Inequality Benefits All, OECD Publishing, Paris.

OECD (2015f), PISA 2015 Results, OECD Publishing, Paris.

OECD (2016a), 2016 Ministerial Council Statement Enhancing Productivity for Inclusive Growth C/MIN(2016)8/FINAL.

OECD (2016b), NAEC Mainstreaming Report: Chapter 2 Mainstreaming Well-being and Resilient, Inclusive and Sustainable Growth, C/MIN(2016)4 C/MIN(2016)4.

OECD (2016c), OECD Regional Outlook 2016: Productive Regions for Inclusive Societies, OECD Publishing, Paris.

OECD (2016d), OECD Economic Surveys: Greece, OECD Publishing, Paris.

OECD (2016e), OECD Regional Outlook 2016: Productive Regions for Inclusive Societies, OECD Publishing, Paris.

OECD (2016f), 2016 Report on the OECD Guidelines for Multinational Enterprises, OECD Publishing, Paris.OECD (2017a), Ministerial Council Statement "Making Globalisation Work: Better Lives for All", C/MIN(2017)9/FINAL.

OECD (2017b), Going for Growth 2017: Chapter 2 Integrating Inclusiveness into Going for Growth, ECO/CPE/WP1(2016)30.

OECD (2017c), OECD International VAT/GST Guidelines, OECD Publishing, Paris.

OECD (2017d), OECD Skills Strategy Update, EDU/EDPC(2017)12/REV1.

OECD (2017e), The OECD Study on Measuring Distance to the SDG Targets, OECD Publishing, Paris.

OECD (2017f), OECD Economic Surveys: Japan, OECD Publishing, Paris.

OECD (2017g), OECD Economic Surveys: United Kingdom, OECD Publishing Paris.

OECD (2017h), Towards a Stronger and More Inclusive Mexico: An Assessment of Recent Policy Reforms, OECD Publishing Paris.

OECD (2017i), The Productivity-Inclusiveness Nexus, C/MIN(2016)3.

OECD (2017j), Investing in Climate, Investing in Growth, OECD Publishing, Paris.

OECD (2017k), Green Growth Indicators 2017, OECD Publishing, Paris.

OECD (2017l), Going Digital: Making the Transformation Work for Growth and Well-Being, Meeting of the OECD Council at Ministerial Level, Paris 7-8 June 2017.

OECD (2017m), Entrepreneurship at a Glance 2017, OECD Publishing, Paris.

OECD (2017n), Health at a Glance 2017, OECD Publishing, Paris.

OECD (2017o), OECD Digital Economy Outlook 2017, OECD Publishing, Paris.

OECD (2017p), A Fiscal Approach for Inclusive Growth in G7 Countries, OECD Publishing, Paris.

OECD (2017r), Report on the Implementation of the OECD Gender Recommendations, Meeting of the OECD Council at Ministerial Level, OECD Publishing, Paris.

OECD (2017s), Recommendation of the Council on Open Government, OECD Publishing, Paris.

OECD (2017t), Preventing Policy Capture: Integrity in Public Decision Making, In OECD Public Governance Reviews, OECD Publishing, Paris.

OECD (2017u), OECD Recommendation of the Council on Public Integrity, OECD Publishing, Paris.

OECD (2018a), Additional Guidance on the Attribution of Profits to a Permanent Establishment under Base Erosion and Profit Shifting (BEPS) Action 7, OECD Publishing, Paris. See http://www.oecd.org/ctp/beps-2015-final-reports.htm.

OECD (2018b), Draft Annual Report on the OECD Guidelines for Multinational Enterprises 2017, DAF/INV(2018)19/CORR1.

OECD (2018c), Embracing Innovation in Government, Global Trends 2018, OECD Publishing, Paris.

OECD (2018d), OECD Due Diligence Guidance for Responsible Business Conduct, DAF/INV(2018)17.

OECD (2018e), Standard for Automatic Exchange of Financial Account Information in Tax Matters: Implementation Handbook, OECD Publishing, Paris.

OECD (2018f), New OECD Jobs Strategy, OECD Publishing, Paris.

OECD (2018g), OECD Employment Outlook 2018, OECD Publishing, Paris.

OECD (2018h), Interim Economic Assessment: Getting Stronger, but Tensions are Rising, OECD Publishing, Paris.

OECD (2018i), Going for Growth 2018: An Opportunity that Governments Should not Miss, OECD Publishing, Paris.

OECD/G20 (2016), G20 Guiding Principles for Global Investment Policy making.

OECD/G20 (2018), Achieving Inclusive Growth in the Face of Digital Transformation and the Future of Work, OECD Report to G-20 Finance Ministers, OECD Publishing, Paris.

Annex 3.A. Main results and potential policies for growth and inclusiveness

1. Sustaining growth and equitably sharing the benefits from growth

Indicators	Key results in OECD countries
1.1 GDP per capita growth	• GDP per capita increased by 1.5% p.a over 2010-2015.
1.2 Median income growth and level	• Median income increased by 0.6% p.a over 2010-2015.
1.3 S80/20 share of income	• The ratio between the top 20% and lowest 80% income earners remained stable at 5.5 in 2015 compared to 2010.
1.4 Bottom 40% wealth share and top 10% wealth share	• The bottom 40% held on average less than 3% of total wealth; the top 10% owned a half and the richest 1% one fifth of the total wealth in 2014.
1.5 Life Expectancy	• Life expectancy increased to 81 years in 2014.
1.6 Mortality from outdoor air pollution	• Outdoor air pollution has contributed to 411 deaths per million inhabitants in 2014, up from 386 in 2010.
1.7 Relative poverty rate	• About 11% of the population were poor, with income below 50% of the median income in 2014.

Figure 3.A.1. OECD trends by indicator: Growth and ensuring equitable sharing of benefits from growth

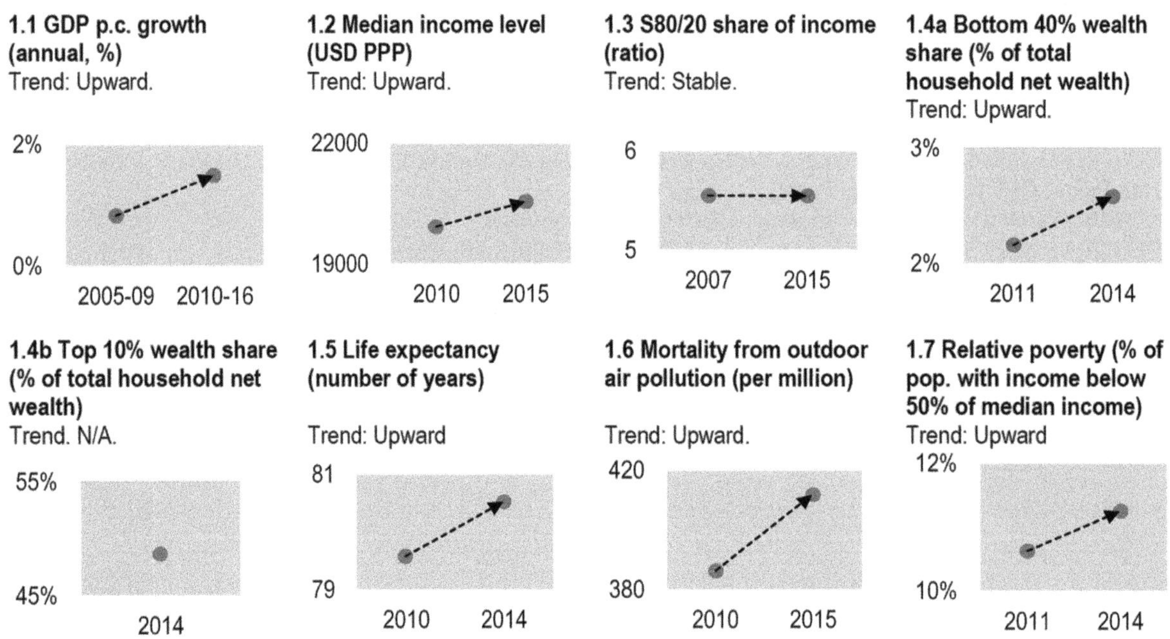

Note: OECD unweighted average is depicted by dots with trend lines, by each indicator.
Source: OECD Secretariat.

StatLink http://dx.doi.org/10.1787/888933724442

2. Supporting business dynamism and inclusive labour markets

Indicators	Key results in OECD countries
2.1 Annual labour productivity growth and level	• Annual labour productivity has increased on average by 1% over 2005-2016.
2.2 Employment-to-population ratio	• Employment-to-population increased from 65% in 2010 to 68% in 2016.
2.3 Earnings dispersion	• The top 10% of earnings were more than 3 times higher than earnings of the bottom 10% in 2014.
2.4 Female wage gap	• Women earn significantly less than men, with a 15% female wage gap in 2015.
2.5 Involuntary part-time employment	• Workers contract are unstable with 4% involuntary part-time labour in 2016.
2.6 Digital access	• Digital opportunities are not fully seized: ¼ of companies use CCS in 2016.
2.7 Share of SME loans in total business loans	• 47% of total business loans are allocated to SMEs in 2016, unchanged since 2010.

Figure 3.A.2. OECD trends by indicator: Inclusive and well-functioning markets

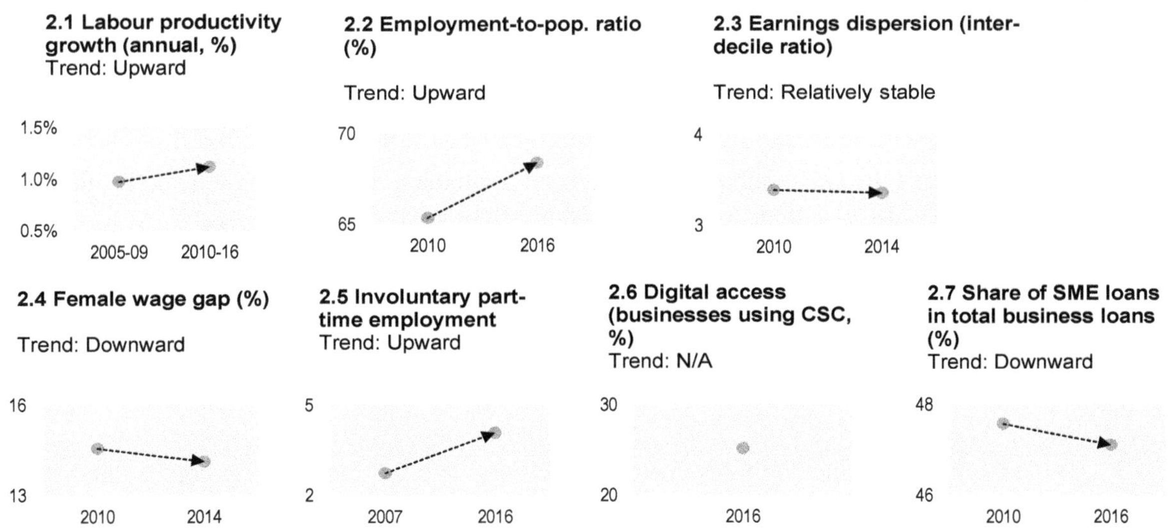

Note: OECD unweighted average is depicted by dots with trend lines, by each indicator.
Source: OECD Secretariat.

StatLink http://dx.doi.org/10.1787/888933724461

Potential policies for growth and inclusiveness

Structural and regulatory policies

- Improve the business environment and facilitate entrepreneurship.
- Facilitate reallocation of workers and capital and allow easy transitions to new jobs for workers that have been made redundant.
- Strengthen competition.
- Promote organisational change and diffusion of technologies.

- Incentivise businesses and governments to invest in new business and governance models.

Labour market policies and employment protection

- Strengthen and better coordinate social dialogue and collective bargaining.
- Adapt and design labour market institutions and social protection systems for emerging forms of work; link entitlements to individuals rather than jobs, make them portable.
- Stimulate job mobility and opportunities for placement and retention of quality jobs.
- Foster employment protection legislation with predictable contract termination costs, not to differentiate in job security across contracts and protect workers against possible abuses.
- Consider new policy approaches, such as individual accounts, universal basic income programmes, and new technological tools that enable better service delivery, administration, identification of needs, and encourage labour mobility.

Taxes and transfers

- Reinforce the redistributive capacity of the tax and benefit systems.
- Strengthen the design of tax policies to ensure inclusive growth and deliver sustainable revenues; for example through their impact on labour market participation, skills development and use, savings behaviours and business dynamism.
- Apply the OECD Guidelines for MNEs and implement the Base Erosion and Profit Shifting (BEPS) actions to level the playing field internationally.
- Shift part of the financing of social programmes to general tax revenue to raise labour market participation, reduce labour market duality and boost labour productivity and economic growth, while at the same time extending support to a larger fraction of society and atypical jobs.

Data exchange, trade and competition policy enforcement

- Enact open trade well-designed product and labour market regulations, and insolvency regimes that do not inhibit corporate restructuring and penalise entrepreneurial failure.
- Promote regulatory policies that improve the business environment for SMEs and entrepreneurship.
- Strengthen fair (cross-border) competition and promote entrepreneurship policies that provide opportunities to all to access the labour market as entrepreneurs.
- Address data access, security and use by individuals and firms.

Territorial policies

- Promote regional infrastructure policies that facilitate innovation diffusion across regions; with housing and land use policies that facilitate resource reallocation within and across regions.

Policies supporting a low-carbon and resource-efficient economy

- Align policies beyond climate policy mechanisms to create new markets and jobs.

3. Investing in people and places left behind, providing equal opportunities

Indicators	Key results in OECD countries
3.1 Variation in science performance explained by students' socio-economic status	• 13% of variation in students' science performance was due to their socio-economic status in 2015.
3.2 Correlation of earnings outcomes across generations	• Limited intergenerational mobility: 38% of earnings explained by parent's situation in 2014.
3.3 Childcare enrolment rate	• 1/3 of children enrolled in childcare in 2014.
3.4 Young people neither in employment nor in education & training (NEET)	• In 2016, 15% of the OECD population aged 18-24 NEET.
3.5 Share of adults who score below Level 1 in both literacy and numeracy	• 1/4 of adults performed badly in literacy and/ or numeracy in 2015.
3.6 Regional life expectancy gap	
3.7 Resilient students	• 29% of resilient students among disadvantaged students in 2015.

Figure 3.A.3. OECD trends by indicator: Equal opportunities and foundations of future prosperity

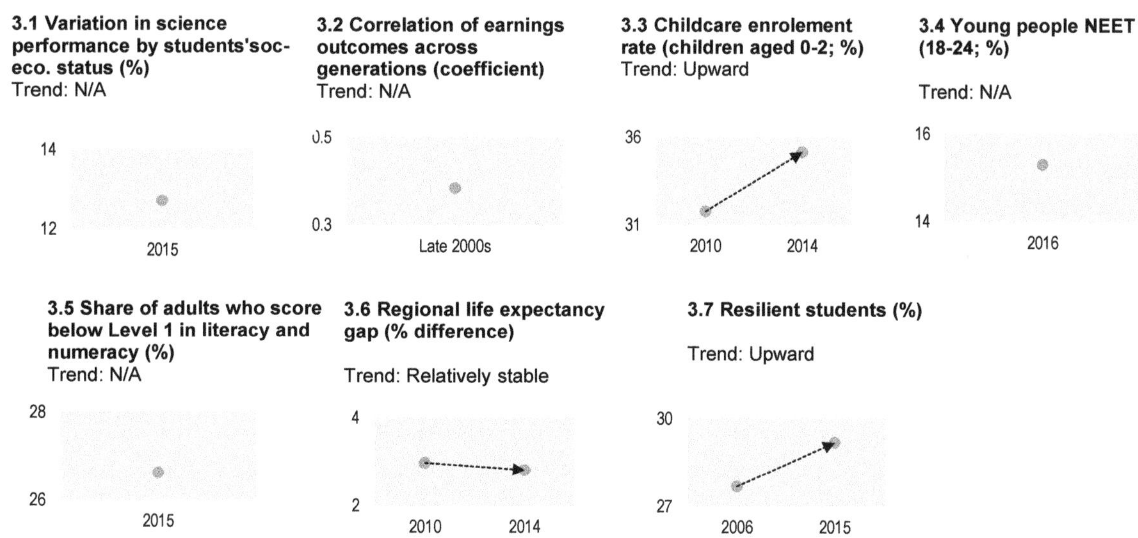

Note: OECD unweighted average is depicted by dots with trend lines, by each indicator.
Source: OECD Secretariat.

StatLink http://dx.doi.org/10.1787/888933724480

Potential policies for growth and inclusiveness

Education and skills policies

- Develop an integrated skills system, covering vocation and tertiary education policies to improve workers' competencies (e.g. through expanded apprenticeship programs), promote increased labour force participation (e.g. by designing social welfare programs that encourage work) and provide adult education, job training and career guidance.

- Implement high-quality initial education and training systems from early childhood through school and beyond.
- Adapt social protection systems to provide high levels of non-routing cognitive skills, problem solving creativity and strong socio-emotional skills.
- Adapt social protection systems to the individualisation and diversification of work in the future.
- Improve the capacity of public authorities and other relevant stakeholders to develop and implement financial literacy and consumer protection measures; also for digitally delivered financial products and services.
- Enable access to all for the best possible start in the labour market by providing them with strong basic skills, socio-emotional skills and specific skills required by employers.
- Support girls' and women's participation in STEM (science, technology, engineering and maths) as an aspect of creating foundations for new types of work.

Labour market policies

- Coordinate labour and product market polices and regulations to lower barriers to mobility of labour and reducing discrimination.
- This requires actions in range of areas: giving all children equal opportunities through health, education and family policies; giving youth a right start in the labour market; ensuring access to lifelong learning, especially for the least skilled; promoting career mobility; helping people back to work when needed; support through the tax and benefit systems; and reducing spatial segregation, improving housing support and transport.

Health policies

- Develop a strategy to address the wide range of social determinants of health inequalities; expand health spending allocated to prevention targeted at key risk factors and population groups; especially for children.

Investment policies

- Stimulate investment in social capital (e.g. volunteering) and incentivise private investments in public goods (social housing, educational policies that promote diversity, cultural policies).
- Invest in disadvantaged schools.
- Improve provision of reliable, safe and sustainable transportation and care services to facilitate access to good schools and reduce exposure to risks (crime, accidents, health, and pollution).
- Step up investment in low-emission technologies and smart and clean infrastructure.
- Invest in high quality local administration in line with the national inclusive growth agenda to encourage action by local communities to create a common purpose for the society (e.g. by fostering the connectedness of people and increasing the "civic sense" as well as equal access to key public services and amenities; such as health, education, nutrition, utility services (e.g. water, energy and transport) and access to nature and green areas.

Taxes and transfers

- Adapt the tax system to encourage skills development and use for all types of students and workers, men and women and young and older workers; as for example, gender gaps are intrinsically linked to educational, family, tax and benefit and retirement policies.
- Break the links between socio-economic disadvantages and health status.

Territorial policies

- Develop regional economic development policies that build economic potential in lagging regions, with regional infrastructure policies, transport, housing and land use policies that facilitate resource reallocation within and across regions.

4. Building efficient and responsive governments

Indicators	Key results in OECD countries
4.1 Confidence in government	• Less than 50% trusted the government in 2016.
4.2 Voter turnout	• About 70% cast their ballots in the latest election.
4.3 Female participation in politics	• No gender parity in politics and institutions, below one third in total in 2017.

Figure 3.A.4. OECD trends by indicator: Governance

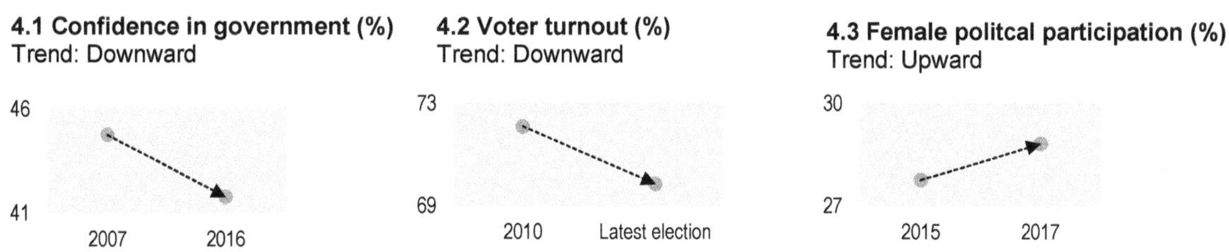

Note: OECD unweighted average is depicted by dots with trend lines, by each indicator.
Source: OECD Secretariat.

StatLink http://dx.doi.org/10.1787/888933724499

Potential policies for growth and inclusiveness

- Coordinate and align action to strengthen institutional frameworks for diversity and gender mainstreaming and budgeting.
- Ensure that public policy-making is protected from undue influence, where a public decision is captured by a narrow interest group to reflect its own interest.
- Strengthen stakeholder engagement to implement policies, standards and projects that are closer to the broader public interest.
- Improve budget transparency, government reliability and the capacity of reaction to adverse events as well as responsiveness and openness to citizen input.

- Provide citizens with the data, resources and information to allow them to make informed decisions about their own lives, professional development and public participation.
- Consider a citizen-driven approach to make data more open and useful for collaboration with and among citizens in light of their rights and obligations.
- Evaluate the transaction costs and accountability of citizen-state interactions in the advent of increasingly personalised services and use of social media.
- Map, understand and integrate citizens' behaviour, demands and needs in the design and delivery of public service strategies in light of digitalisation and open government principles; improve public procurement systems (including e-procurement).
- Empower the role of state to promote cultural aspects of education beyond the classrooms and support active participation of citizens, while enabling youth engagement strategies.

Annex 3.B. Definition of indicators by inclusive growth dashboard categories

Growth and ensuring equitable sharing of benefits from growth

Data sources used are: Income Distribution and Poverty Database; OECD Wealth Distribution Database; OECD Regional Well-Being Database; OECD Health Status Database; OECD Productivity Database; OECD Green Growth Indicators. The analysis is informed by the following but non-exhaustive OECD policy work: policy recommendations from the OECD Jobs Strategy; OECD Job Quality; OECD Skills; OECD Regional Development Policy. The indicators are:

- GDP per capita growth is a measure of a country's economic output that accounts for its number of people. It divides the country's gross domestic product by its total population, available for all OECD countries until 2016.
- Median income refers to the real median household disposable income in dollars PPP, available until 2014 for all OECD countries.
- Income gap refers to the ratio of the top and bottom quintile household income share, available until 2014 for 17 OECD countries.
- The bottom 40% and the top 10% wealth shares capture inequality at the bottom and the top of the wealth distribution. Wealth gap refers to the wealth share of the bottom 40% of the population, available until 2014 for 18 OECD countries. Household net wealth includes financial and non-financial assets and liabilities.
- Life expectancy at birth captures the overall health outcomes and represents one of the core indicators of the human capital and citizens preferences. Life expectancy refers to the life expectancy at birth, available until 2015 for all OECD countries.
- The mortality from outdoor air pollution measures the number of deaths per million inhabitants associated with people's exposure to air pollution (i.e. $PM_{2.5}$), available until 2015 for all OECD countries.
- Poverty rate corresponds to the share of households with equivalised disposable income after taxes and transfers below 50% of the median disposable income. Available until 2014 for 34 OECD countries.

Inclusive and well-functioning markets

Data sources used are: OECD Productivity Statistics; OECD Labour Force Statistics database; OECD Employment Database (with EU-SILC and national statistical sources); OECD Education at a Glance; OECD Financing Entrepreneurs and SMEs 2018. The analysis is informed by the following but non-exhaustive OECD standards and policy work: OECD Productivity-Inclusiveness Nexus; OECD Innovation Strategy; OECD Going for Growth; OECD Going Digital; OECD Tax Policies for Inclusive Growth; BEPS; OECD Guidelines for MNEs, including Responsible Business Conduct; OECD Policy Framework for Investment; OECD Base Erosion and Profit Shifting; OECD Policy Guidance on Circular Economy; OECD Green Growth Strategy. The indicators are:

- Labour productivity refers to the productivity level at USD constant PPP 2010, available until 2015 for all OECD countries;

- Employment-to-population ratio provides information on the ability of an economy to create jobs, available until 2015 for all OECD countries.
- Earnings dispersion refers to the ratio of the earnings top and bottom deciles, available until 2014 for all OECD countries.
- Female wage gap refers to the difference between male and female median wages, available until 2014 for 32 OECD countries.
- Involuntary part-time employment refers to part-time workers who could not find full-time work, for persons aged 15 and over in percentage of total employment, available until 2016 for 31 OECD countries.
- Companies' digital access is proxied by the share of companies using cloud computing services.
- The share of SME loans refers to the share of total business loans allocated to SMEs.

Opportunities and foundations of future prosperity

Data sources used are: OECD PISA; GSOEP (complemented by national statistical sources); OECD Dataset on Transition from School to Work; OECD PIAAC; OECD Regional Well-Being. The analysis is informed by the following but non-exhaustive OECD standards and policy work: OECD Skills Strategy; OECD Education; OECD Health. The indicators are:

- Student performance and status refers to the percentage of variation in science performance explained by students' socio-economic status, available until 2015 for 28 OECD countries.
- Earnings persistence refers to inter-generational earnings elasticities in the late 2000s.
- Child care enrolment refers to child care enrolment rate (children aged 0-2), available until 2014 for 33 OECD countries.
- Inactive young refers to the share of young (NEET) aged 18 to 24 years old neither in employment nor in education and training, available until 2016 for 32 OECD countries.
- The share of adults who score below Level 1 in both literacy and numeracy, available until 2015 for 28 OECD countries.
- Regional life expectancy gap refers to the regional life expectancy gap between the top and bottom 10% regions by population, available until 2015 for 29 OECD countries.
- Resilient students refers to the share of student in the bottom quarter of the PISA index of economic, social and cultural status (ESCS) in the country/economy of assessment that performs in the top quarter of students among all countries/economies, after accounting for socio-economic status. Available in 2006 and 2015.

Governance

Data sources used are: OECD Regulatory Policy Committee; Institute for Democracy and electoral assistance (IDea) Global Database of Quotas for Women: Inter - Parliamentary Union and Un Women's "Women in Politics" database; OECD calculations based on voter turnout data from the International Institute for Democracy and Electoral Assistance (IDEA). The analysis is informed by the following but non-exhaustive OECD standards and policy work: OECD Open Government Initiative; OECD Digital Government Toolkit; OECD Recommendation of the Council on Public Integrity [C(2017)5]; OECD Recommendation of the Council on Public Procurement [C(2015)2]; OECD Automatic Exchange of Information; OECD Recommendation of the Council on the Governance of Critical Risks [C/MIN(2014)8/FINAL]; OECD Recommendation on Gender Equality in Public Life [C(2015)164].[3] The indicators are:

- The level of confidence over the government, available until 2016 for all OECD countries.
- Voter turnout refers to the last election turnout rate, available until 2014.
- Gender participation refers to the share of women parliamentarians and legislated gender quota, available until 2017 for all OECD countries.

End notes

3 In the tax area, there are two OECD recommendations currently in force: Recommendation of the Council on the Use of the OECD Model Memorandum of Understanding on Automatic Exchange of Information for Tax Purposes [C(2001)28/FINAL] and Recommendation of the Council on the Standard for Automatic Exchange of Financial Account Information in Tax Matters [C(2014)81/FINAL] as well as Declaration on Automatic Exchange of Information in Tax Matters. There is also the Convention on Mutual Administrative Assistance in Tax Matters (MAAC) negotiated at and administered by the OECD; as well as the Multilateral Competent Authority Agreement on Automatic Exchange of Financial Account Information (MCAA CRS) and the Multilateral Competent Authority Agreement on the Exchange of Country-by-Country Reports (MCAA CbC).

Part II. Analysis underpinning the Framework for Policy Action on Inclusive Growth

Chapter 1. Sustain growth that benefits all

The upswing in the global economic outlook creates opportunities to make economic growth beneficial to all. This chapter charts the outcomes of growth for people to understand better whether economic growth is being translated into rising living standards across different groups of population in terms of income, gender, age and region of residence.

Despite recent improvements in some countries, more progress is needed to transform productivity gains and job creation into increased living standards for all. Income and wealth inequality remains at high levels in some OECD countries and the spread is growing. The bottom of the distribution remains at high risk of falling further behind, while the top 1% are pulling further ahead. Gaps emerge and are growing in other areas too. These trends are also prevalent across regions and indeed, age-groups, which is of particular concern given ageing societies, principally in developed countries.

Responding to these challenges requires an emphasis on policies that put inclusive growth at the centre, with an emphasis on: product and labour market policies and educational policies that are key for equitably sharing productivity gains; fair and efficient redistribution systems; ensuring the finance sector works for everyone in society; promoting regional catching up, and providing youth with a strong start to their educational and working lives.

Charting growth outcomes for people

Trends in median income and inequalities of income and wealth

Real median income has stagnated. Real median household disposable income remains at or below pre-crisis levels in many OECD countries, despite a recent recovery in most OECD countries. During 2007-2010, median disposable incomes decreased by an average of 1.3% in OECD countries (Figure 1.1), although countries faced uneven patterns over this period. In recent years, real median disposable incomes increased by an average 3.5% in the OECD area but continue to remain below 2007 levels in Greece, Spain, Iceland and Mexico. Even in the countries where real median disposable incomes have been on a positive trend in recent years; those improvements often fell short of GDP per capita trends (Figure 1.2). This suggests that the benefits of recent economic recovery have not been shared equally in terms of income distribution. However, the measurement of household's income distribution raises important issues. In particular, more work is needed to integrate survey-based data with tax record-based data to improve the measurement of income and income inequality.

Figure 1.1 Growth in real median disposable income

OECD countries, 2007-2016 or latest, %

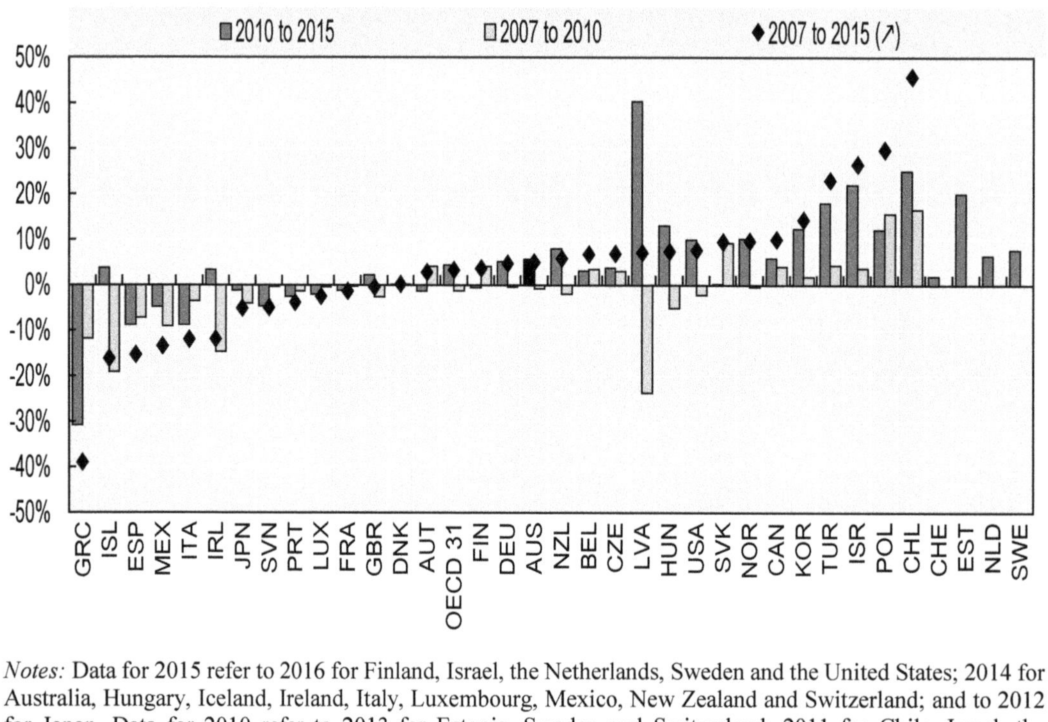

Notes: Data for 2015 refer to 2016 for Finland, Israel, the Netherlands, Sweden and the United States; 2014 for Australia, Hungary, Iceland, Ireland, Italy, Luxembourg, Mexico, New Zealand and Switzerland; and to 2012 for Japan. Data for 2010 refer to 2013 for Estonia, Sweden and Switzerland; 2011 for Chile, Israel, the Netherlands, New Zealand, and Turkey; and to 2009 for Hungary, and Japan. Data for 2007 refer to 2008 for Germany, Australia, Chile, France, Norway, Israel, and Mexico; and to 2009 for Switzerland. 2016 data for the Netherlands are provisional. The OECD average excludes Estonia, the Netherlands, Sweden and Switzerland due to a break in the time series for these countries.
Source: OECD Income Distribution Database, OECD National Accounts database.

StatLink http://dx.doi.org/10.1787/888933724518

Figure 1.2 Growth in GDP per capita and real median disposable income

OECD countries, 2010-2016 or latest, %

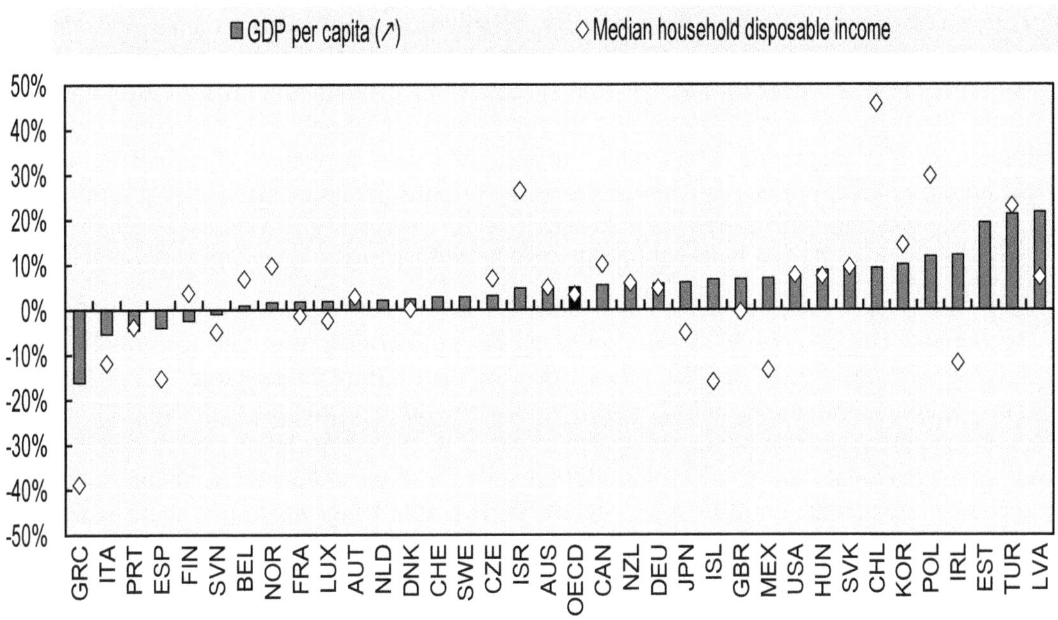

Notes: Median disposable income data for 2015 refer to 2016 for Finland, Israel, the Netherlands, Sweden and the United States; 2014 for Australia, Hungary, Iceland, Ireland, Italy, Luxembourg, Mexico, New Zealand and Switzerland; and to 2012 for Japan. Data for 2007 refer to 2008 for Germany, Australia, Chile, France, Norway, Israel, and Mexico; and to 2009 for Switzerland. 2016 median disposable income data for the Netherlands are provisional. The OECD median disposable income average excludes Estonia, the Netherlands, Sweden and Switzerland due to a break in the time series for these countries.
Source: OECD Income Distribution Database, OECD National Accounts database.

StatLink http://dx.doi.org/10.1787/888933724537

Labour productivity improvements have not led to significant improvements in wages. Aggregate labour productivity growth has decoupled from real median compensation growth in most OECD countries over the last two decades. In the long run, raising productivity is critical to improving living standards as real wages are the most direct and most important mechanism through which the benefits of productivity growth are transferred to workers. In the last couple of decades, however, this mechanism has proved particularly weak (Figure 1.3A). Decoupling of real median wages from labour productivity can be explained by declines in labour income shares and declines in the ratio of median to average wages. Excluding sectors which are driven by changes in commodity and housing prices (primary and real-estate sectors) and reflect imputations in the national accounts (non-market sectors) only marginally decreases the contribution of lower labour income shares to decoupling (Figure 1.3B).[4]

Box 1.1. OECD and national initiatives for improving the measurement of the income distribution

The measurement of household's income distribution from survey data raises three important issues: i) there is a discrepancy between household disposable income as measured from household surveys (micro data) and through the lens of Systems of National Accounts (macro data); ii) the measurement of income inequality can be improved by integrating household surveys and administrative data; iii) due to differences in local prices, income imperfectly proxies the concept of living standards, and complementary measures such as consumption inequality can be useful. This box describes the OECD and national initiatives that address these three issues.

The OECD and Eurostat launched a joint Expert Group on Disparities in National Accounts (EG DNA) in 2011 - followed up by an OECD Expert Group in 2014 - to develop a methodology for the compilation of distributional measures of household income, consumption and saving within the framework of National Accounts. National accounts data are taken as a starting point, while micro information from surveys and administrative data are used for breaking down the household sector of the national accounts into income quintiles and other socio-demographic groups, such as those based on main source of income or household type. So far, the expert group has engaged in two exercises to compile experimental distributional results on the basis of the methodology as developed by the group, one of which has been finalised in 2012 (Fesseau and Mattonetti, 2013) and the other one in 2015 (Zwijnenburg et al., 2017).

While several countries (e.g. Australia, Canada, the Netherlands and the United Kingdom) have already started publishing distributional results on the basis of this methodology, the expert group is further improving the methodology to broaden country coverage and to improve the timeliness of the results. Furthermore, EG DNA also develops a methodology for the compilation of the distribution of household wealth in order to obtain a comprehensive overview of distributional results for the household sector. Looking at the results of the exercises, EG DNA shows that inequality in consumption is indeed lower than on the basis of income, probably related to smoothing of individual consumption over time as explained by the life-cycle hypothesis and the permanent income hypothesis. This also explains some of the negative savings results for specific household groups as obtained in the exercise.

The measurement of income inequality can be improved by linking several databases. Household surveys have a number of limitations when it comes to the representation of both the very top and bottom of the income distribution. These include issues related to sampling (under-representation of the very rich), data collection (under- or non-reporting of different forms of income including investment income and social transfers, survey non-response and other measurement errors), and data preparation (top coding trimming or censoring, provision of subsamples). For the estimation of income inequality, having good data on both top incomes and those at the bottom of the distribution is crucial. Data from tax files are well suited to capture the incomes of the very rich, although they are not without limitations.

First, many countries face problems of tax evasion and tax avoidance, leading to the under-declaration of income. Second, tax-exempt income, such as fringe benefits or imputed rent, is left out of analysis based on tax data (e.g. if a growing share of capital income is tax exempt or subject to a withholding tax, this can affect the analysis of top income shares). Third, tax-return data may provide an accurate picture for top incomes but remain mute about how top incomes fit into the overall distribution. Similarly, administrative data can potentially provide more accurate and complete information on social transfers provided by the state than can be obtained from household surveys, but on their capacity to tell us anything about the distribution of income on their own is limited. For these reasons, there is increasing interest in the potential to combine both survey and administrative data to produce income inequality estimates, thereby drawing on the strengths of each source, rather than relying on either on their own. The extent to which statistical compilers are able to do this depends on a number of factors, in particular the national legislative environment with respect to access to and linking administrative records.

However, even where access to record-level administrative data is not possible, statistical compilers can supplement survey data. For example in the UK, survey data are treated with a 'SPI adjustment', which involves replacing income values for 'very rich' individuals in the survey by the mean income of a corresponding group of individuals obtained from tax data, as well as recalibrating the survey weights (DWP, 2017). This approach has been built upon in a number of recent academic papers (e.g. Burkhauser et al., 2018). Where national legislation allows, more ambitious approaches may be possible. For example, facilitated by recent UK legislation (Digital Economy Act, 2017), UK statisticians are now working to move beyond the approach described above, to develop data on the distributions of income, consumption and wealth based on linked survey and non-survey sources (including tax and other administrative records). Under this approach non-survey data will not only be used to replace some information currently collected by survey, but also to improve survey sampling, imputation and weighting, thereby improving both the representation and precision of the tails of the distribution and as a consequence, the estimation of inequality. Linking tax record data to a survey data set can on the one hand improve cross-national comparisons of the US and UK in the top income literature by comparing like-to-like in terms of sharing unit and unit of analysis and on the other hand improve UK measures of income inequality in the survey based literature based on the entire income distribution.

Standard economic theory suggests that living standards are better reflected through consumption than income (Blundell and Preston, 1998). Individuals are better able to smooth consumption rather than income over their lifetimes, making consumption a more informative indicator of current and lifetime well-being. Unlike income, consumption remains relatively steady throughout life since individuals can borrow during years with low income and save in high-income years (Hassett and Mathur, 2012). Despite this conceptual case for studying consumption data, household well-being indicators (such as poverty and inequality measures) are typically based on income rather than consumption. This is partly due to a widespread presumption that household income is easier to measure than expenditure, at least in OECD countries (Browning, Crossley and Winter, 2014).

Findings about trends in consumption inequality are significantly influenced by methodological issues. Early studies based on the US Consumer Expenditure Survey (CEX) found that consumption inequality had grown more modestly than income inequality (Krueger and Perri, 2006; Slesnick, 1994; Hassett and Mathur, 2012). More recently, studies correcting for measurement problems afflicting the CEX, using alternative data sources, or measuring consumption in alternative ways, have found that consumption inequality (particularly in nondurables and services) has increased more and tracked the rise in income inequality (Aguiar and Bils, 2015; Attanasio and Pistaferri, 2016). An emerging literature is also creating consumption-based poverty measures (Meyer and Sullivan 2013, Meyer et al., 2015), which find distinct patterns for income and consumption inequality. For example, studies have tended to find that consumption inequality has risen less than income inequality in recent decades (Krueger and Perri 2006; Meyer and Sullivan 2013), some studies find that the rise has been fairly similar (Attanasio, Hurst, and Pistaferri 2012).

Furthermore, Larrimore et al. (2016) make an effort to link additional administrative records and survey data to unit record tax data to address the issue of tax record data's inability to capture non-taxable income. This paper is among the first using tax record data as a base to make clear that "taxable realized capital gains" as used in most studies based on tax record data alone produce results that are quite different from those using "accrued capital gains" with these same tax record data. As Larrimore et al. (2017) point out, this issue is not entirely solved by Piketty, Saez, and Zucman (2018), which attempts to address some of these same issues within a National Accounts framework. There are increasing calls for improving existing survey data or complementing them with newly collected survey data. Technological change has moreover opened up new possibilities for the collection of consumer expenditure data, such as from credit card companies or handheld scanners (Browning, Crossley and Winter, 2014; Pistaferri, 2015). Currently, the OECD is collecting and analysing consumption expenditure data from several countries in order to study the consumption patterns of the middle class.

Sources: Aguiar, M. and M. Bils (2015), "Has Consumption Inequality Mirrored Income Inequality?", American Economic Review, Vol. 105/9, pp. 2725-2756, http://dx.doi.org/10.1257/aer.20120599; Attanasio, O. and L. Pistaferri (2016), "Consumption Inequality", Journal of Economic Perspectives—Volume, Vol. 30/2, pp. 2016-3, http://dx.doi.org/10.1257/jep.30.2.3; Attanasio, O., E. Hurst, and L. Pistaferri (2012), "The Evolution of Income, Consumption, and Leisure Inequality in The US, 1980-2010." National Bureau of Economic Research Working Paper 17982.; Blundell, R. and I. Preston (1998), "Consumption Inequality and Income Uncertainty*", The Quarterly Journal of Economics, Vol. 113/2, pp. 603-640https://doi.org/10.1162/003355398555694.; Browning, M., T. Crossley and J. Winter (2014), "The Measurement of Household Consumption Expenditures", Annual Review of Economics, Vol. 6/1, pp. 475-501, http://dx.doi.org/10.1146/annurev-economics-080213-041247.; Burkhauser R.V., N. Hérault, S.P. Jenkins and R. Wilkins (2018), "Survey under-coverage of top incomes and estimation of inequality: what is the role of the UK's SPI adjustment?", Fiscal Studies , Vol. 00, No. 0, pp. 1-28.; Digital Economy Act, 2017 – Available at: http://www.legislation.gov.uk/ukpga/2017/30/contents/enacted; DWP (2017) - Households Below Average Income (HBAI): quality and methodology information report, 2015/16; Fesseau, M. and M. Mattonetti (2013), "Distributional Measures across Household Groups in a National Accounts Framework: Results from an Experimental Cross-country Exercise on Household Income, Consumption and Saving", OECD Statistics Working Papers, No. 2013/04, OECD Publishing, Paris.; Hassett, K. and A. Mathur (2012), "A New Measure of Consumption Inequality", AEI Economic Studies, https://www.aei.org/wp-content/uploads/2012/06/-a-new-measure-of-consumption-inequality_142931647663.pdf (accessed on 22 February 2018).; Krueger, D. and F. Perri (2006), "Does Income Inequality Lead to Consumption Inequality? Evidence and Theory1", Review of Economic Studies, Vol. 73/1, pp. 163-193.; Meyer, B., A. Bee and J. X. Sullivan (2013), "Consumption and Income Inequality and the Great Recession", American Economic Review, Papers and Proceedings, May 2013, 178-183.; Meyer, B., A. Bee and J. X. Sullivan (2015), "The Validity of Consumption Data: Are the Consumer Expenditure Interview and Diary Surveys Informative?" in Improving the Measurement of Consumer Expenditures, Christopher Carroll, Thomas Crossley, and John Sabelhaus, editors. University of Chicago Press, 2015, 204-240.; Piketty, T., E. Saez and G. Zucman (2018), Distributional National Accounts: Methods and Estimates for the United States, Quarterly Journal of Economics, 2018, 133(2): 553-609.; Pistaferri, L. (2015), "Household consumption: Research questions, measurement issues, and data collection strategies", Journal of Economic and Social Measurement, Vol. 40/1-4, pp. 123-149.; Slesnick, D. (1994), "Consumption, Needs and Inequality", International Economic Review, Vol. 35/3, pp. 677-703.; Zwijnenburg, J., S. Bournot and F. Giovannelli (2017), "Expert Group on Disparities in a National Accounts Framework: Results from the 2015 Exercise", OECD Statistics Working Papers, No. 2016/10, OECD Publishing, Paris.

Figure 1.3 Decoupling between labour productivity and wages

OECD countries, 1995-2013, Index 100=1995

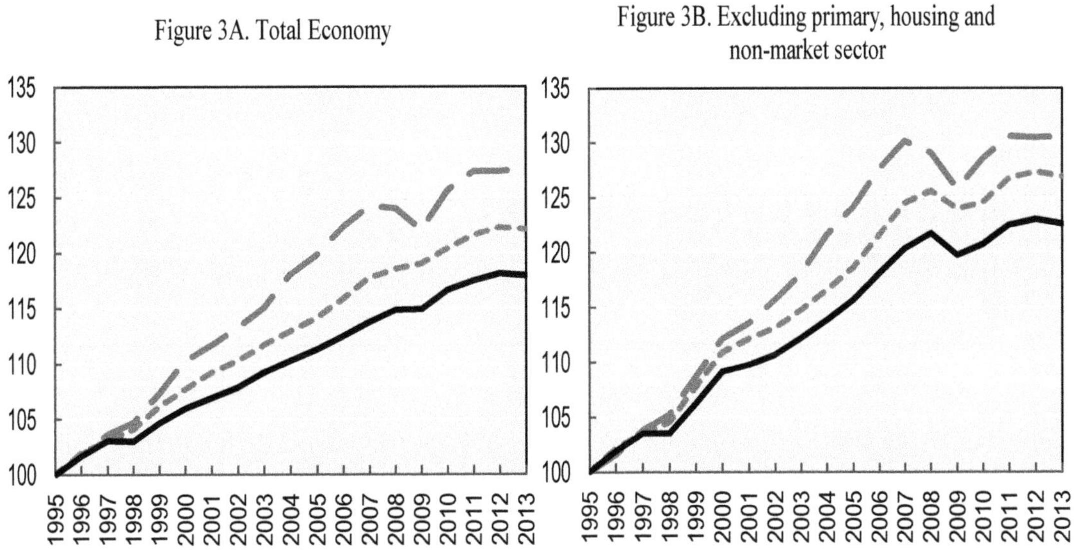

Note: The trends reflect the declines in labour income shares and increases in wage inequality. Macro-level decoupling between compensation growth of the typical worker and labour productivity growth can be decomposed into (1) the growth differential between average labour compensation and labour productivity, which is fully accounted for by evolutions in the labour income share, and (2) the growth differential between median and average wages, which is a partial measure of wage inequality (Panel A). Unweighted average of 24 OECD countries; 1995-2013 for Austria, Belgium, Germany, Finland, Hungary, Japan, Korea, United Kingdom; 1995-2012 for Australia, Spain, France, Italy, Poland, Sweden; 1996-2013 for Czech Republic, Denmark; 1997-2012 for Canada, New Zealand; 1997-2013 for Norway, US; 1998-2013 for Ireland; 1995-2010 for Netherlands; 2001-2011 for Israel; 2002-2013 for Slovak Republic. In Panel A, all series are deflated by the total economy value added price index. In Panel B, all series are deflated by the value added price index excluding the primary, housing and non-market sectors. The sectors excluded in panel B are the following (ISIC rev. 4 classification): (1) Agriculture, Forestry and Fishing (A), (2) Mining and quarrying (B), (3) Real estate activities (L), (4) Public administration and defence, compulsory social security (O), (5) Education (P), (6) Human health and social work activities (Q), (7) Activities of households as employers (T), and (8) Activities of extraterritorial organisations and bodies (U). "Wage inequality" refers to total economy due to data limitations.

Source: OECD National Accounts Database, OECD Earnings Database, Schwellnus et al. (2017).

StatLink http://dx.doi.org/10.1787/888933724556

Labour shares have declined in most OECD countries, while the ratio between median to average wages has decreased in all but two. Labour share developments have been very heterogeneous across OECD countries, but around two-thirds saw a decline (Figure 1.4). Most of the decline occurred prior to the crisis, while in the immediate aftermath the labour shares picked up (partly reflecting the business cycle). However, in the most recent years the labour shares have broadly stabilised with large differences across countries depicted by first and third quartiles of countries (Figure 1.5).

Figure 1.4 Labour income share evolutions

OECD countries, 1995-2014, % points

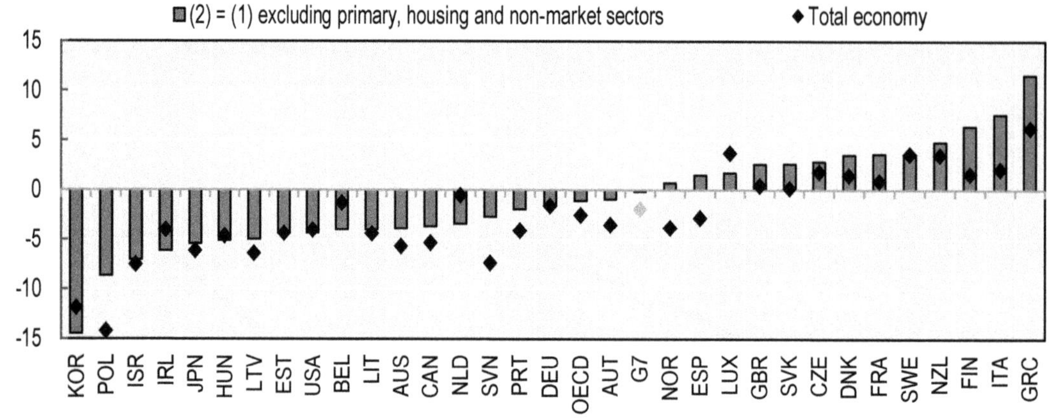

Note: Three-year averages starting and ending in indicated years. OECD and G7 refer to un-weighted averages for the relevant countries included in the Figure; 1995-2013 for Australia, France, Korea and Portugal; 1995-2012 for New Zealand; 1997-2012 for Canada; 1997-2014 for United Kingdom; 1998-2014 for Ireland and US. Increases in wage inequality have contributed to aggregate decoupling by reducing the ratio of median to average wages in a wide range of OECD countries. The average decline in the ratio of median to average wages was around 2 percentage points over the period 1995-2014, but for a number of countries, including the Czech Republic, Hungary, Korea, New Zealand Poland and the US, declines in this ratio were significantly more pronounced. Only Chile, Italy and Spain bucked the trend of increasing wage inequality. These results derive from the OECD Earnings Database; available for 23 OECD countries.
Source: OECD National Accounts Database, Schwellnus *et al.* (2017).

StatLink http://dx.doi.org/10.1787/888933724575

Figure 1.5 Trends in labour income share evolutions

Unweighted average of 31 OECD countries, % points

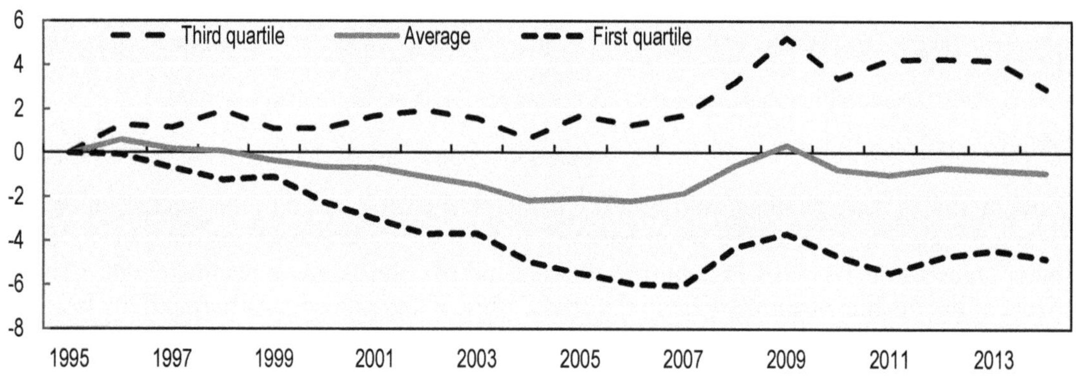

Note: 1995-2014 for Austria, Belgium, Czech Republic, Germany, Denmark, Spain, Estonia, Finland, France, United Kingdome, Greece, Hungary, Israel, Italy, Japan, Lithuania, Latvia, Luxembourg, Netherlands, Norway, Poland, Portugal, Slovakia, Slovenia and Sweden; 1995-2012 for New Zealand; 1995-2013 for Australia and Korea; 1997-2012 for Canada; 1998-2014 for Ireland and US. Labour income share evolutions are presented in OECD average, first and third quartiles that refer to groups of 31 OECD countries to show dispersion across countries.
Source: OECD National Accounts Database.

StatLink http://dx.doi.org/10.1787/888933724594

The decline in the ratio of median to average wages is driven by high wage growth of top earners. The increase in wage inequality as measured by the decoupling between median from average wage growth reflects disproportionate wage growth at the very top of the wage distribution. This is supported by Alvaredo et al. (2016) that show that the most striking development over the past two decades has been the divergence of wages of the top 1% of income earners from both the median and the 90th percentile (Figure 1.6; Figure 1.7).

Figure 1.6 The ratio of median to average wages has declined

OECD countries, 1995-2013, % points

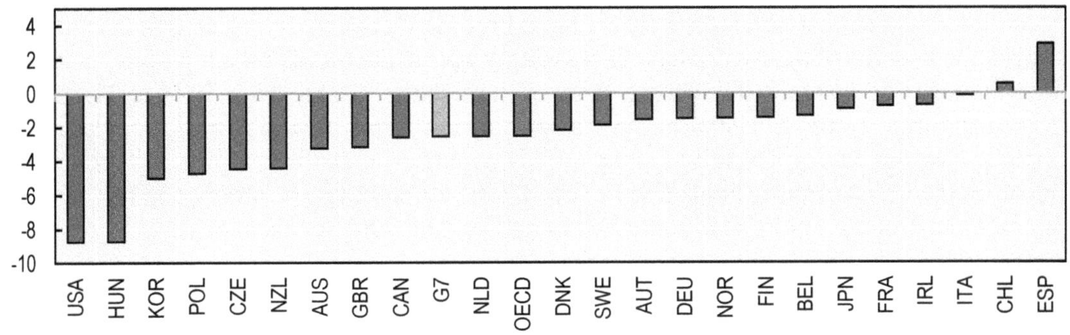

Note: Three-year averages starting and ending in indicated years. OECD and G7 refer to unweighted averages for the relevant countries included in the Figure. 1996-2013 for Chile, Czech Republic, Denmark; 1995-2012 for Australia, Spain, France, Italy, Poland, Sweden; 1997-2013 for Norway, New Zealand; 1998-2013 for Canada; 1995-2010 for Netherlands.
Source: OECD Earnings Database, Schwellnus et al. (2017).

StatLink http://dx.doi.org/10.1787/888933724613

Figure 1.7 Wages of top income earners diverged from the average and median

Unweighted OECD average of 9 countries, 1995-2011, Index 1995=100

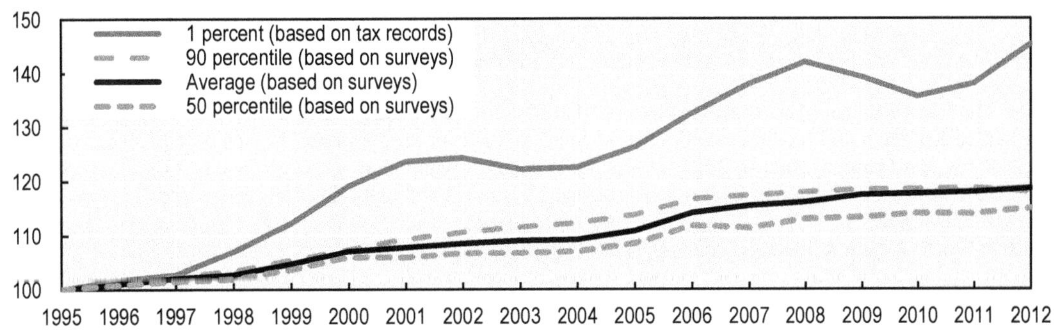

Note: Indices based on unweighted average for nine OECD countries: Australia (1995-2010), Canada (1997-2000), Spain (1995-2012), France (1995-2006), Italy (1995-2009), Japan (1995-2010), Korea (1997-2012), Netherlands (1995-1999) and US (1995-2012), for which data on wages of the top 1% of income earners are available. All series are deflated by the same total economy value added price index.
Source: OECD Earnings Database, Alvaredo et al. (2016), Schwellnus et al. (2017).

StatLink http://dx.doi.org/10.1787/888933724632

The share of the top 1% has increased since 2007. The Gini coefficient is commonly used to measure overall income inequality; however, it cannot reveal the extent to which the wealthy few are pulling ahead of the rest of the population. The latest evidence from tax records depicts substantial increases in the income share of the top 1% in many OECD countries (Figure 1.7)

The wage growth has lagged behind the labour productivity growth in emerging and developing countries. Most of the post-crisis period has seen an overall decline in the wage growth: from 2.5% in 2012 to 1.7% in 2015 globally, and from 6.6% in 2012 to 2.5% in 2015 in emerging and developing countries in Asia and the Pacific (ILO, 2017). This trend only partly reflects differences among workers and firms. In most countries, wages spiked for the top 10%, particularly for the top 1% earners (ILO, 2017). In Europe, the highest-paid 10% receive about one quarter of the total wages; and further more in the emerging market economies like Brazil (35%), India (43%) and South Africa (49%). Altogether, these trends mean that although workers have become increasingly productive across the world, the benefits of their work have increasingly accrued to those at the top of the income distribution. For example, the income share of the richest 1% rose from 7.5% to 11.2% in Korea and from 16.6% to 19.9% in the US between 2007 and 2014 (Figure 1.8). While the income share of the top 1% fell in many OECD countries in 2010, it reverted to pre-crisis levels in the US, Australia, Poland and a few others. By contrast, in Turkey and Korea, the income share of the top 1% has continued to rise beyond 2007 levels in 2014.

Figure 1.8 Income share of the top 1%

Selected OECD countries, 1997, 2007 and 2016 or latest, %

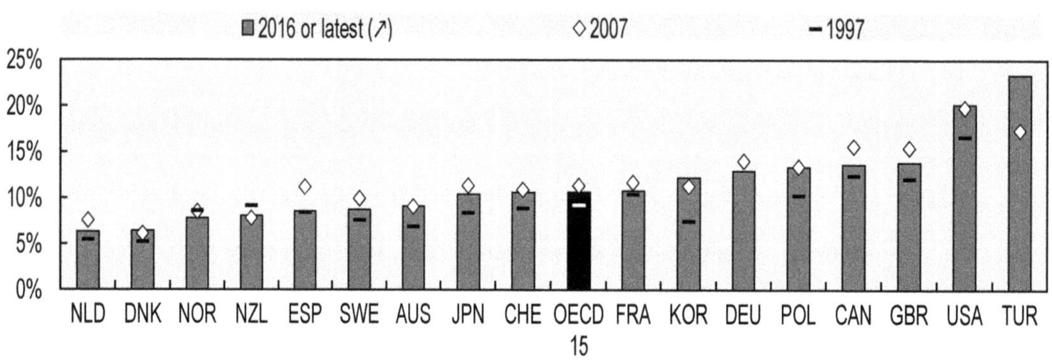

Note: The latest available year refers to 2016 for Turkey; 2015 for Poland; to 2014 for New Zealand, France, the United Kingdom and the US; to 2013 for Sweden; to 2012 for the Netherlands, Spain and Korea; to 2011 for Norway and Germany; and to 2010 for Denmark, Japan, Switzerland and Canada. The OECD average is the simple average of the countries shown in the chart with available data for all three periods (i.e. excluding Turkey and Germany).
Source: World Wealth & Income Database.

StatLink http://dx.doi.org/10.1787/888933724651

Overall market income inequality stalls at record levels; and remained one of the highest between 2007 and 2015. In terms of disposable income before taxes and benefits, income inequality has risen in several countries since 2007 (Figure 1.9), including the US (2% points) and Spain (2% points), while it has fallen by more than 2% points in Iceland, Chile and Latvia.

Wealth is concentrated in the hands of a few, regardless of how it is measured. Wealth held by the average household in the top 10% is 15 times that of the median household in OECD countries (Figure 1.10, left vertical axis); it is much higher in the US (68 times), the

Netherlands (58 times) and Denmark (30 times), partly reflecting the fact that in each of these countries the source data provides comprehensive coverage of very wealthy households, which are often under-sampled in conventional household surveys. By contrast, the difference between the wealth of the median household and the average wealth of households in the bottom quintile of the distribution is 1.3 in the OECD area (Figure 1.10, right axis), about twelve-times smaller. Inequality in the lower half of the distribution is the largest in Denmark and the Netherlands (partly because the source data captures better the very wealthy).

Figure 1.9 Gini coefficient of disposable income

Total population, OECD countries, 2016 or latest, 2010 and 2007

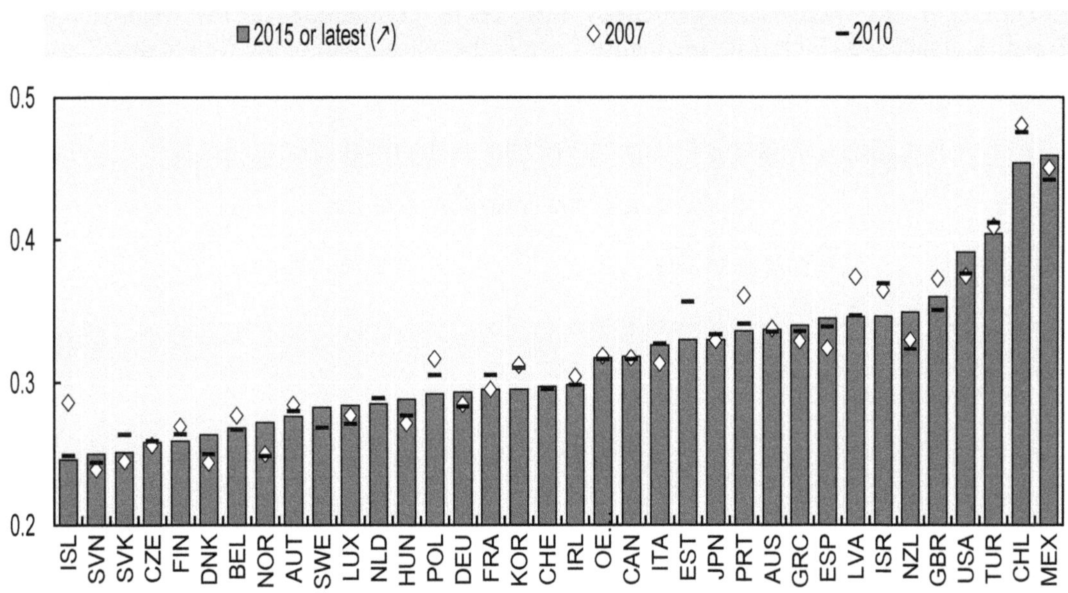

Note: Data for 2015 refer to 2016 for Finland, Israel, the Netherlands, Sweden and the United States; 2014 for Australia, Hungary, Iceland, Ireland, Italy, Luxembourg, Mexico, New Zealand and Switzerland; and to 2012 for Japan. Data for 2010 refer to 2013 for Estonia, Sweden and Switzerland; 2011 for Chile, Israel, the Netherlands, New Zealand, and Turkey; and to 2009 for Hungary, and Japan. Data for 2007 refer to 2008 for Germany, Australia, Chile, France, Norway, Israel, and Mexico; and to 2009 for Switzerland. 2016 data for the Netherlands are provisional. The OECD average excludes Estonia, the Netherlands, Sweden and Switzerland due to a break in the time series for these countries.
Source: OECD Income Distribution Database.

StatLink http://dx.doi.org/10.1787/888933724670

The wealthiest 5% held more than one third of wealth; the wealthiest 1% held nearly one fifth of the wealth.[5] As shown in Figure 1.11, wealth inequality is the highest in the Netherlands and the US (with, respectively, 52% and 68% shares in terms of the top 5%, and 28% and 42% in terms of the top 1%) and the lowest in the Slovak Republic and Greece (with respectively, 23% and 29% shares in terms of the top 5%, and 7% and 8% in terms of the top 1%). In the OECD average country, wealth inequality remained around the same levels between 2010 and 2014 (in terms of 1% and 5% metrics) while it increased in the US, United Kingdom and Greece and fell in Luxembourg, Canada, Italy and Portugal.

The post-crisis rebound in the financial markets has brought less benefit to the young and less-educated. The growth in net wealth since the financial crisis has been lower for households with a younger and a less educated head. In Canada, median net wealth has increased more rapidly than in the upper percentiles of the distribution, lowering wealth inequality at the top of the distribution (Figure 1.11, at least, in part, reflecting better performance of the young (Figure 1.12), whose growth in average net wealth outpaced that of aged. Wealth growth of the highly skilled, however, significantly outpaced that of the lower skilled. In Australia on the other hand, growth in wealth of the median household was significantly outpaced by that of the top 10%, in part reflecting growing disparities between the young and old. In Italy, median net wealth decreased at a slower rate than the wealth of the top 10%, lowering wealth inequality, as net wealth of the highly skilled fell at a faster pace than that of lower-skilled but, at the same time, net wealth among the young contracted at a significantly higher pace than of the old. Conversely in the United Kingdom and the US, where median net wealth also fell, net wealth of the top percentiles increased; mirrored by contractions in net wealth of the young and increases in the old. Inequalities within the bottom end of the wealth distribution remained fairly stable in all countries except the US, where it increased.

Figure 1.10 Top and bottom wealth inequality

OECD countries, 2016 or latest available year

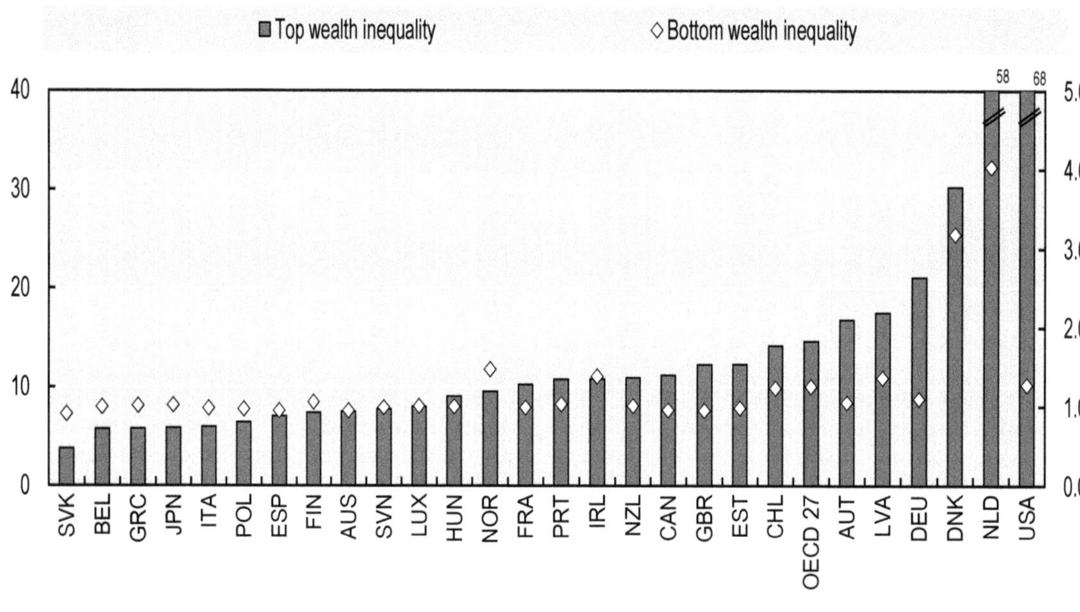

Note: Top wealth inequality refers to the difference between the mean wealth of the top 10% and the median wealth, divided by the median wealth. Bottom wealth inequality refers to the difference between median wealth and the mean wealth of the bottom quintile, divided by the median wealth. Data refer to 2016 for the US; to 2015 for Denmark, the Netherlands, and the United Kingdom; to 2013 for Estonia, Ireland and Portugal; and to 2012 for Canada and Spain. Data for 2010 refer to 2013 for Korea; to 2012 for Norway; to 2011 for Australia, Austria, Chile, Germany, Italy, Luxembourg, and the United Kingdom; and to 2009 to France, Greece and Spain. In Denmark and the Netherlands the share held by the bottom 60% of households is negative reflecting that, on average, these households have liabilities exceeding the value of their assets. In Norway and Ireland it is the share held by the bottom 40% to be negative.
Source: OECD Wealth Distribution Database.

StatLink http://dx.doi.org/10.1787/888933724689

Figure 1.11 Wealth shares of top percentiles of the net wealth distribution

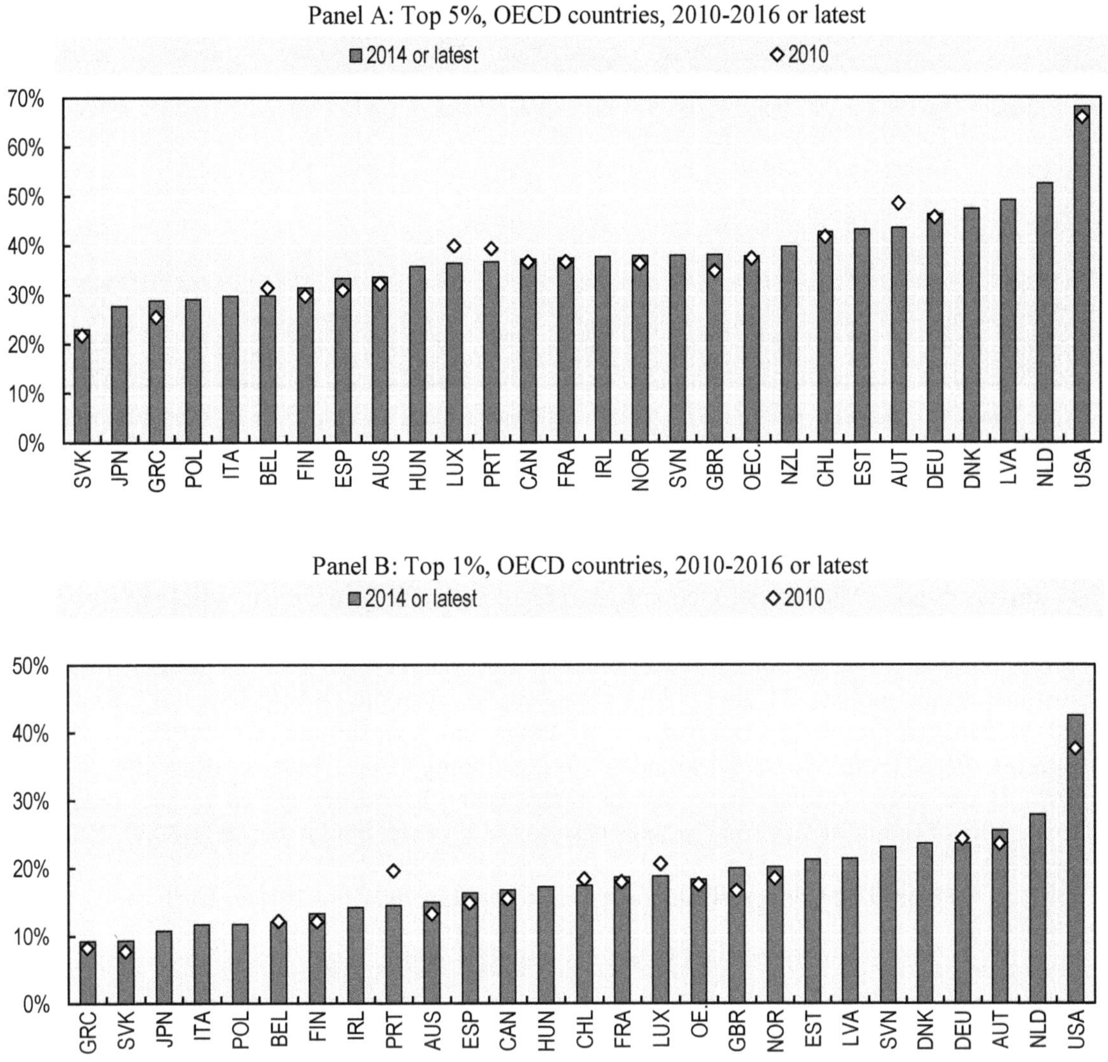

Note: In each Panel, countries are ranked in ascending order of the wealth share of the top 5% in 2014. Data for 2014 refer to 2016 for the US; to 2015 for Denmark, Korea, the Netherlands and the United Kingdom; to 2013 for Estonia, Ireland and Portugal; and to 2012 for Canada and Spain. Data for 2010 refer to 2013 for Korea; to 2012 for Norway; to 2011 for Australia, Austria, Chile, Germany, Italy, Luxembourg and the United Kingdom; and to 2009 to France, Greece and Spain. In each Panel, the OECD average is the simple average of the countries with available data in both 2010 and 2014. For countries in grey, data are based on registers or surveys that typically better capture the very rich and which are often under-sampled in conventional household surveys

Source: OECD Wealth Distribution Database.

StatLink http://dx.doi.org/10.1787/888933724708

Table 1.1. Changes of net wealth at different points of distribution

Selected OECD countries, between 2006 and 2016 or latest, annual percentage change.

	Mean	Median	Bottom quintile	Middle three quintiles	Top quintile	Top 10%	Top 5%	Top 1%	Top wealth inequality	Bottom wealth inequality	Observed period
Australia	0.9	0.2	-2.5	-0.1	1.1	1.1	0.8	-0.6	3.9	0.0	2006-2014
Canada	3.2	3.5	4.4	3.4	3.1	2.9	2.6	1.9	1.5	-0.2	2005-2016
Italy	-1.4	-1.0	1.3	-1.2	-1.6	-1.8				0.0	2006-2014
United Kingdom	1.7	-1.5	0.7	-1.1	2.8	3.1	3.4	5.4	9.5	-0.2	2007-2015
United States	0.7	-3.3	-9.9	-3.2	1.3	1.6	1.6	2.4	8.4	2.0	2007-2016

Note: Top wealth inequality refers to the difference between the mean wealth of the top 5% and the median wealth, divided by the median wealth. Bottom wealth inequality refers to the difference between median wealth and the mean wealth of the bottom quintile, divided by the median wealth.
Source: OECD Wealth Distribution Database

Income and wealth inequalities have also increased in emerging and developing countries. Since 1980, income inequality has increased rapidly in China, India, and Russia. Inequality has stabilised in Latin America and the Caribbean, although remained at high levels. Globally, the poorest 50% are estimated to receive less than 9% of the world's income and the richest 1% above 20% of the world's income (World Inequality Report, 2018). Most of the world's poorest live in Africa and Asia (around 70% of the world's poorest 10% in terms of per capita incomes; not including China). In terms of wealth, about 50% of the world's wealth is owned by the richest 1%, largely driven by the unequal ownership of capital and shifting balance between private and public wealth (UNDP, 2014).

Figure 1.12 Change of mean net wealth between 2006 and 2016 or latest

Selected OECD countries, annual percentage change

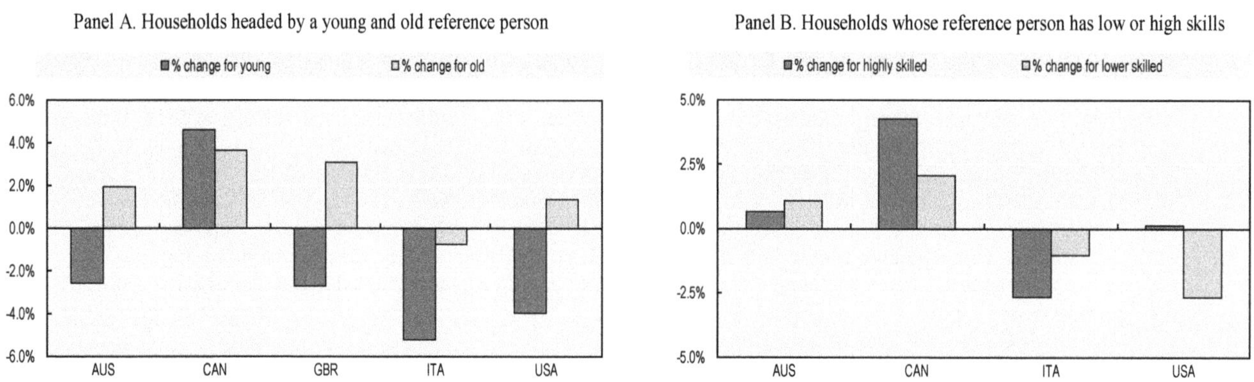

Note: 1. Young household heads are those under 34 years of age, while the old heads are those above 65.
2. The low education group refers to household heads with lower secondary education or below (ISCED 0-2), while the high education group refers to household heads with tertiary education (ISCED 5 & 6).
Figures for 2006 relate to 2005 for Australia and Canada, and 2007 for the United Kingdom and United States. Figures for 2014 refer to 2015 for the United Kingdom and to 2016 for Canada and the United States.
Source: OECD Wealth Distribution Database.

StatLink http://dx.doi.org/10.1787/888933724727

Trends in regional disparities

There are large economic differences across regions within the same country. The income disparities within regions of the same country are now larger in some countries than the disparities between OECD countries. In many OECD countries, citizens in the richest regions have a significantly higher disposable income than households in the poorest regions. In the US, Italy, Turkey, Spain or Mexico, disposable household incomes in the richest region are between 30 and 50% higher than in the respective country's poorest region (Figure 1.13). The most prosperous region in the US, the District of Columbia, recorded a mean disposable income of USD 47 320, significantly above the income level of USD 28 967 in Mississippi, the least prosperous region in the US.

Regional convergence or divergence in disposable household income is context-specific. There has been no clear overall trend in regional disparities in disposable household income per capita during 2010-2014 across OECD countries. In roughly half of them, income disparities between the richest and poorest regions increased, especially in Greece, Canada and the Netherlands (Figure 1.14). Disparities decreased in a few other countries, most notably in Chile, Portugal and Slovenia. In countries with decreasing regional disparities, the income convergence was predominantly driven by faster growth in the bottom regions than in the top regions. Analogously, a divergence in regional income disparities was driven by larger decreases in disposable income in the poorest regions. In Greece, for example, income in relatively poor Eastern Macedonia (Thrace) declined more than in the more affluent region Attiki.

Figure 1.13 Regional disparities in mean disposable household income

OECD countries, 2013 or latest year available, USD PPP

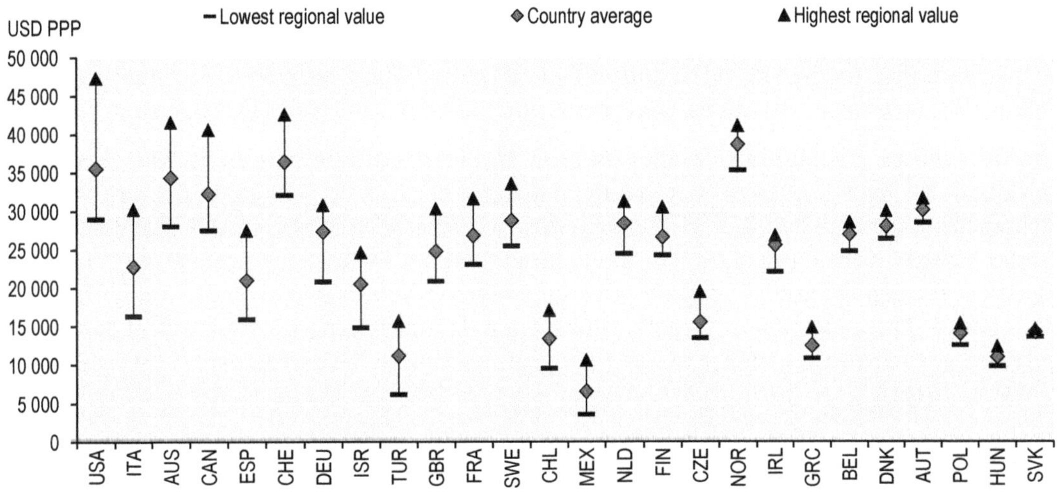

Note: The figure shows the equalised mean disposable household income in the richest and poorest regions (large TL2 regions) in OECD countries, 2013 or latest. Data are expressed in USD constant prices, PPP (reference year 2010). Ceuta and Melilla regions are not included in Spanish regions.
Source: OECD Regional Statistics database.

StatLink http://dx.doi.org/10.1787/888933724746

Figure 1.14 Change in disposable income regional disparity

OECD countries, 2010 to 2014, %

Evolution of the ratio top 10% over bottom 10% region in each country, and reason of the change

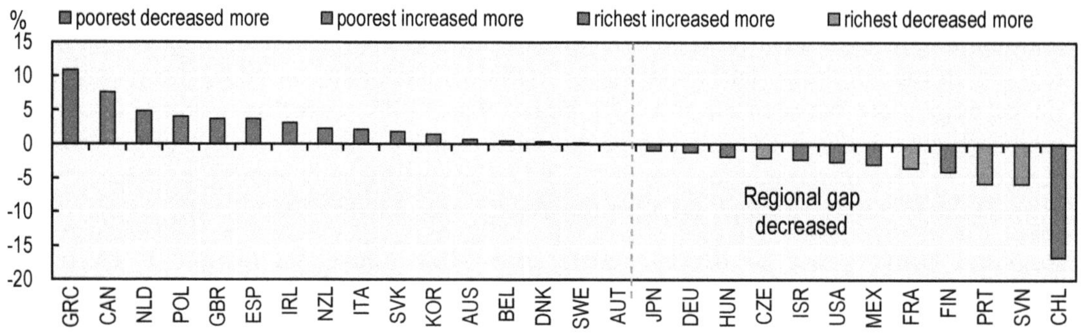

Note: The figure shows the change between 2010 and 2014 in the ratio of average disposable income per capita of the richest 10% and poorest 10% TL2 regions. Richest and poorest regions are the aggregation of regions with the highest and lowest income per capita and representing 10% of national population. Ceuta and Melilla regions are not included in Spanish regions

Source: Authors' calculations based on OECD Regional Statistics (database), http://dx.doi.org/10.1787/region-data-en.

StatLink http://dx.doi.org/10.1787/888933724765

Widening productivity gaps across regions resulted in higher output inequality. Differences in income inequalities across regions are driven by differences in labour productivity growth (Figure 1.15). Indeed, countries where regions that were catching up to their country's frontier were the major contributors to total productivity growth (Type I) retained fairly constant interregional income inequality while countries where the contribution to productivity growth was concentrated in regions that were already more productive than the rest of the country (Type II) experienced an increase of inter-regional inequality in terms of per capita GDP between 2000 and 2014 (OECD, 2018a).

Some regions risk falling further behind if the productivity gap is not closed. If productivity growth rates do not change, catching-up regions will close the gap to their frontier, on average, by 2050. However, without a change, this also means that during the same period diverging regions will have fallen to about 50% of the productivity frontier. To close the gap in the next 34 years, diverging regions would need to outgrow their frontier by about 1.2% points. Put differently, the average labour productivity growth in diverging regions would need to increase to 2.8% per year, quadruple the current rate (OECD, 2016a; OECD, 2016b).

Firms and workers in larger cities are generally more productive than in smaller cities or rural regions. A variety of channels create this productivity benefit. One of them is the concentration of highly educated workers. These workers are not only more productive themselves, but create additional "human capital spillovers"; that is, a higher percentage of highly educated workers increases productivity (measured by individual earnings) for all workers (Moretti, 2004). In a sample of five OECD countries (Germany, Mexico, Spain, the United Kingdom and the US) a 10 percentage point increase in a city's share of university graduates, is associated with productivity increases of about 3% (Ahrend et al., 2017). In addition, knowing that there are greater returns to education provides an incentive for further investment in one's education, creating a virtuous circle. Spillovers are not limited to highly educated workers. Co-location of workers and firms, in general, creates "agglomeration economies". Agglomeration economies confer a productivity "bonus" to workers that depends on the size of the city.

Figure 1.15 Inequalities grow when regions fail to catch up

Per capita GDP inequality (Gini coefficient) in TL3 regions, OECD countries, 2000-14

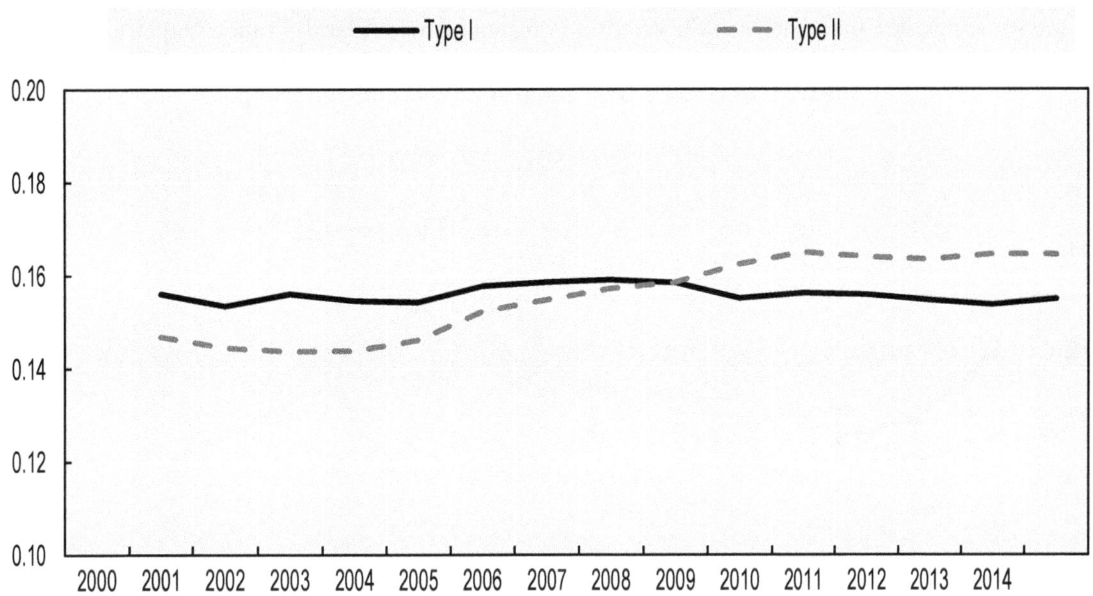

Note: Type I countries are those with strong regional catching up dynamics in terms of labour productivity across regions, while Type II countries experienced divergence of most regions and the productivity advantage in the most productive "frontier" regions increased. Type I countries are AUT, CZE, DEU, ESP, ITA, POL, PRT, and ROU; Type II countries are BGR, DNK, FIN, FRA, GBR, GRC, HUN, NLD, SVK, and SWE. Per capita GDP inequality with GDP measured in USD at constant 2010 prices and purchasing power parities.
Source: OECD (forthcoming), Bachtler et al. (2017).

StatLink http://dx.doi.org/10.1787/888933724784

Rural growth does not only occur in rural regions that are close to cities, but proximity is an important predictor for rural growth. Proximity allows stronger linkages between urban and rural places that allows for agglomeration benefits to be shared beyond the borders of a city. Rural residents have easier access to advanced public and private services that are only found in cities and commuting flows can help alleviate the congestion within cities. Indeed, more than 75% of rural residents live in close proximity to a (functional) urban area (OECD, 2016b).

Trends in ageing unequally

Inequalities are increasing across generations too. Income inequality typically rises with age within cohorts, generally peaking between 55 and 60 years old in OECD countries and declining thereafter (OECD, 2017a). However, inequality has evolved differently from one birth cohort to the next. The1940s-born experienced a particularly pronounced rise and fall in income with age, as shown by the hump corresponding to the 1940s cohort (Figure 1.16). For this generation, the Gini index rose from an OECD-wide average of 0.245 among 30-to-34 year-olds to 0.315 when, 25 years later, they reached 55 to 59 years. The increase was much more gradual for the 1960s cohort (for which data are available only up to 50-54) albeit from a higher level of inequality at younger ages. For the youngest cohorts, the Gini index even declines up to around age 35, in contrast to the initial increase that had prevailed up to the 1950s-born cohort.

Overall income inequality at the same ages across cohorts has increased. The cumulative increase (between the 1920s and 1980s birth cohorts) has been very large – greater than 10% points– in Belgium, the Slovak Republic, Austria, Israel, the US, Poland, the United Kingdom, Finland, the Czech Republic and Australia. By contrast, inequality at the same age declined between the cohorts in Ireland, Switzerland, France and Greece.

Figure 1.16 Income Gini index by cohort and age group

OECD-wide averages, Gini index

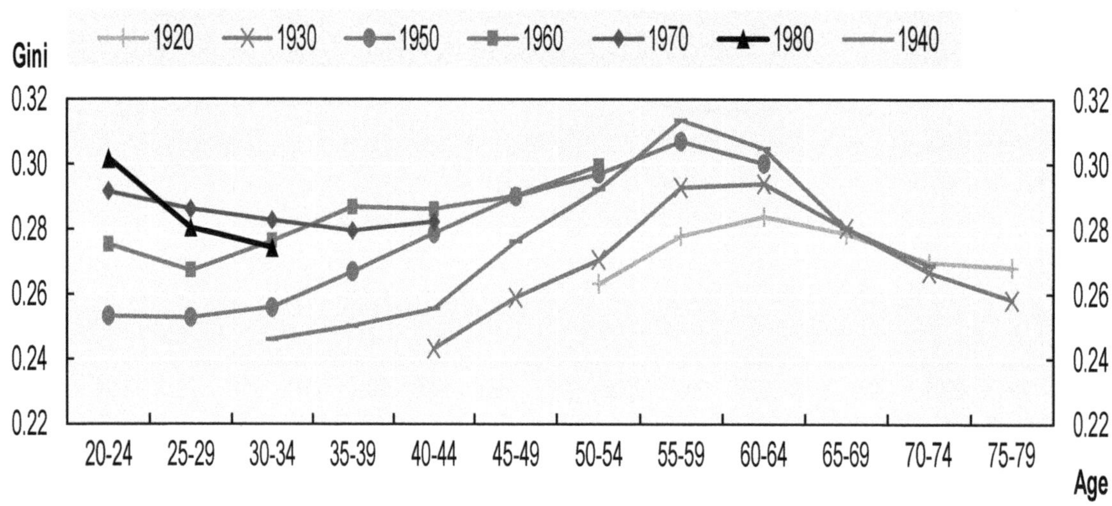

Source: Figure 3.18 in OECD (2017a), Preventing Ageing Unequally, OECD Publishing, Paris.

StatLink http://dx.doi.org/10.1787/888933724803

Income inequality at the same age has increased steadily in all cohorts born between the 1920s and 1980s. Income inequality for those born in the 1980s is much higher than among their parents at the same age, which in turn was higher than for their parents. More precisely, on average the Gini coefficient at the same age between generations born in the 1920s and in the 1950s increased by 1.5% points (Figure 1.17). Between the 1950s and 1980s birth cohorts, the Gini index at the same age increased by further 3 percentage points (or 10%) on average. In other words, at a given age, income inequality climbed by about 0.3% per birth year on average among people born from 1950 onwards. If the age patterns of the past prevail among the younger cohorts, they will suffer from great inequality in old age. Population ageing could heighten the difficulties that the disadvantaged elderly of the future may experience.

Figure 1.17 Income inequality at the same age has increased from one generation to the next

Changes in Gini indices across birth cohorts in percentage points, average across age groups, cohort reference = 1920s

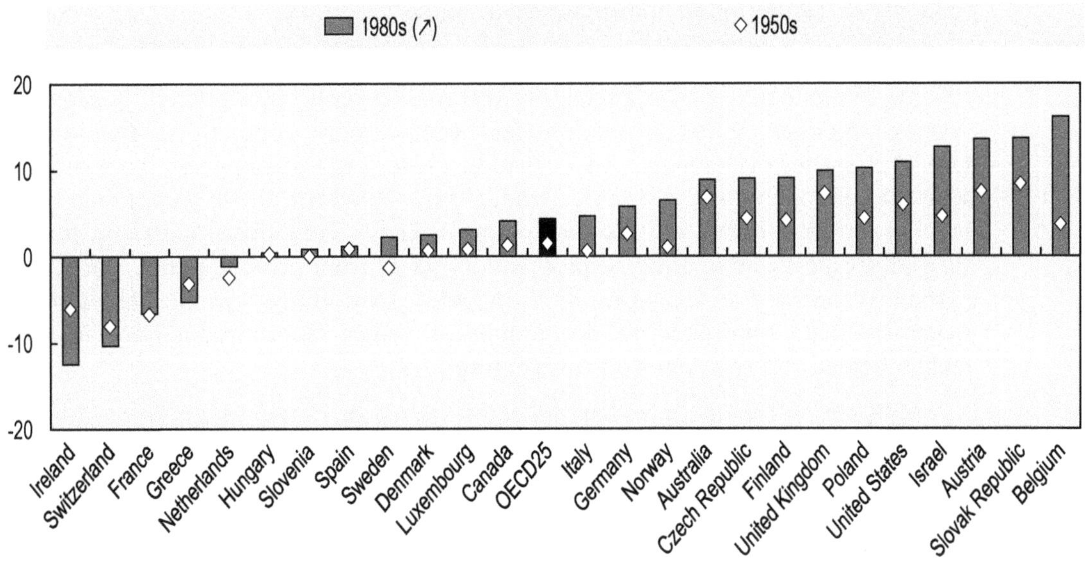

Note: For each country, reported figures are derived from a specification that includes cohort and age fixed effects. Older cohorts tend to be observed at old ages only and younger cohorts at young ages. Due to quality issues, data from Mexico have not been used.
Source: Figure 3.19 in OECD (2017a), Preventing Ageing Unequally, OECD Publishing, Paris.

StatLink http://dx.doi.org/10.1787/888933724822

Key dynamics and policies to enhance inclusive outcomes from growth

Addressing the decoupling between productivity and wages and ensuring a fairer sharing of productivity gains

The decoupling of real wage growth from productivity growth partly reflects global mega-trends, including capital-enhancing technological change and the rise in global value chains. Increasing productivity is not always enough to raise wages of a typical worker in real terms. Declines in relative investment prices –a measure of capital-enhancing technological change– and the rise of global value chains have reduced labour shares and may have raised wage inequality by increasing relative demand for high-skilled workers while squeezing the wages of low-skilled workers (OECD, 2017b; De Serres and Schwellnus, 2018). This explains the decoupling between labour productivity and real median wages.

Large cross-country heterogeneity in decoupling suggests that national policies and institutions matter. Recent evidence indicates that three broad policy areas are key to a wider sharing of productivity gains (OECD, 2018b):

- **Skills policies.** High skills can support the wider sharing of productivity gains by limiting capital-labour substitution. Empirically, capital-labour substitution is more pronounced in countries and industries specialising in high-routine activities. However, even at given levels of specialisation in high-routine activities, capital-labour substitution is lower when skills are high - with numeracy skills being particularly important (OECD, 2018b). This may be because high-skilled workers are reassigned to non-routine tasks more easily than low-skilled workers. Moreover, skills appear to shift specialisation patterns; with high skills typically reducing specialisation in high-routine activities.

- **Product market policies.** Pro-competitive product market reforms raise wages relative to productivity by reducing product market rents appropriated by capital. Average product market regulation has become more competition-friendly in OECD countries over the past two decades. *Prima facie* this appears inconsistent with the decoupling of wages from productivity. However, the evidence suggests that in a number of countries the technological change and globalisation have more than offset the wider sharing of productivity gains from pro-competitive product market reforms. For example, this includes reinforcing "winner-take-most" dynamics that contributed to decoupling of wages from productivity in the technologically most advanced firms (Figure 1.18).

Figure 1.18 Average wages and productivity in the best firms and the rest, 2001=100

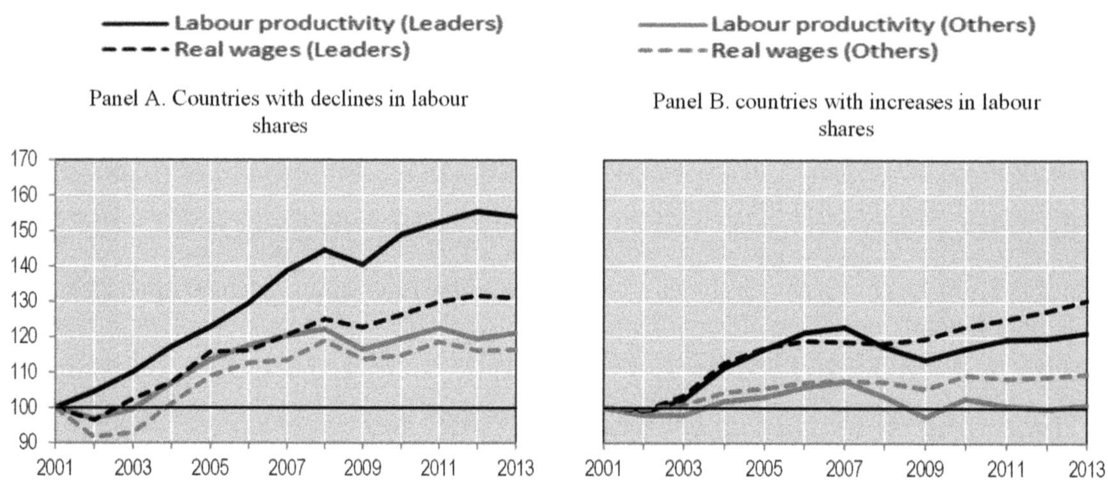

Note: Labour productivity and wages are computed as the unweighted mean across firms of real value added per worker and labour compensation per worker. Leaders are defined as the top 5% of firms in terms of labour productivity within each country group in each industry and year. The countries with a decline in the labour share (excluding the primary, housing, financial and non-market industries) over the period 2001-2013 are: Belgium, Denmark, Germany, Ireland, Korea, Sweden, United Kingdom and US. The countries with an increase are: Austria, Czech Republic, Estonia, Finland, France, Italy, Netherlands and Spain.
Source: OECD calculations based on OECD-ORBIS.

StatLink http://dx.doi.org/10.1787/888933724841

- **Labour market policies and institutions.** Labour market policies and institutions can support a fairer sharing of productivity gains through their impact on the relative cost of labour; for instance, by influencing the wage formation process or altering the cost of hiring and firing (OECD, 2018b; OECD, 2018c), and also by influencing the distribution of product market rents. In the imperfectly competitive labour market (e.g. in a labour market that is characterised by monopsony where the employer has leeway to set the level of wages), workers and capital owners bargain over the distribution of rents formally or informally. Labour market policies such as minimum wages or collective bargaining institutions can influence the distribution of rents between workers and capital-owners.

Figure 1.19 Trends in collective bargaining coverage and trade union density

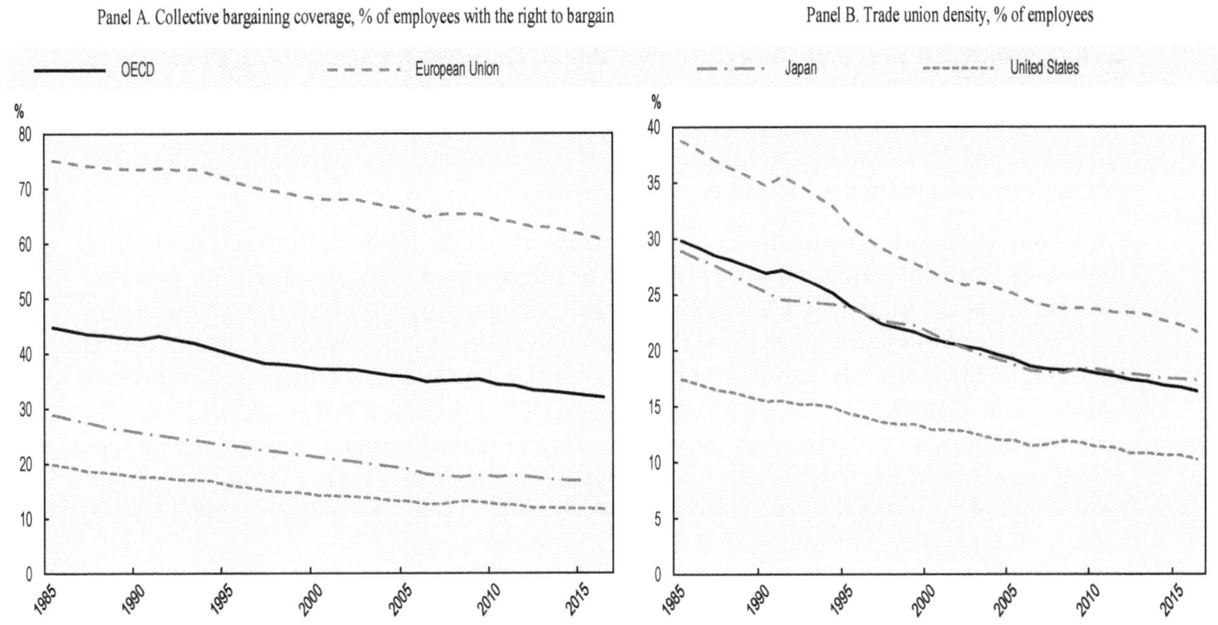

Source: OECD/ICTWSS Database.

StatLink http://dx.doi.org/10.1787/888933724860

Labour market policies and institutions that strengthen workers' bargaining position, especially at the lower end of the wage distribution, without unduly raising labour costs, are most conducive to the wider sharing of productivity gains. Well-designed active labour market policies support a wider sharing of productivity gains by helping people who lost their jobs find new and better ones (OECD, 2018b). Minimum wages can also help to ensure that low-wage workers benefit from growing economic prosperity, although need to be moderate in countries where relative cost competitiveness is an issue, and well-designed to avoid capital-labour substitution. In particular, the floor set by minimum wages could avoid that low-skilled workers are priced out of jobs by carefully considering interactions with taxes and transfers. For example, reductions in social security contributions around the minimum wage can enhance the effectiveness of the minimum wage as a tool to raise pay and reduce poverty, while limiting the rise in labour costs for firms. Minimum wages could be revised regularly, based on accurate, up-to-date and impartial information and advice that considers labour market conditions and the views of different stakeholders. Coverage of and compliance with minimum wage legislation could often be improved. Collective bargaining institutions can help to promote a broad sharing of productivity gains and raise wages of low-income workers. However, they would not need to push up wages only for a small group of workers covered by the agreements. For collective bargaining institutions to be effective for a majority of workers, coverage needs to be high. Over the past decades, however, collective bargaining coverage has been declining in most OECD countries (Figure 1.19; OECD, 2017b).

Collective bargaining coverages can be improved through well-organised social partners based on broad memberships. In order to extend social dialogue to all segments of the economy, including small firms and non-standard forms of employment, governments can put in place a legal framework that promotes social dialogue in large and small firms alike and allows labour relations to adapt to new emerging challenges. In the absence of broad memberships, another way to maintain high coverage is the use of administrative extensions that extend the coverage of collective agreements beyond the members of signatory unions and employer organisations to all workers and firms in a sector. Parties that negotiate the agreements should represent the interests of all groups of firms and workers, that is, to avoid that extensions harm the economic prospects of start-ups, small firms or vulnerable workers. This can be achieved by subjecting the extension requests to reasonable representativeness criteria or providing well-defined procedures for exemptions and opt-outs in case of economic hardship.

Collective bargaining institutions need to strike the right balance between providing high coverage and sufficient coordination to align wages with productivity growth. Centralisation can improve the sharing of productivity gains by increasing the labour share, especially for low-wage workers, and by reducing wage inequality. Recent research by the OECD (2018d) shows that forms of centralised and/or coordinated bargaining systems can improve labour market performance compared to (fully) decentralised bargaining systems or where there is no collective bargaining. The former record higher employment rates are able to integrate vulnerable workers more into the labour market while at the same time improving the sharing of productivity gains by increasing the labour market share, especially for low-wage workers, and reducing wage inequality.

Fair and efficient redistribution

The tax and transfer system is a central means of redistributing in a fair and impartial manner the gains of growth to promote equity. Designing these systems to foster inclusive growth requires a holistic approach. The labour income tax system and transfers need to reduce poverty for those at the bottom of the income and wealth distribution. At the same time, it is important to ensure that capital income taxes are coherently taxed and tax evasion and avoidance is addressed to ensure effective taxation of those with high levels of income and wealth. However since the mid-1990s, the redistributive effect of taxes and transfers has declined (Causa and Hermansen, 2018; Figure 1.20A). This redistributive effect is more pronounced in the pre-crisis period during the mid-2000s.

Declines in the size of personal income taxes (PITs) tended to reduce redistribution. PITs have become slightly more progressive in particular because of the cuts in PITs on lower incomes. These counteracting changes in size and progressivity of personal income taxes tended to shape redistribution with fairly equal forces, in contrast to transfers for which changes in size tended to dominate over changes in targeting. In particular, income support provided by social transfers to workless households in the bottom 40% has declined in the majority of OECD countries for which data are available. Given the overwhelming weight of transfers relative to market income among that group, their disposable income declined markedly relative to median income. In the majority of countries for which data are available, cash transfers have become increasingly ineffective at preventing workless households from falling into relative poverty, especially in the presence of children. In contrast to workless households, income support provided by taxes and transfers to bottom 40% working households has increased in the majority of OECD countries. The increase in net transfer support was largely driven by declines in income taxes and social security contributions that tended to mitigate declines in market incomes Figure 1.20B), although significant variation across OECD countries can be found (see also Box 1.2).[6] The trend towards less redistribution was most pronounced over the pre-crisis period (1995-2007), and was temporarily reversed during the first period of the crisis (2007-2010); reflecting the cushioning impact of automatic stabilisers and fiscal discretionary measures.

Figure 1.20 Redistribution has declined in OECD countries since mid-1990s

Change in redistribution for the working-age population

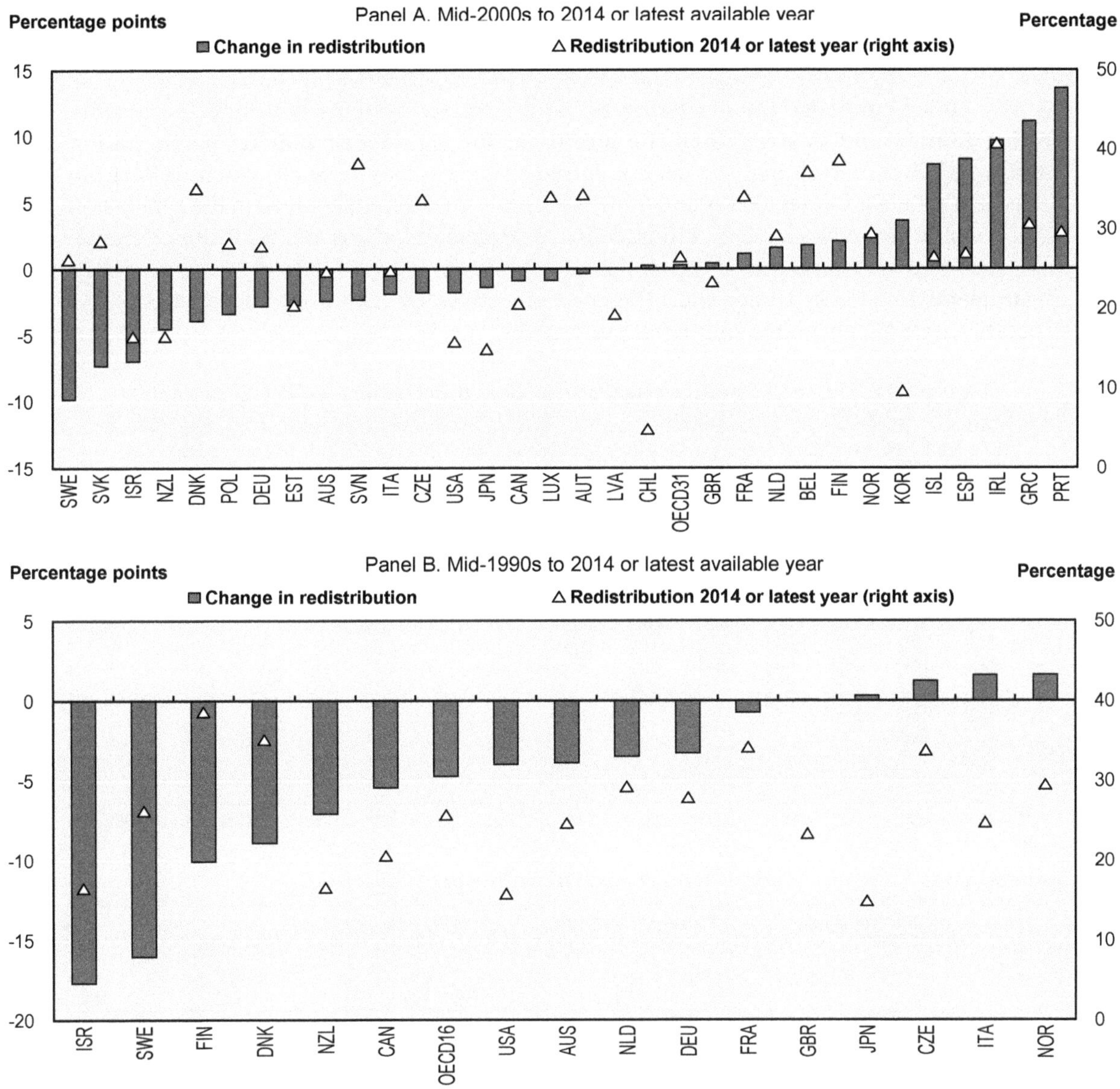

Note: Coverage over time varies across countries. For Panel A: data refer to 2003-2012 for Japan; 2003-2014 for New Zealand; 2004-2015 for Finland and the United Kingdom; 2005-2014 for Denmark, France and Poland; 2005-2015 for Israel, the Netherlands and the United States; 2006-2015 for Chile and Korea; and 2004-2014 for the rest. For Panel B data refer to 1994-2015 for the United Kingdom; 1995-2012 for Japan; 1995-2015 for Finland, Israel, the Netherlands and the United States; 1996-2014 for Czech Republic and France; and 1995-2014 for the rest. Further details are provided in Causa and Hermansen (2017).
Source: Causa and Hermansen (2017).

StatLink http://dx.doi.org/10.1787/888933724879

A decline in redistribution by cash transfers has driven the decline in overall redistribution across the majority of OECD countries over the last decade; since cash transfers account for the bulk of redistribution. Personal income taxes also contributed to this decline but played a less important and more heterogeneous role across countries

(Figure 1.21A). The decline in transfer redistribution was largely driven by insurance transfers (e.g. unemployment insurance, work-related sickness and disability benefits). This was partly mitigated by assistance transfers (e.g. minimum income transfers, means- or income-tested social safety net) in about half of the countries for which information is available (Figure 1.21B). Assistance transfers are less redistributive than insurance transfers in OECD countries.

A key policy challenge for designing tax and transfer systems is to achieve income redistribution and to strengthen the incentives for e.g. labour market participation and up-skilling. Given that the decline in redistribution may to some extent reflect the effects of efficiency-oriented tax and transfer reforms, this should not lead to the conclusion that countries have no choice but to trade more efficiency for less equity. Rather, reforms of taxes and transfers should be designed within an array of complementary policy instruments to address equity and efficiency objectives by taking into account country-specific context, constraints and social preferences.

Figure 1.21. The redistributive effect of transfers has declined in OECD countries

Change in redistribution for the working-age population, mid-1990s to 2013 or latest available year

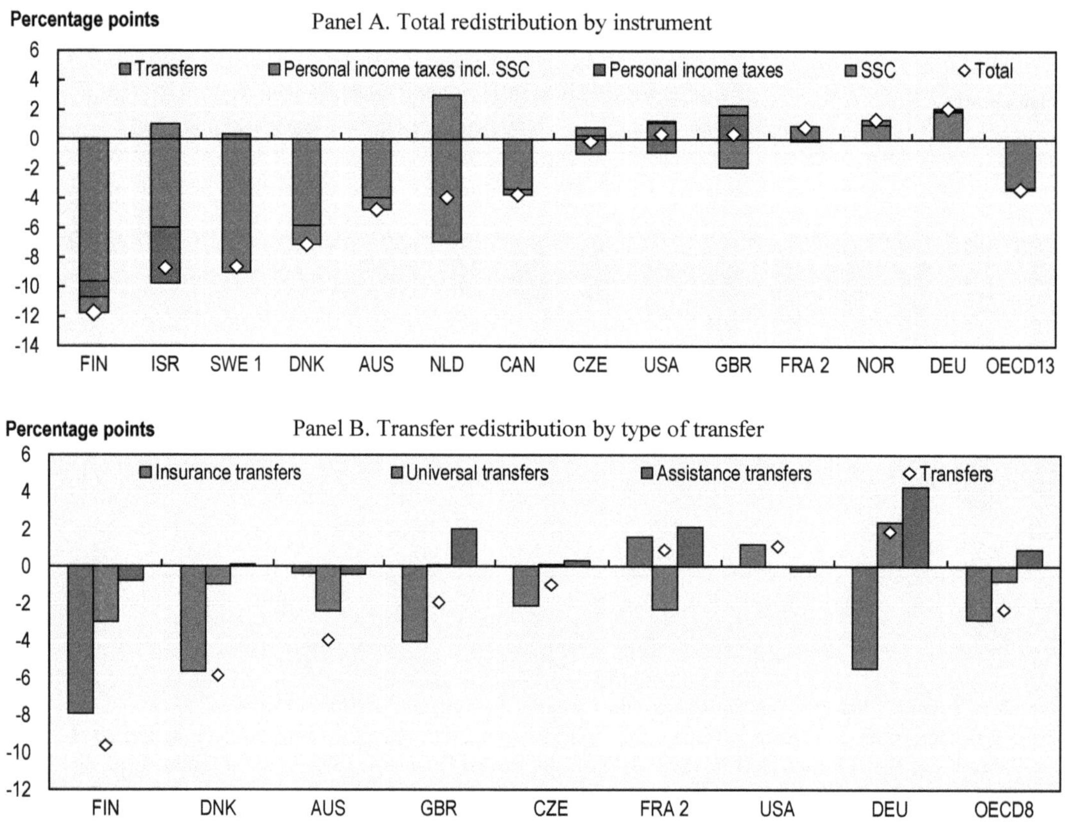

Note: See Causa and Hermansen (2017), Box 4 for the approach to assess the redistributive impact of individual parts of the tax and transfer systems. Coverage over time varies across countries. Further details are provided in Causa and Hermansen (2017).
Source: Causa and Hermansen (2017).

StatLink http://dx.doi.org/10.1787/888933724898

Box 1.2. The empirical analysis of the income redistribution drivers in OECD countries

Recent OECD research used the cross-country time-series regression analysis to examine the main drivers of income redistribution to working-age households. Causa et al. (2018, forthcoming) define redistribution as the relative reduction in market income inequality achieved through personal income taxes, employees' social security contributions and cash transfers. Using the household-level micro data, the empirical results so far indicate that the changes in the size of tax and transfer systems are likely to have contributed to the decline in income redistribution. This finding is related to widespread declines in social spending on cash support for the working-age population and to the diminishing role of personal income taxes in reducing inequality in the context of trade (Causa et al., 2018 forthcoming).

The underlying drivers and other changes in specific tax and transfer policy instruments include: i) the decline in the progressivity of personal income taxes, driven by a flattening of the tax schedule in the upper-part of the wage distribution as well as by a decline in top personal income tax rates and in the taxation of dividend income at the personal level, ii) the decline in the generosity and duration of unemployment-related transfers, including cuts to social assistance for the long-term unemployed, in combination with an increase in spending on active labour market policies, and iii) the reforms of pensions to encourage longer working life, for instance increases in the age of full pension eligibility and reductions in replacement rates. The impact of these factors has been partly mitigated by progressive family-friendly policies, such as widespread increases in spending on early education and childcare, as well as by tax cuts to low wage earners.

Source: Causa, O. A. Vindics and O. Akgun (2018), An empirical investigation on the drivers of income redistribution across OECD countries.

Strengthening the progressivity of the tax system should also occur through more effective taxation of capital income at the personal level. The share of income earned by capital is rising (Autor et al., 2017). At the same time, there are widespread calls for higher levels of capital taxation both domestically and internationally in response to increasing levels of income and wealth inequality, and drops in statutory corporate income tax rates. The move to Automatic Exchange of Information creates important new opportunities to tax capital effectively. However, savings rates generally lack coherence in most OECD and G20 countries (Figure 1.22). Tax differentials across assets are likely to result in significant distortions to the allocation of savings, as well as expanded opportunities for tax planning (OECD, 2018b). This means that the taxation of capital is often inefficient and regressive (Aghion et al., 2017).

Broadening the base of capital taxation is needed to improve the efficiency and fairness of their tax systems, although countries do not necessarily need to tax capital more (for example, to raise statutory rates). Some countries have tax expenditures for capital that have non-distributional policy rationales (such as the desire to increase levels of home ownership in the case of mortgage interest deductibility and the objective of increasing national savings for retirement in the case of the deductibility of pension contributions). However, these tax expenditures –particularly where they are uncapped– can have regressive consequences.

Figure 1.22. The tax burden on savings varies widely by asset type

Effective tax rates on savings across asset types on average across 40 OECD and associate countries

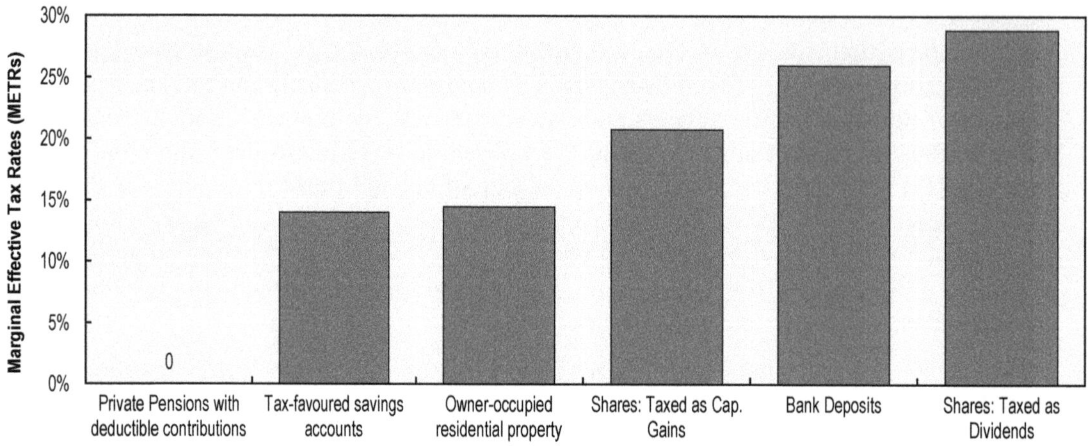

Note: METRs are based on a taxpayer earning the average wage, holding an asset for ten years. Inflation rates are set at the OECD average level. The average is calculated for Argentina, Australia, Austria, Belgium, Bulgaria, Canada, Chile, Colombia, Czech Republic, Denmark, Estonia, Finland, France, Germany, Greece, Hungary, Iceland, Ireland, Israel, Italy, Japan, Korea, Latvia, Lithuania, Luxembourg, Mexico, Netherlands, New Zealand, Norway, Poland, Portugal, Slovak Republic, Slovenia, South Africa, Spain, Sweden, Switzerland, Turkey, United Kingdom, and United States.
Source: OECD, Taxation of Household Savings.

StatLink http://dx.doi.org/10.1787/888933725924

Caution needs to be exerted with wealth taxes. When combined with personal tax rates on capital income, they can result in extremely high effective tax rates being imposed on certain assets. Wealth taxes can be substitutes where a country for other policy reasons does not have a broad-based capital income tax, including a tax on capital gains, and a well-designed inheritance tax (OECD, 2018b). However, in the presence of these taxes, the case for net wealth taxes is not that strong.

Policymakers should consider the progressivity of the entire tax system to deliver inclusive growth rather than the progressivity of each tax in isolation. This includes rebalancing the tax mix towards those tax categories that can improve both the equity and efficiency of the tax system, and reforming taxes other than income tax to ensure progressivity (Akgun et al., 2018). The OECD has focused on the positive growth consequences of consumption taxes and property taxes.

Continued reform of VAT is necessary to deliver both progressivity and efficiency. The reform should focus on the removal of those tax expenditures that benefit higher income earners, particularly in the case of non-essential goods and services such as in the case of hotels, restaurants, and certain cultural products (Figure 1.23). Where base broadening does make some households worse off, it is important for the success of such reforms to ensure that losers are adequately compensated.[7]

Figure 1.23. Taxes on income have risen since the crisis, while corporate taxes have fallen

Changes in the tax mix in OECD and selected G20 countries,

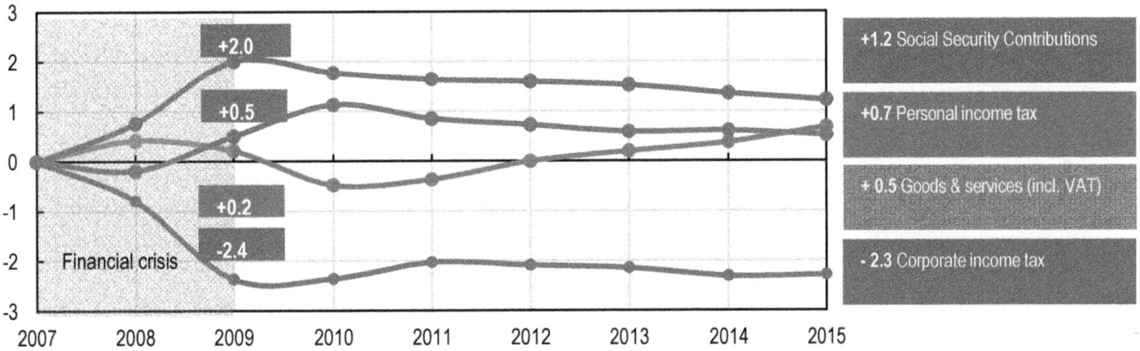

Source: OECD Revenue Statistics.

StatLink http://dx.doi.org/10.1787/888933724917

Taxes on immovable property have positive efficiency and equity consequences (Akgun et al., 2017), but reforms can increase their progressivity. Their progressivity stems from the fact that those with low levels of income and wealth are less likely to own property. In addition, the comparative difficulty in avoiding the tax and the immobility of the tax base creates beneficial characteristics also from an administration perspective. Subsidies for residential property in many OECD countries have adverse distributional effects and are not outweighed by property taxes (OECD, 2018b; OECD, 2018c). This is particularly true for mortgage interest deductibility that is uncapped in some OECD and G20 countries (OECD, 2018b).

Figure 1.24. Many VAT tax expenditures provide more support to high income households

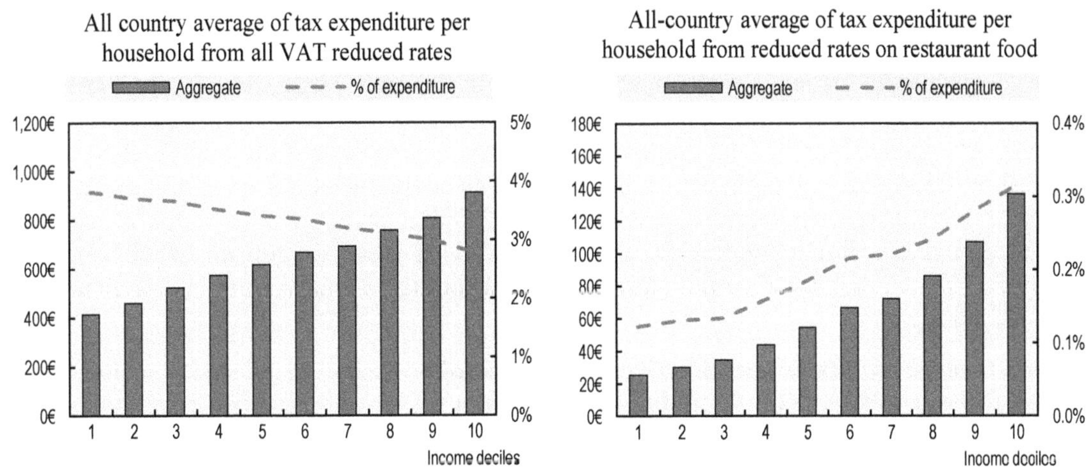

Source: The Distributional Effects of Consumption Taxes in OECD Countries (OECD, 2014).

StatLink http://dx.doi.org/10.1787/888933724936

Tax transparency through peer reviews and exchange of information agreements are vital to maximise the effectiveness, integrity and progressivity of tax systems. Avoidance and evasion can undermine the integrity and progressivity of the tax system. Tax evasion is a particularly acute problem for many developing countries with weak governance and lower levels of tax capacity. While the development of exchange of information marks a step change in global tax transparency, there must be a continued focus on the peer-review process and the development of the network of exchange of information agreements for these new systems to maximise their effectiveness.

More work is needed to ensure that tax authorities have the capacity to use the information being exchanged to effectively address informality and tax evasion. Increased international cooperation is required. Policymakers need to be vigilant for any efforts to frustrate or circumvent new systems for exchanging information on tax matters, including the attempts to claim residency in low or no-tax jurisdictions. Informality can be addressed through a combination of tax policy and tax administration initiatives; including through targeted tax measures to induce taxpayers to enter the formal economy, such as EITCs or the phasing in of tax and SSCs.

Policies enhancing inclusive outcomes in developing countries

Strong and well-designed social protection is a powerful lever of inclusive growth in developing countries. Over the past decades, a growing number of developing countries have invested in social protection. Today about 2 billion people in the developing world have access to social safety net programs (World Bank, 2015). Virtually all countries, even some in fragile political contexts, have interventions in place that aim to address consumption deficits. Some middle income countries, especially in Latin America, have introduced cash transfers to encourage human capital development. Social protection can contribute to poverty reduction, resilience and economic development (World Bank, 2015; WIR, 2018).

Developing countries need to expand their social protection systems, either in terms of expenditure or coverage. Most developing countries spend only 5% of GDP or less on social protection, compared to 20% and above in OECD countries (ILO, 2017). Significant under-investment in social protection is associated with large coverage gaps. In low-income and lower-middle-income countries, in particular in Africa, a large share of the extreme poor population is not at all covered by social assistance. In more advanced countries, inadequate social insurance coverage means that the near poor and the middle class is at risk from falling back into poverty in the event of an economic shock or of an unforeseen loss of income due to sickness, for example. Besides coverage, the scope of social protection is also limited, with only a small number of life-cycle related benefits being provided – such as child benefits, unemployment benefits for the working age or pension for the elderly.

Long-term solutions to the effective and sustainable financing of social protection need to be found. A number of challenges stand in the way to effective functioning of social protection: from limited fiscal space and large informality to fragmented responsibilities and weak implementation mechanisms, poor governance and administrative capacity, the absence of appropriate management and information systems, insufficient knowledge and data, and the lack of policy coherence.

The effect of tax and transfers on inequality and poverty are mixed. In advanced OECD countries, taxes and transfers reduce the Gini coefficient on average by 15 Gini points

(OECD, 2011). In Latin America (OECD, 2009) and some countries in Asia (OECD, 2015a; OECD, 2015b), this effect is far less pronounced with a reduction of less than 2 Gini points. Other evidence for developing countries shows that tax and transfers tends to reduce slightly inequality but increases poverty (Lustig, 2017). In both advanced and developing countries, public spending is found to have a bigger impact on reducing inequality than taxation (IMF, 2014). Additional evidence for OECD countries (OECD, 2011; OECD, 2012) and Asia (Claus and al., 2014) indicates that social security contributions and consumption taxes tend to be regressive.

Reconciling tax and social protection policy objectives is crucial to promoting inclusive growth. This involves reassessing the equity-efficiency trade-off that exists at the heart of every tax system (Brys and al., 2016). In the case of developing countries whose tax systems are still evolving, it is important to get this right at the start. In many developing economies, social security contributions are very high. In Latin America, social security contributions account for the majority of the tax wedge due to the very-low level of personal income tax payments (OECD/CIAT/IDB, 2016). Social security and tax administration systems are often not integrated, which opens the door for tax evasion. Companies will maximise their payroll to the tax administration to minimise their corporate tax liability, while they will minimise their payroll for the social security system to minimise their contributions.

The way taxes and expenditures are allocated in a society is at the heart of the social contract, so is public confidence in fiscal institutions. The level of trust in the government is often determined by the extent to which fiscal policies such as taxes and transfers are perceived to be effective and equitable (OECD, 2008). When the fiscal system fails to reduce the gap between richer and poorer individuals it undermines fiscal legitimacy, damages the social contract and compromises the building of more inclusive societies.

While tax and transfers can be a powerful instrument for tackling inequality and poverty, ensuring sustainable funding for social policy and public investments requires strong mobilisation of domestic revenues. International evidence on the impact of fiscal policy on inequality and poverty demonstrates the need to look at tax and benefit systems as a whole (Brys and al., 2016). It further raises specific policy questions for developing countries that remain largely unanswered, for instance, on the appropriate balance between increased taxes to fund public social spending and poverty reduction and the need to maintain an internationally competitive tax system and attractive investment environment.

End notes

4 In several OECD countries, declines in total-economy labour income shares reflect increases in housing rents, which are related to increases in housing prices. Similarly in commodity-producing countries, declines in total-economy labour shares largely reflect increases in commodity prices. It should be noted that the GVA price index used to deflate labour income does not fully reflect the worker perspective (as it would for instance using a CPI). The GVA price index, for example (although convenient for decomposition analysis), presupposes that price changes in the cost of capital (services) and labour are the same.

5 Wealth concentration at the top of the distribution is likely to be significantly understated for countries whose data rely on household surveys that do not oversample the very rich (as it is done in the US) relative to those that rely on registers (such as Nordic countries and the Netherlands).

6 These results are based on country averages and in the majority of OECD countries for which data are available.

7 VAT is more beneficial for growth compared to other taxes in the tax mix in part because VAT is not levied on exports, and the tax base is relatively immobile (Akgun et al., 2017). High VAT rates are a characteristic of countries that have highly developed transfer systems. VAT is well-adjusted to a world characterised by increasing levels of globalisation and digitalisation. New international standards – the OECD/G20 VAT/GST VAT Guidelines have led the way in ensuring the ability of VAT to adapt to the challenges of digitalisation.

References

Aghion P, Akcigit U, Lequien M, Stantcheva S. (2017), "Tax Simplicity and Heterogeneous Learning", Working Paper available at: https://scholar.harvard.edu/aghion/publications/does-self-employment-respond-simpler-fiscal-incentives-evidence-france.

Aguiar, M. and M. Bils (2015), "Has Consumption Inequality Mirrored Income Inequality?", American Economic Review, Vol. 105/9, pp. 2725-2756, http://dx.doi.org/10.1257/aer.20120599.

Ahrend, R. et al. (2017), "What Makes Cities More Productive? Evidence From Five OECD Countries on the Role of Urban Governance", Journal of Regional Science, Vol. 57/3, pp. 385-410.

Akgun, O., B. Cournede and J.-M. Fournier (2017), "The Effects of the Tax Mix on Inequality and Growth", OECD Economics Department Working Papers, ECO/WKP(2017)79, OECD Publishing, Paris.

Alvaredo F., A. B. Atkinson, S. Morelli (2016), "The Challenge of Measuring UK Wealth Inequality in the 2000s", Fiscal Studies, Vol. 37, No. 1, pp. 13-33.

Andrews, D., C. Criscuolo and P. Gal (2015), "Frontier Firms, Technology Diffusion and Public Policy: Micro Evidence from OECD Countries", OECD Productivity Working Papers, No. 2, OECD Publishing, Paris.

Attanasio, O., E. Hurst, and L. Pistaferri (2012), "The Evolution of Income, Consumption, and Leisure Inequality in The US, 1980-2010." National Bureau of Economic Research Working Paper 17982.

Attanasio, O. and L. Pistaferri (2016), "Consumption Inequality", Journal of Economic Perspectives—Volume, Vol. 30/2, pp. 2016-3, http://dx.doi.org/10.1257/jep.30.2.3

Autor, D., Dorn, D., Katz, L. F., Patterson, C., & Van Reenen, J. (2017), "The Fall of the Labour Share and the Rise of Superstar Firms", No. dp1482, Centre for Economic Performance, LSE.

Bartolini, D. (2015), "Municipal Fragmentation and Economic Performance of OECD TL2 Regions", OECD Regional Development Working Papers, No. 2015/2, OECD Publishing, Paris.

Berlingieri, G., P. Blanchenay and C. Criscuolo (2017), "The Great Divergence(s)", OECD Science, Technology and Innovation Policy Papers, No. 39, OECD Publishing, Paris.

Blundell, R. and I. Preston (1998), "Consumption Inequality and Income Uncertainty*", The Quarterly Journal of Economics, Vol. 113/2, pp. 603-640, https://doi.org/10.1162/003355398555694.

Boulant, J., M. Brezzi and P. Veneri (2016), "Income Levels And Inequality in Metropolitan Areas: A Comparative Approach in OECD Countries", OECD Regional Development Working Papers, No. 2016/6, OECD Publishing, Paris.

Browning, M., T. Crossley and J. Winter (2014), "The Measurement of Household Consumption Expenditures", Annual Review of Economics, Vol. 6/1, pp. 475-501, http://dx.doi.org/10.1146/annurev-economics-080213-041247.

Burkhauser R.V., N. Hérault, S.P. Jenkins and R. Wilkins (2018), "Survey under-coverage of top incomes and estimation of inequality: what is the role of the UK's SPI adjustment?", Fiscal Studies , Vol. 00, No. 0, pp. 1-28.

Causa, O. and M. Hermansen (2017), "Income redistribution through taxes and transfers across OECD countries", OECD Economics Department Working Papers, No. 1453, OECD Publishing, Paris.

Claus, I., J. Martinez-Vasquez, and V. Vulovic (2014), "Government Fiscal Policies and Redistribution in Asian Countries", In R. Kanbur, C. Rhee, and J. Zhuang, eds. Inequality in Asia and the Pacific: Trends, Drivers, and Policy Implications, London and New York: Routledge and Manila: Asian Development Bank.

De Serres, A. and C. Schwellnus (2018), "Decoupling of Wages and Productivity: Micro-level Mechanisms", OECD Economics Department Working Papers, OECD Publishing, Paris.

Digital Economy Act, 2017 – Available at: http://www.legislation.gov.uk/ukpga/2017/30/contents/enacted

DWP (2017) - Households Below Average Income (HBAI): quality and methodology information report, 2015/16

Fesseau, M. and M. Mattonetti (2013), "Distributional Measures across Household Groups in a National Accounts Framework: Results from an Experimental Cross-country Exercise on Household Income, Consumption and Saving", OECD Statistics Working Papers, No. 2013/04, OECD Publishing, Paris. http://dx.doi.org/10.1787/5k3wdjqr775f-en

Hassett, K. and A. Mathur (2012), "A New Measure of Consumption Inequality", AEI Economic Studies, https://www.aei.org/wp-content/uploads/2012/06/-a-new-measure-of-consumption-inequality_142931647663.pdf (accessed on 22 February 2018).

ILO (2017), "Global Wage Report 2016/2017", ILO, Geneva.

IMF (2014), "Fiscal Policy and Income Inequality", IMF Policy Paper, Washington DC.

Krueger, D. and F. Perri (2006), "Does Income Inequality Lead to Consumption Inequality? Evidence and Theory1", Review of Economic Studies, Vol. 73/1, pp. 163-193, http://dx.doi.org/10.1111/j.1467-937X.2006.00373.x.

Lustig N. (2017), "Fiscal Policy, Income Redistribution and Poverty Reduction in Low and Middle Income Countries", Commitment to Equity (CEQ) Working Paper Series 54, Tulane University, Department of Economics.

Meyer, B., A. Bee and J. X. Sullivan (2013), "Consumption and Income Inequality and the Great Recession", American Economic Review, Papers and Proceedings, May 2013, 178-183.

Meyer, B., A. Bee and J. X. Sullivan (2015), "The Validity of Consumption Data: Are the Consumer Expenditure Interview and Diary Surveys Informative?" in Improving the Measurement of Consumer Expenditures, Christopher Carroll, Thomas Crossley, and John Sabelhaus, editors. University of Chicago Press, 2015, 204-240.

Moretti, E. (2004), "Estimating the Social Return to Higher Education: Evidence from Longitudinal and Repeated Cross-sectional Data", Journal of Econometrics, Vol. 121, pp. 175-212.

O'Farrell, R., Ł. Rawdanowicz and K. Inaba (2016), "Monetary Policy and Inequality", OECD Economics Department Working Papers, No. 1281, OECD Publishing, Paris.

OECD (2009), "Latin American Economic Outlook 2009", OECD Publishing, Paris.

OECD (2011), "Divided We Stand: Why Inequality Keeps Rising", OECD Publishing.

OECD (2012), "Income Inequality and Growth: The Role of Taxes and Transfers", OECD Economics Department Policy Notes, No.9. January 2012.

OECD (2014), "The Distributional Effects of Consumption Taxes in OECD Countries", OECD Publishing, Paris.

OECD (2015a), "In It Together: Why Less Inequality Benefits All", OECD Publishing, Paris.

OECD (2015b), "Social Cohesion Policy Review of Vietnam", OECD Development Centre Studies, OECD Publishing, Paris.

OECD (2016a), "Investing in Integrity for Productivity", Working Party of Senior Public Integrity Officials, GOV/PGC/INT(2016)6.

OECD (2016b), "OECD Regional Outlook 2016: Productive Regions for Inclusive Societies", OECD Publishing, Paris.

OECD (2016c), "The Governance of Inclusive Growth", OECD Publishing, Paris.

OECD (2017a), "Preventing Ageing Unequally", OECD Publishing, Paris.

OECD (2017b), "The Productivity-Inclusiveness Nexus", C/MIN(2016)3.

OECD (2018a), "Productivity and Jobs in a Globalised World: (How) Can All Regions Benefit?", OECD Publishing, Paris.

OECD (2018b), "The Role and Design of Net Wealth Taxes in the OECD", OECD Tax Policy Studies No. 26, OECD Publishing, Paris.

OECD (2018c), "The Taxation of Household Savings", OECD Tax Policy Studies No. 25, OECD Publishing, Paris.

OECD (2018d), OECD Employment Outlook 2018, OECD Publishing, Paris.

OECD/CIAT/IDB (2016), "Taxing Wages in Latin America and the Caribbean", OECD Publishing, Paris.

Piketty, T., E. Saez and G. Zucman (2018), Distributional National Accounts: Methods and Estimates for the United States, Quarterly Journal of Economics, 2018, 133(2): 553-609.

Pistaferri, L. (2015), "Household consumption: Research questions, measurement issues, and data collection strategies", Journal of Economic and Social Measurement, Vol. 40/1-4, pp. 123-149, http://dx.doi.org/10.3233/JEM-150401.

Schwellnus C., Kappeler A., Pionnier P.-A. (2017), "Decoupling of Wages from Productivity: Macro-level Facts", OECD Economics Department Working Paper No. 1373.

Slesnick, D. (1994), "Consumption, Needs and Inequality", International Economic Review, Vol. 35/3, http://www.jstor.org/stable/2527080 (accessed on 22 February 2018), pp. 677-703.

UNDP (2014), "The 2014 Human Development Report - Sustaining Human Progress: Reducing Vulnerabilities and Building Resilience", Human Development Report Office, United Nations, NYC.

WIR (2018), "World Inequality Report", Available at: http://wir2018.wid.world/files/download/wir2018-full-report-english.pdf

World Bank (2015), "The State of Social Safety Nets 2015", Washington, DC: World Bank.

Zwijnenburg, J., S. Bournot and F. Giovannelli (2017), "Expert Group on Disparities in a National Accounts Framework: Results from the 2015 Exercise", OECD Statistics Working Papers, No. 2016/10.

Chapter 2. Support business dynamism and inclusive labour markets

This chapter starts from the trend of sluggish productivity growth that is slowing wage growth, and then elaborates on how ongoing economic transformations are likely to impact the productivity-inclusiveness nexus. While some countries have made progress, high levels of income and non-income inequalities hamper economic growth in most OECD countries. In the context of weak productivity growth in OECD countries, growing wage differences between and within firms have spurred market-income inequality. Concentration has increased in the manufacturing and services sectors in many OECD countries. While employment-to-population rates have increased in several OECD countries, some groups have been left behind. Women, young people and the older population, in particular, do not participate equally in labour and capital markets and find it difficult to start and run business in most countries.

Both structural and fiscal policies are needed to align better growth and inclusiveness objectives - for example, to foster competition and enabling policy frameworks that can open up markets and encourage investment in people, cities, infrastructure and skills. Better coordination of product and labour market policies (also at the international level) would ease implementation of reforms, maximise their impact on growth, job-creation and equity. Labour market policies and institutions are needed to strengthen workers' bargaining position. Shifting part of the financing of social programmes to general tax revenue can help to raise labour market participation, reduce labour market duality and boost labour productivity and economic growth, while at the same time extending support to a larger fraction of society and also covering atypical jobs. The new OECD Jobs Strategy sets out a state of policy principles for promoting a more inclusive labour market that is more resilient and adaptable and built upon more and better jobs.

The Inclusive Growth Framework for Policy Action on Inclusive Growth consolidates some of the key policy recommendations to sustain and more equitably share the gains of economic growth from related OECD work, around broad principles to support business dynamism and inclusive labour markets through:

(i) broad-based innovation and technology diffusion;

(ii) strong competition and vibrant entrepreneurship;

(ii) access to good quality jobs, especially for women and under-represented groups; and

(iv) enhanced resilience and adaptation to the future of work.

Jobs, productivity and equality in the face of digitalisation and trade

The future of production

Innovation is key to drive long-term productivity and income growth. Digitalisation can improve the methods of production process; however, new technologies and know-how require time to get adopted and adapted for business use to strengthen productivity growth (Box 2.1).

Box 2.1. A dynamic business environment is key for employment growth

The OECD work on the productivity-inclusiveness nexus has shown that the gap between high-productivity firms and those lagging behind has increased, even within the same country and narrowly defined industries. This slowdown in productivity growth divergence and increasing inequality are interrelated (Berlingieri et al., 2017). This implies that policy responses that can tackle the increasing productivity divergence could potentially produce a "double dividend" in terms of both greater productivity growth and reduced income inequality.

The heterogeneity in productivity performance has increased across firms within sectors, both at the global level and within countries. At the global level, broad measures of business dynamism that capture the reallocation of resources have worsened significantly over time (Andrews et al., 2016).

At the global level this divergence is also linked to the slowdown in aggregate productivity and hints at some of its potential deeper causes: (i) insufficient diffusion of the technology and knowledge to the laggard firms that find it increasingly difficult to catch up; and (ii) slowing down the process of "creative destruction" with lesser exit of inefficient firms and slower reallocation of resources to growing new firms (Andrews et al., 2016). This has implications for aggregate productivity growth but also for employment growth. Small start-ups and young firms contribute twice as much to job creation than to job destruction or total employment. Older SMEs and older large firms account for the bulk of employment across countries, but - on aggregate - create fewer jobs than they destroy (Criscuolo et al., 2014).

Within countries and sectors (Berlingieri et al., 2017), the productivity has dispersed substantially over time. The within-sector productivity dispersion has increased for both labour and multi-factor productivity, with a remarkably similar pattern across all productivity measures. This divergence in productivity is found to be linked to a divergence in wages across firms. In turn, these firm-level patterns can account for a significant part of the increase in overall earnings inequality.

Sources: Criscuolo et al. (2014); Andrews et al. (2016); Berlingieri et al. (2017a; 2017b).

Digital transformation is not just about the technology, but about how technology is combined with other changes and investments within firms. For digitalisation to strengthen in overall growth performance, the divide between frontier and lagging firms needs to be closed by firms investing in the intangible capital and adapting their business models; workers acquiring new skills; and countries developing their digital infrastructure and adopting favourable framework policies (OECD, 2018a). As advanced economies converge towards the frontier, growth should become increasingly innovation-driven;

while for emerging and developing countries that have come less far along the convergence process, the ability to adopt technologies is key to raising productivity and speed up structural change.

Digitalisation has not yet materialised in higher aggregate productivity growth. Business dynamism has declined across OECD countries, contributing to a slowdown against slow capital deepening and weak multi-factor productivity growth (Figure 2.1). Recent analysis suggests that the contribution from entrants to aggregate productivity growth has declined over the last decade, both because of the reduced role of entrants in aggregate output and because of a decline in the relative productivity of entrants compared to incumbents (Figure 2.2).[8] Declining business dynamism implies a lower share of young firms and a higher share of low-productivity incumbents (Andrews et al, 2016; Figure 2.3). This relative ageing of the firm population indirectly affects the productivity performance of incumbent firms as it makes it easier for weak firms to survive, without adopting best practices emerging from digitalisation.

Firms' uptake of new technologies is uneven. While digital technologies offer new opportunities for businesses to participate in global markets, innovate and scale up, many firms are not yet using the productivity-enhancing applications that can drive productivity and improve performance (Figure 2.4). Effective use of new technology requires that firms invest in new business models, managerial and organisational change; which also drives competition for talent and new skills. Most SMEs and large firms are connected to broadband network and have their own website. However, advanced ICT applications such as enterprise resource planning software, cloud computing and big data are used only by some businesses, typically the largest ones.

Figure 2.1 Declining business dynamism across 20 OECD and non-OECD economies

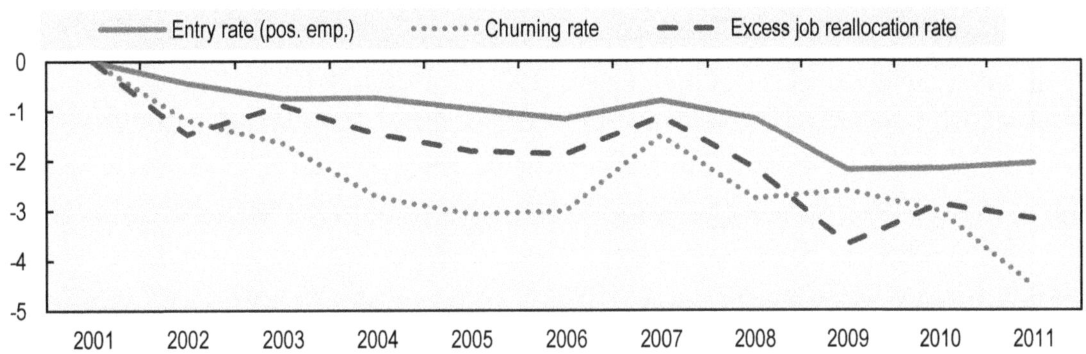

Note: The entry rate is defined using the number of units with positive employment (number of entering units with positive employment over total number of units with positive employment). The churning rate is defined as the sum of the gross job creation rate and the gross job destruction rate. The excess job reallocation rate is defined as churning rate less the absolute value of net employment growth for the period. Excess job reallocation thus reflects the job reallocation that occurs over and above the minimum necessary to accommodate the net employment changes. The figure reports regression coefficients of within-sector country regressions of the relevant variable on year dummies with 2001 being the reference year. Years before 2001 and after 2011 are excluded due to the more limited data coverage. Estimates are based on data for 20 countries (AUT, BEL, BRA, CRI, DNK, ESP, FIN, FRA, GBR, HUN, ITA, JPN, LUX, NLD, NOR, NZL, PRT, SWE, TUR, USA).
Source: OECD DynEmp v.2 and OECD DynEmp v.3. database.

StatLink http://dx.doi.org/10.1787/888933724955

Figure 2.2 Business dynamism and productivity growth

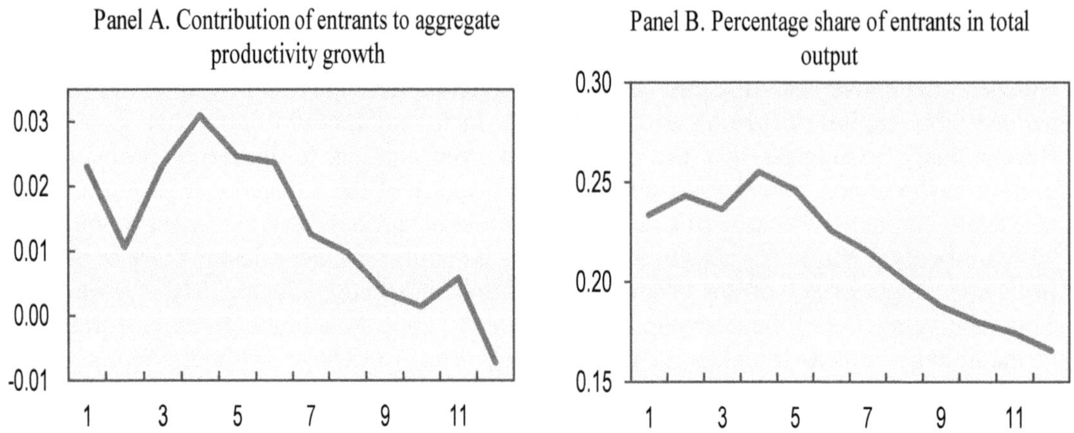

Note: The figure relies on multi-factor productivity computed as a Solow residual, using external, industry specific labour shares from OECD STAN. Entrants are defined as firms which are 0-5 years old. The figure corresponds to a regression-adjusted weighted mean across countries and A38 industries. It is based on the following countries: Austria, Belgium, Chile, Denmark, Hungary, Italy, Japan, Netherland, Norway and Portugal.
Source: OECD Multiprod, May 2017.

StatLink http://dx.doi.org/10.1787/888933724974

Figure 2.3 Changes in the composition of firms in the economy

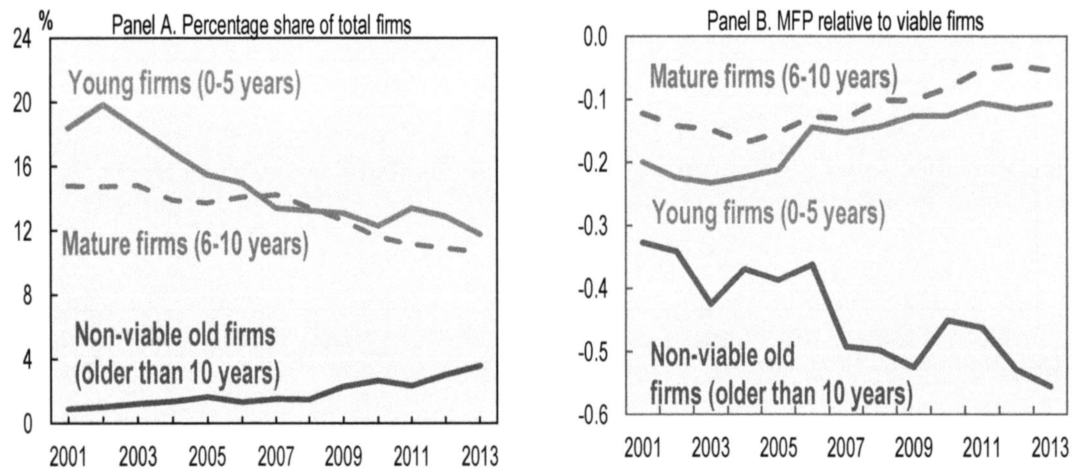

Note: Non-viable old firms are firms older than 10 years that record negative profits over at least two consecutive years. Viable old firms (i.e. older than 10 years that do not record negative profits over at least two consecutive years) are omitted. The age of the firm is inferred from the incorporation date. The estimates are unweighted averages across industries in the non-farm non-financial business sector.
Source: Andrews, Criscuolo and Gal, 2016.

StatLink http://dx.doi.org/10.1787/888933724993

Figure 2.4 Diffusion of selected ICT tools and activities in enterprises

As a percentage of enterprises with ten or more employees, OECD countries (average, min., max.), 2016

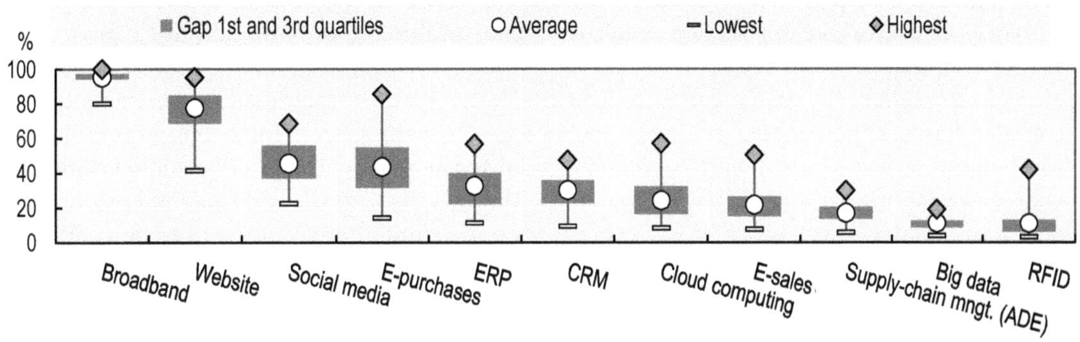

Note: See Source for variables definition and country coverage. Source: OECD, 2017b, http://dx.doi.org/10.1787/888933585457.

StatLink http://dx.doi.org/10.1787/888933585457

Figure 2.5 Enterprises using cloud computing services by firm size

As a percentage of enterprises in each employment size class, 2016

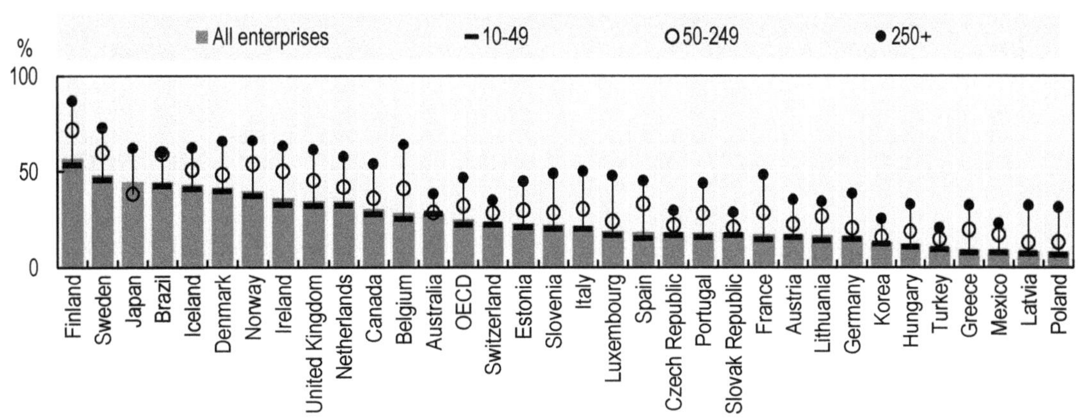

Note: See Source for variables definition and country coverage. Source: OECD, 2017b, http://dx.doi.org/10.1787/888933585495.

StatLink http://dx.doi.org/10.1787/888933585495

Digitalisation and globalisation can reinforce each other. The fragmentation of production in global value chains (GVCs) has been enabled by a decline in the ICT-related costs and strengthened knowledge-sharing. Firms can now specialise in activities within production networks, benefit from complementary investments in technology, process innovation or organisational change, and access new varieties of inputs and knowledge spillovers from foreign frontier firms (Criscuolo and Timmis, 2017). However, a number of factors are needed to realise the growth potential, particularly in enabling younger firms to scale up. Rapid scaling of firms expansion seems to be more of a feature of the US than of other OECD countries (Calvino, Criscuolo and Menon, 2016). Country differences depend on the industrial structure and country size, although can also be affected by institutional and policy settings as well as trade costs and restrictions. High growth is a result of a mix of factors, which include the entrepreneurs' growth ambitions, skills and experience, and access to knowledge networks (Richbell, Watts, & Wardle, 2006; Moen, Heggeseth, & Lome, 2016). Since the most ICT-intensive firms tend to concentrate in a few regions, a digital divide is also opening up between regions (OECD, 2017a). A similarly uneven development or reach of digital-enabled economic activity can occur within countries as well. Focusing solely on reducing the digital divide between countries or regions might not be sufficient to ensure that underserved communities *within* countries can also harness the benefits of digital technology. In particular, efforts to digital include rural communities, women, and youth are critical for increasing the likelihood that digital-enabled economic activity will be inclusive. Limited access to skills and financial resources and high reallocations costs (for example, due to employment protection legislation, insolvency regimes and tax policies) can further reduce the ability of firms to tap into the emerging opportunities of digitalisation.

Figure 2.6 Use of enterprise resource planning by firm size

OECD countries, 2015, %

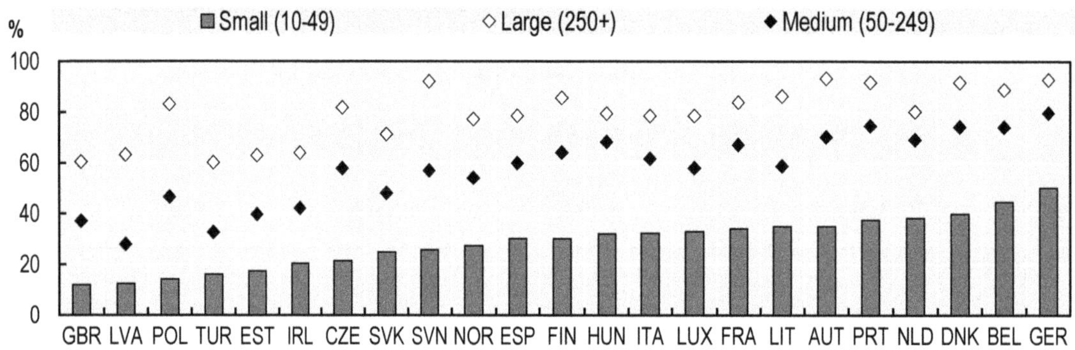

Source: OECD ICT Database.

StatLink http://dx.doi.org/10.1787/888933725012

Digital technologies present both opportunities and challenges for SMEs. The intangible nature and low costs replicability of digital technologies is reducing the need for large upfront investments. In particular, cloud computing and other digital technologies have given SMEs access to computing power, better possibilities for online commerce and advertising without having to incur high transportation, communication and marketing costs. While the costs of adopting basic digital technologies have fallen dramatically, small firms with 10-49 employees are only half as likely as large firms to have business websites and only one third as likely as large firms to use the Enterprise Resource Planning (ERP) platform that integrates core business processes in real-time (Figure 2.6).

Start-ups that grow represent only a tiny fraction of all start-ups. However, it is the rapid scaling up of this small number of successful start-ups that drives the large share of overall job creation by young firms. Most start-ups either fail in the first years of activity or remain very small. This is due to the distinctive "up-or-out" dynamics of start-ups, where high average growth rates co-exist with low survival rates. The majority of enterprises (between 75% and 90%) remain micro-businesses with fewer than ten employees (Figure 2.7).

Figure 2.7 Enterprises by size in terms of employment, business economy

Percentage of all enterprises, 2014, or latest available year

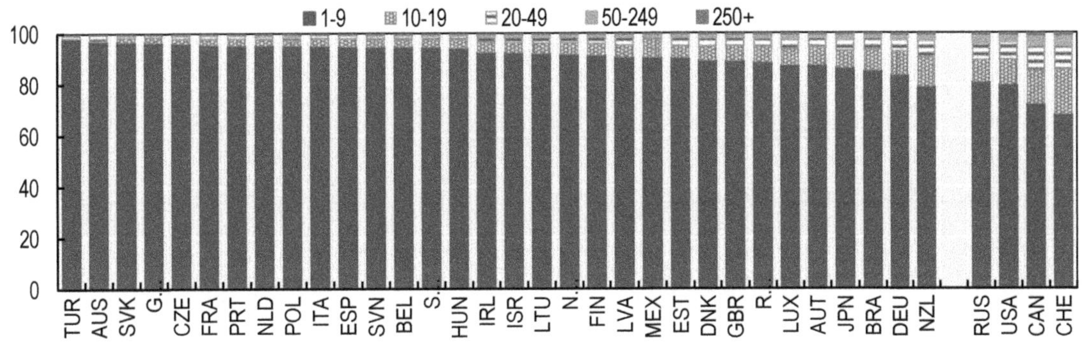

Source: OECD (2017d), Entrepreneurship at a Glance 2017.

StatLink https://doi.org/10.1787/entrepreneur_aag-2017-graph16-en

Emerging and developing countries are also tapping on the growth potential of digitalisation, but large informal sectors hamper progress. Informal firms are often characterised by low managerial skills and face acute difficulties to access finance (La Porta and Shleifer, 2014). The lack of access to credit may constrain their ability to invest in physical and intangible capital as well as training of their workers. Some aspects of the digital transformation, for instance e-payments and mobile payments, have enabled entrepreneurs and start-ups to leapfrog the traditional development path and may have encouraged some business to formalise (McKinsey, 2017). In several countries in Africa, Asia and Latin America, entrepreneurship and start-ups have increased (OECD, 2012). Global talent mobility and production unbundling have helped workers to acquire relevant skills and entrepreneurial culture. The spread of ICT has created opportunities for knowledge exchange, making start-up companies a commercially viable business option. Youth entrepreneurship has gained in importance, helped by policies to support good quality jobs for youth, with successful young entrepreneurs having distinct profiles from low-educated youth (OECD, 2017e).

The digital economy features large economies of scale, potentially creating winner-takes-most dynamics in a range of industries (Brynjolfsson and McAfee, 2011). This may be reinforced by the growing importance of a role in ownership and access to data for competitiveness, as well as strong reputation and network effects. Concentration has increased in the manufacturing and services sector in OECD countries. Recent OECD evidence from the MultiProd database points to an increase in concentration across OECD countries in both the manufacturing and services sector, both when focusing on firms at the top of the sales and those at the top of the productivity distribution (Figure 2.8). Employment concentration has grown more slowly than both gross output and value added concentration is in line with existing evidence (e.g. Autor, et al., 2017 and Berlingieri at al., 2017a): the firms can "scale without mass", that is, attain large market shares with a relatively small workforce, especially in the services sector.

Figure 2.8 The increase in concentration across OECD countries

Share of Gross Output, Employment and Value added at the top of the sales and Labour productivity distribution

a. Sales Distribution

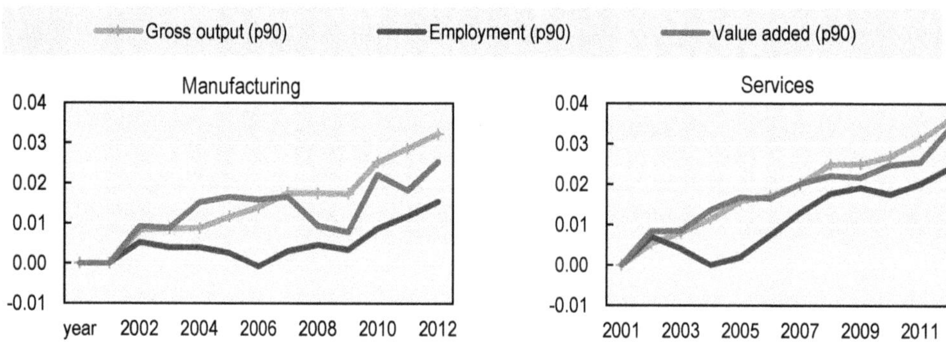

b. Labour Productivity Distribution

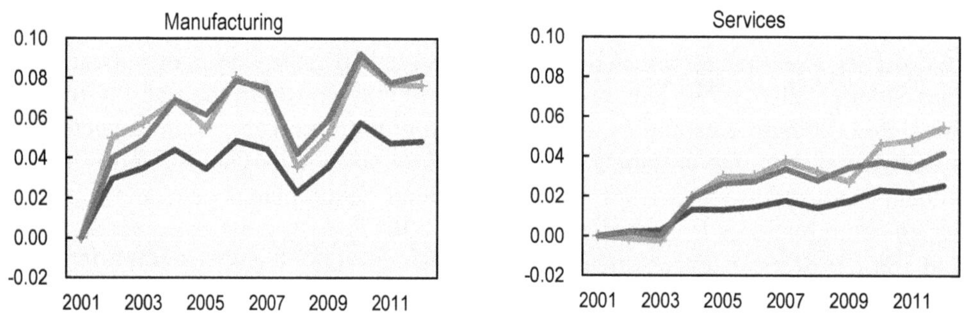

Note: Countries included: Australia, Austria, Belgium, Switzerland, Denmark, Finland Japan, Hungary, Norway Portugal and Sweden. The graphs can be interpreted as the cumulated growth rates of the share of gross output (GO), employment (L), value added (VA) in the top decile of the sales (top panel) and labour productivity (bottom panel) distribution within each country and sector over the period. The estimates reported in the graph are those of year dummies in a cross-country regression of the share of GO, L and VA in the top decile of the distribution with year=2001 being the reference year.

Source: MultiProd database (see http://www.oecd.org/sti/ind/multiprod.htm), December 2017.

StatLink http://dx.doi.org/10.1787/888933725031

New technologies have enabled productive "superstar firms" to gain a large slice of the market share and often also realise high price-cost margins. Recent OECD research confirmed that global frontier firms in the ICT services sector have increased their share over the past decade and that these firms had a significantly larger gap in multi-factor productivity not only vis-à-vis non-frontier firms but even within the group of global frontier firms, that is, between the very top firms (top 2%) and other frontier firms (Figure 2.9; Andrews et al., 2016). Specifically, it focused on the relative performance of frontier firms in ICT services (computer programming, software engineering, data storage, and so on) vis-à-vis other sectors. If the incumbents are more likely to innovate than the rest, then Acemoglu and Hildebrand, (2017) suggest their market shares also increase with innovation.

Figure 2.9 Revenues and multifactor productivity of frontier and laggard firms

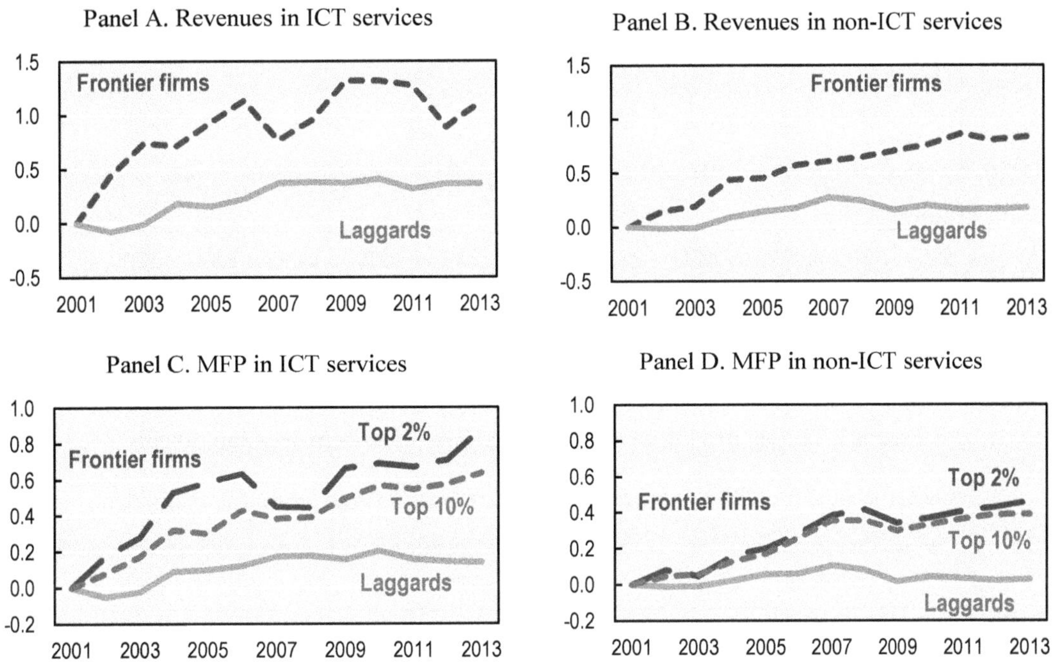

Note: In Panels A and B, the global frontier group of firms is defined by the top 5% of companies with the highest MFP levels within each 2-digit industry, while Panels C and D employ two definitions of the global frontier based on the top 2%, and 10% of the MFP distribution to emphasize a growing dispersion at the top of the productivity distribution. Laggards capture all the other firms. Unweighted averages across 2-digit industries are shown for sales and MFP, separately for services and ICT services, normalized to 0 in the starting year. Time period is 2001-2013. Services refer to non-financial business services. ICT-intensive services refer to the information and communication sector (industry code J in NACE Rev. 2) and postal and courier activities (53). MFP is based on the Wooldridge (2009) methodology for production function estimation.
Source: Andrews, Criscuolo and Gal, 2016.

StatLink http://dx.doi.org/10.1787/888933725050

The productivity-inclusiveness nexus is also influenced by a number of recent trends. For example, non-digital firms' cross-border acquisition of digital assets is increasing rapidly; from USD 16.6 billion in 2014 to USD 22.2 billion in 2015 (a 34% increase) and to USD 73.6 billion in 2016 (a 230% increase) (Figure 2.10). Traditional industries are increasingly using M&A activity to expand into the digital economy. The benefits of such activity can include increased R&D investment and the elimination of duplicative margins for products that rely on digital technology inputs.

Figure 2.10 Cross-border acquisition of digital assets by non-digital firms

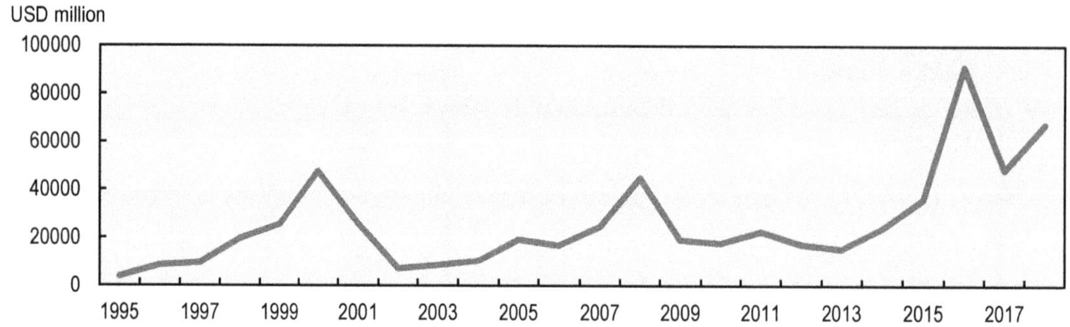

Source: Dealogic database.

StatLink http://dx.doi.org/10.1787/888933725069

Figure 2.11 Fast growth in number of M&As of data processing targets

Change in number of M&As per year relative to 2005, top 5 fastest growing 3-digit sectors

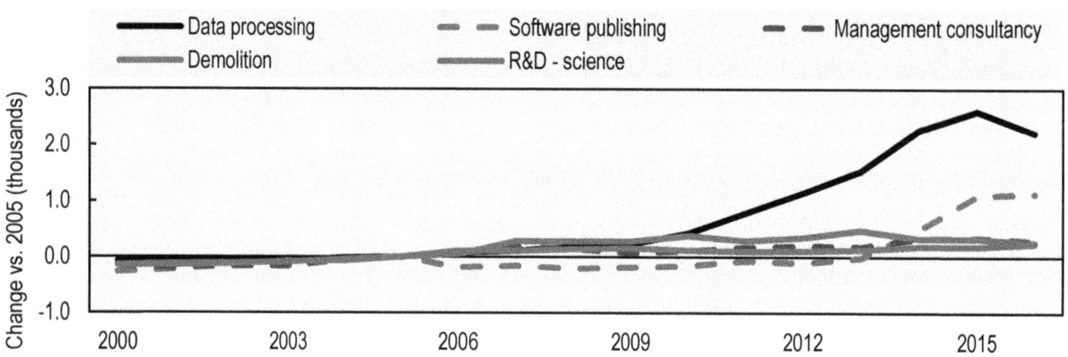

Note: Industry reflects the primary NACE rev.2 industry of the target firm. Show for the top 5 3 digit industries with the fastest growth in number of deals over 2005-2016.
Source: BvD Zephyr M&A Database.

StatLink http://dx.doi.org/10.1787/888933725088

Mergers and acquisitions have increased rapidly for some digital sectors over the past years. In particular, the number of acquisitions of data processing services firms has grown more than any other digital or non-digital sectors (Figure 2.11). Strong increase in purchases of ICT firms may have varied implications for competition and the diffusion of digital technologies. When an acquirer is itself in the digital sector, it may acquire new technologies and skills, facilitate the diffusion of complementary digital technologies, but also acquire potential future competitors.

State-owned enterprises are dominating mergers and acquisitions. The sale of state-owned assets to private firms amounted to only US$ 0.2 billion, while SOE acquisitions of private businesses reached approximately USD 113.2 billion in December 2017 (Figure 2.12). This could be an indication of uneven market access. Large SOEs that are dominant in their home jurisdiction (and not subject to the principles of competitive neutrality) can engage in M&A overseas, while foreign competitors would have limited merger and acquisitions (M&A) opportunities to enter the SOE's home market. This could have significant implications for the competitive dynamics of industries undergoing restructuring, for example the steel industry in view of excess capacity.

Figure 2.12 Asymmetry between state-owned and private-owned enterprises in M&A

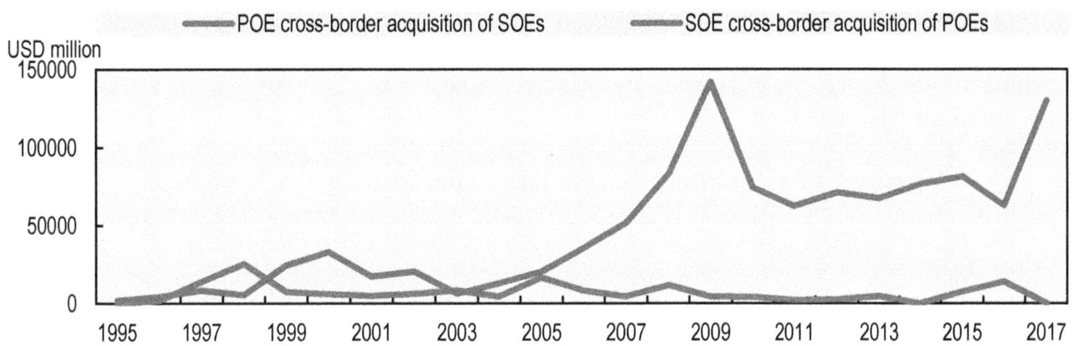

Source: Dealogic database.

StatLink http://dx.doi.org/10.1787/888933725107

The future of work

Globalisation is facilitating the diffusion of innovation and technological advances, which are reshaping the labour markets in all countries and creating new challenges and opportunities for promoting inclusive growth. Advanced economies remain central in services value chains, although the reconfiguration of GVCs could create disruptions for emerging economies that rely on industrialisation as a path to catch-up. There are concerns that digitalisation could reorient global production and trade back towards advanced countries ("reshoring"). Evidence of reshoring is limited at this stage, but concerns are rising that robotics, automation, computerised manufacturing and artificial intelligence could in the future reduce the cost advantages of production in emerging economies. At the same time, new technologies such as 3D printing could tip the scales towards small-scale localised production and erode the cost advantage of emerging economies in low-tech manufacturing as a source of jobs and growth (DeBacker and Flaig, 2017). On the other hand, digitalisation could provide large emerging economies with new opportunities to "leapfrog" the traditional development path.

New technologies will affect the availability, nature and quality of jobs. The future of work will generate opportunities for new and more productive jobs, but will also lead to wide-ranging disruptions and risks for the inclusiveness of growth, as some skills become obsolete while others may be in shortage. In advanced countries, there are concerns about job opportunities lost to offshoring in manufacturing and increasingly in services, although new opportunities for "reshoring" are opening up. At the same time, globalisation has led to new, more skilled jobs as firms sought to increase their competitiveness by moving up the value-added chain by investing in a more skilled workforce. Likewise, the impacts of technological change on jobs will depend on a host of economic, legal and social factors, as well as on the availability of the requisite skills.

Thus far, increased import penetration has only had a minor impact on manufacturing employment and trade has provided opportunities for manufacturing jobs in a few advanced countries and many emerging market economies (OECD

2017b). Likewise, greater use of ICT has thus far had little impact on employment growth in the economy as a whole (OECD 2017c). ICT and automation have led to restructuring but have not resulted in greater unemployment at the aggregate level (Bessen, 2016; Gaggle and Wright, 2015; Graetz and Michaels, 2017; Cortes and Salvatori, 2016; Autor, 2015; Autor et al., 2015) and may even have contributed to job creation (e.g. Mann and Püttman, 2017). This may be because the decline in the cost of ICT capital has reduced labour demand per unit of output, but at the same time progressively led to lower prices and new products, higher aggregate demand and higher employment. This offsets at least some of the initial job displacement.

Figure 2.13 A significant share of jobs will be affected by automation

Percentage of jobs at high risk of automation and at risk of significant change

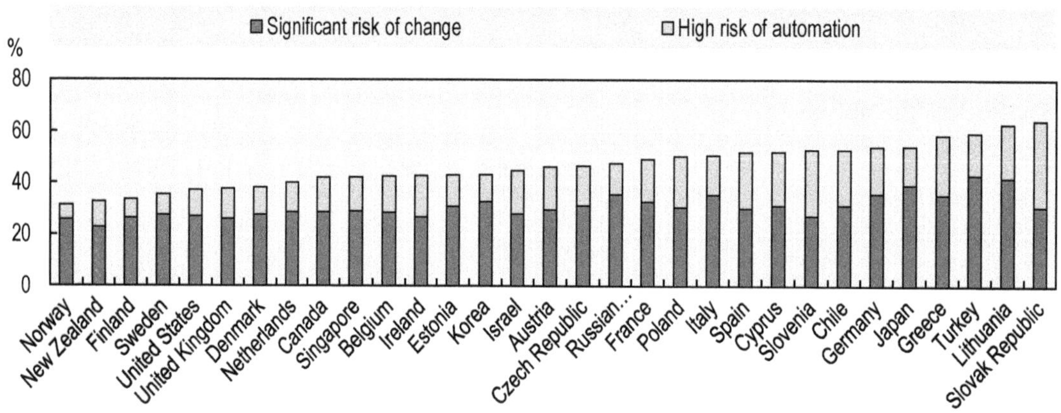

Source: OECD (2018a).

StatLink http://dx.doi.org/10.1787/888933725126

New forms of employment and tasks are emerging. Automation can lead to job losses in the short-term, particularly in the exposed industries as new technologies makes some jobs redundant, but in the long-term can raise the demand for other jobs and encourage the creation of new tasks (Acemoglu and Restrepo, 2016 and 2017; Autor and Salomons, 2017; Gregory et al., 2016; Figure 2.13). While recent estimates suggest that about 14% of today's jobs in OECD countries have a high risk of automation in the next 15-20 years, a further 32% could see substantial change in the way they are carried out and the tasks performed (Nedelkoska and Quintini, 2018 forthcoming). This implies that incentives and opportunities to re-skill and upgrade existing skills will need to be strengthened, especially for low-skilled workers who face the highest risk of seeing their jobs either partially or totally automated and yet participate least in training.

Globalisation and technological change are leading to a significant reallocation of employment between activities. This may give rise to complicated transitions for workers and create distress in the sectors and regions that have fewer opportunities to adapt. The regional concentration of manufacturing employment makes regions less resilient when hit by sector-specific shocks to the manufacturing sector; whether originating from a technological change, import competition or other factors. Moreover, in the context of ongoing climate change, jobs will shift as emission-intensive activities change business profiles and technologies, even if the impact on overall employment is likely to be modest

(OECD, 2017f). On the one hand, additional jobs could be created elsewhere, for example, in the manufacturing of pollution-control devices and renewable energy production (ILO, 2018), when shifting from fossil fuels to renewables, or from truck manufacturing to rail car manufacturing, or from land filling and waste incineration to recycling. On the other hand, some jobs may disappear without direct replacement, if for example packaging materials are discouraged or banned and their production is discontinued. Large impacts in individual sectors may not translate into a large overall reallocation of activity and jobs because the most carbon-intensive industries represent only a small share of total value-added and employment. The modest aggregate effect on jobs of the low-carbon transition hides substantial job losses and geographical dislocation in some sectors, in addition to significant creation of new jobs, some of which require new skills.

A more general concern expressed by workers is that globalisation and digital transformation are contributing to poorer working conditions and lower quality jobs. New forms of employment are emerging that can promote greater labour market inclusiveness if concerns about job quality are addressed. Both a more digitalised and globalised world have given rise to the "platform economy", in which workers carry out "gigs" either in person (for example, delivering food and providing rides) or online (such as transcription and product categorisation). Workers that can carry out individual tasks required by consumers over online platforms, often perform these tasks or "gigs" as independent contractors. There is an increasing number of non-standard workers who may only work occasionally and have multiple jobs and income sources, with frequent transitions between dependent employment, self-employment and work-free periods (Figure 2.14). These new forms of employment can offer much flexibility – both regarding where and when the work is carried out – and therefore provide opportunities for people who have been excluded from the labour market due to caring responsibilities or because they live in remote areas. Yet some of these jobs raise concerns about job quality, for example, the remuneration received may be low with little or no employment protection and social security coverage (OECD, 2018a; OECD, 2018b; OECD, 2018c).

No major trade-offs are found between the quantity and quality of jobs in OECD countries. Promoting a more inclusive labour market by helping more people into jobs does not have to be at the expense of lower job quality standards, e.g. lower rates of pay. Figure 2.15 plots different dimensions of job quality – earnings quality, labour market insecurity and the quality of the working environment – against the employment rate in OECD countries. A key message that emerges is that there is no systematic evidence of a trade-offs between higher employment rates and better job quality as a number of countries have achieved both. Nevertheless, job quality levels vary substantially among countries with similar employment levels. For example, Estonia and Denmark have similar employment rates, but earnings quality is much higher in Denmark, reflecting both higher productivity and lower earnings inequality (Box 2.2; OECD, 2018a; OECD, 2018b; OECD, 2018c).

Box 2.2. The OECD Job Quality Framework

Job quality is an inherently multi-dimensional concept that refers to those job attributes that contribute to the well-being of workers. Building on the influential report by the Stiglitz-Sen-Fitoussi Commission (Stiglitz et al., 2009), which identified eight dimensions of well-being, the OECD Job Quality framework was developed (OECD, 2014). It is structured around three of those eight dimensions that are closely related to people's employment situation, namely material living standards, insecurity of an economic as well as physical nature, and personal activities including work.

The development of the OECD Job Quality framework led to the construction of indicators for each of these dimensions, drawing on the existing literature in economics, sociology and occupational health, as well as pragmatic considerations of obtaining measures that could be easily obtained for most countries and were available at the individual level (Cazes et al., 2015). Since this framework has been widely endorsed (for example, by the G20 at the summit in Ankara in September 2015), it is also adopted here as a key component of the labour market performance measurement framework for the new OECD Jobs Strategy.

The OECD Job Quality framework measures job quality along three dimensions:

- Earnings quality. Earnings quality refers to the extent to which the earnings received by workers in their jobs contribute to their well-being by taking account of both the average level as well as the way earnings are distributed across the workforce.
- Labour market security. Labour market security measures the risk of unemployment (the risk of becoming unemployed and the expected duration of unemployment) and the degree of public unemployment insurance (coverage of benefits and their generosity).
- The quality of working environment. The quality of working environment captures non-economic aspects of job quality and measures the incidence of job strain that is characterised by a combination of high job demands and few job resources to meet those demands. The incidence of very long hours of work is also used as an alternative indicator of the quality of the working environment since the data required to measure job strain are not available in most emerging economies.

Sources: Cazes et al. (2015); OECD (2014); OECD (2018a); OECD (2018b).

In line with the productivity-equality nexus, both wage differences between and within firms contribute to income inequality. In fact, the bulk of wage inequality at a given time reflects wage differences within firms (Abowd et al., 1999 for France; Card et al., 2013, for Germany; Torres et al., 2013, for Portugal; Schaefer and Singleton, 2017, for the United Kingdom; Song et al., 2015 for the United States). Workers-related or jobs-related characteristics (e.g. skills, age or tenure, full time versus part time) do not explain all wage differences across workers (ILO, 2017). In Europe in 2010, wage inequality within enterprises accounted for almost half of total wage inequality. Growing inequality within firms has been explained by the decline in wage premium for low-skilled workers in large firms (Song et al., 2015) and the growing wage of corporate managers and high-skilled professionals, who have benefited from much higher wage increases than their co-workers (Piketty, 2013; Sabadish and Michel, 2012). Box 2.3 provides more insights on drivers of inequality in earnings between and within firms from the latest research.

Figure 2.14 The share of non-standard workers is high in some countries

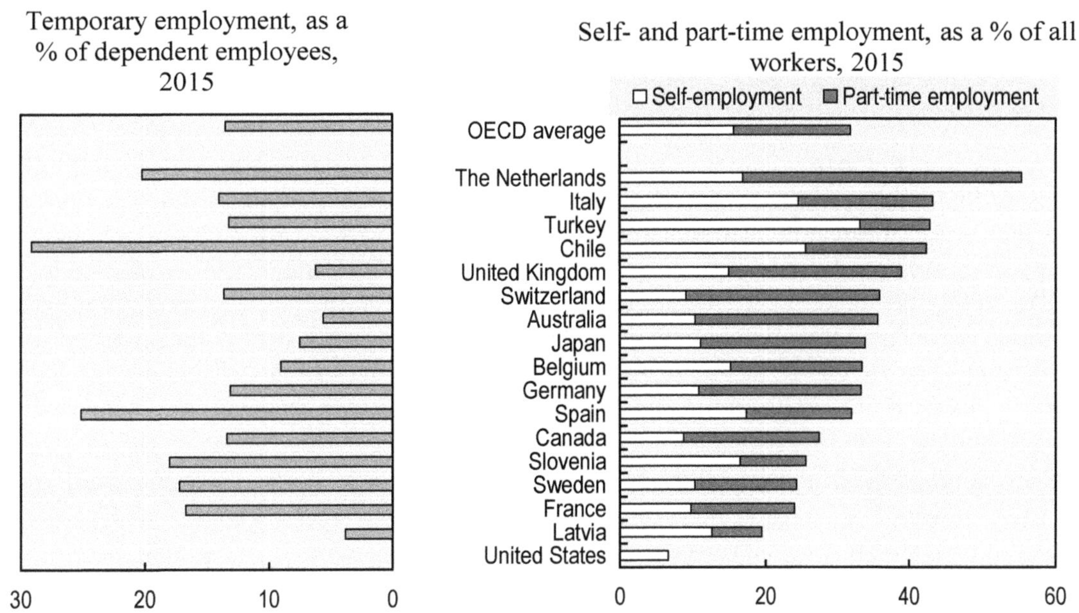

Note: Data on self-employment in France refer to 2011; data on temporary and part-time workers is not available for the US.
Source: OECD Employment and Labour Market Statistics Database and OECD (2017a).

StatLink http://dx.doi.org/10.1787/888933725145

Youth and low-skilled workers are more affected by economic shocks than prime- age workers and high-skilled workers; and perform jobs of lower quality. Looking at job quality outcomes across socio-economic groups reveals that over the past decade, the deep and prolonged economic crisis led to a worsening of labour market security that particularly hit the youth and low-skilled workers (Figure 2.16). These two groups tend to be the most disadvantaged ones – not only do they have the poorest outcomes in terms of employment and unemployment rates, but they also have the worst outcomes with respect to job quality (in terms of lower earnings quality, considerably higher labour market insecurity and higher job strain especially for the low-skilled). By contrast, high-skilled workers perform well on all three dimensions. For women, the picture is mixed: their employment rates are still substantially lower than those for men, and women suffer a large gap in earnings quality (OECD, 2016a). The employment challenge is pressing in developing countries with demographic pressures and scarce wage employment opportunities for youth. Between 2015 and 2020, 60 million jobs would have to be generated to provide jobs for the projected number of youth entering the labour market in South Asia; 42 million in sub-Saharan Africa and 30 million in the Middle East and North Africa to provide jobs for the projected number of youth entering the labour market (World Bank, 2015; WIR, 2018).

Box 2.3. Explaining inequality in earnings between and within firms

Seemingly identical workers may not earn equally on the same jobs. Krueger and Summers (1988) were among the first to document this gap for different sectors of the US economy; although similar findings were found for other countries.

Alvarez et al. (2016) find that almost two-thirds of the overall earnings dispersion in Brazil's formal sector came from between-firm differences in average earnings in 1996. One-third of the overall dispersion in earnings came from within-firm differences in pay. Most of Brazil's decline in earnings inequality between 1996 and 2012 is explained by the falling pay heterogeneity between firms, while a fall in the pay distribution within firms contributed less. By contrast in the US, Song et al. (2015) show that dispersion in earnings has been larger within firms than between firms over 1978-2013. However, for the "mega-firms" with more than 10,000 workers, both inequalities increased substantially over the same period by roughly equal magnitudes.

Following workers across different employers in the longitudinal data, recent empirical work confirms the relative importance of within-firm pay heterogeneity. In general, roughly half of the inequality relates to differences between workers and around one fifth to inherent differences between firms (e.g. Abowd et al., 1999; Andrews et al., 2008). However, Card, Heining and Kline (2013), Alvarez et al. (2016) and Song et al. (2015) attribute a substantial share of the shifts in earnings inequality over time to changes in the distribution of firm pay heterogeneity for some countries ("between firm" wage inequality).

Alvarez et al. (2016) find that close to 60% of the pay heterogeneity across employers is explained by differences in labour productivity, measured by value added per worker at the firm level. The link between productivity and earnings accounts for the largest share of the decline in dispersion of both worker pay and firm pay over time (Alvarez et al., 2016). High-skill workers tend to self-select themselves to high-pay firms (e.g. Song et al., 2015); however, outsourcing should also be taken into account as it has been shown to contribute to high between-firm wage dispersion in Germany (Goldschmidt and Schmieder, 2017).

Sources: Adapted from the literature review by Christian Moser, Columbia University; synthesising among others the work by Krueger and Summers (1988), Song et al. (2015), Alvarez et al. (2016), Abowd, Kramarz and Margolis (1999), Andrews et al. (2008), Card, Heining and Kline (2013), Goldschmidt and Schmieder (2017), Adalet McGowan et al. (2017).

Figure 2.15 Employment and job quality dimensions

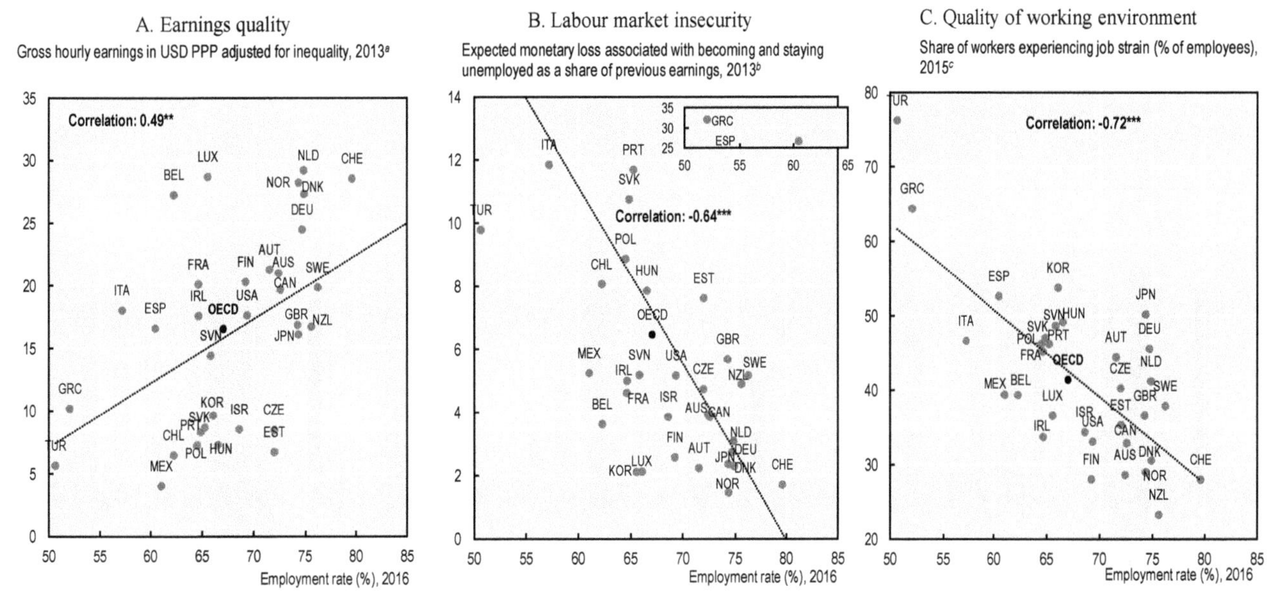

Note: Correlation coefficient is statistically significant at 0.1% level (***) or at 1% level (**). Data for the OECD are unweighted averages for job quality measures and a weighted average for the employment rate. a) Data refer to 2013 except for Estonia, Luxembourg, Netherlands, Slovenia and Turkey (2010); Israel (2011); France, Italy, Poland, Spain, Sweden and Switzerland (2012) and Canada, Czech Republic, Hungary, Korea, Mexico, Norway, Slovak Republic, the United Kingdom and the US (2014). b) Data refer to 2013 except for Chile (2011). c) Data refer to 2015 except for Australia, Canada, Israel, Japan, Korea, Mexico, New Zealand, Switzerland and the US (2005) and Norway and Turkey (2010). No data available for Chile and Iceland.
Source: OECD calculations based on OECD Job Quality database, and the OECD Employment Database.

StatLink http://dx.doi.org/10.1787/888933725164

Rapid population ageing will increase substantially the number of older people, who will need help to remain in work or find new work. Ageing also implies job reallocation. Many countries are undergoing significant demographic change. On average across OECD countries, the share of the population aged 65 and over is estimated to rise from less than one person in six in 2015 to more than one person in four by 2050. China is also on the cusp of experiencing pronounced ageing of its population. Fewer young people will be entering the workforce and shortages of qualified labour could arise as larger cohorts of older workers retire. Longer working lives may be accompanied by more numerous job changes. Population ageing is also likely to lead to reallocations of labour across sectors and occupations as the overall consumption patterns change: demand will continue to shift from durable goods (such as cars) towards services (such as health care).

Figure 2.16 Job quality outcomes by socio-demographic group

Cross-country averages

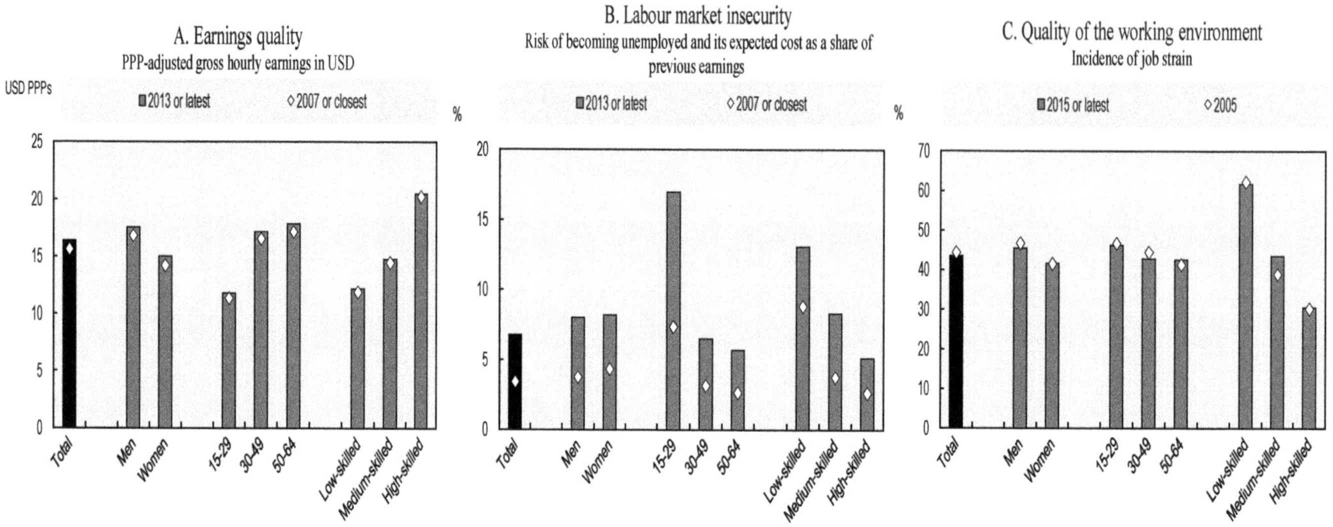

Note: Unweighted averages based on countries for which all information by group is available depending on the indicator reported. Average in Panel A refers to 28 countries (not including Israel, Latvia, Luxembourg, New Zealand, Slovenia, Switzerland and Turkey), to 28 countries in Panel B (not including Chile, Israel, Latvia, New Zealand, Norway, Switzerland and Turkey), and to 23 countries in Panel C (not including Australia, Canada, Chile, Iceland, Israel, Japan, Korea, Latvia, Mexico, New Zealand, Switzerland and the US).
Source: OECD (2017), "Job quality", OECD Employment and Labour Market Statistics (database), http://dx.doi.org/10.1787/e357cdbf-en (Accessed on 13 December 2017).

StatLink http://dx.doi.org/10.1787/888933725183

Figure 2.17 Labour markets have polarised in nearly all OECD countries

Change in percentage point change in share of total employment, 1995 to 2015

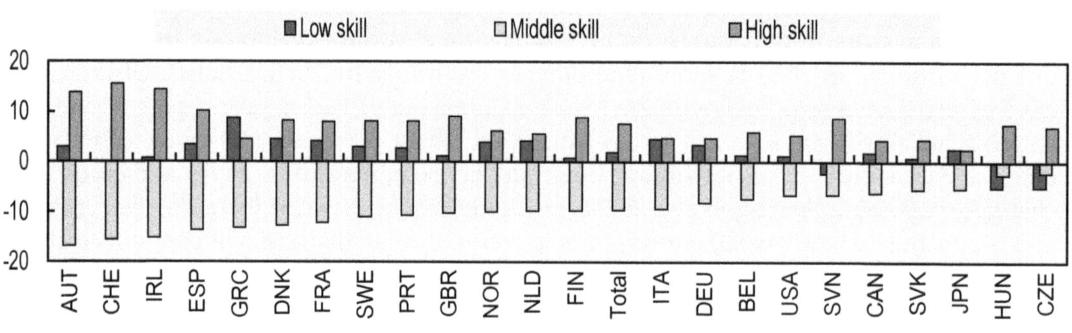

Source: OECD Employment Outlook 2017.

StatLink http://dx.doi.org/10.1787/888933477940

All these mega-trends –digitalisation, globalisation, demographic change and climate change mitigation– are changing demand for skills. For example, technological advances require cognitive skills, such as interpretation, analysis and communication of complex information and problem-solving, while automation is reducing demand for basic skills in numeracy and literacy, and manual skills particularly in the manufacturing sector

(OECD, 2016a; OECD, 2016b; OECD, 2017g; OECD, 2018c). Workers performing "routine" tasks tend to be at a higher risk of losing their jobs to automation. Mega-trends may associate with the labour market polarisation. Over the past two decades, most OECD countries have experienced a process of polarisation away from middle-skill jobs to low-skill and high-skill jobs (Figure 2.17). However, job polarisation does not necessarily result in wage polarisation and greater wage inequality (Acemoglu and Autor, 2011; Mischel, Shierholz and Schmitt, 2013; Dustmann, Ludsteck and Schönberg 2009; Salvatori, 2015).[9] Also, there is evidence that routine jobs are more likely to be offshored and to be associated with wage declines, while imports from low-wage countries contribute to greater wage dispersion across firms (OECD, 2017a). Similarly, Acemoglu and Restrepo (2017) find large negative wage effects in the US regions most exposed to robots, while Dauth et al. (2017) find that exposure to robots results in sizeable negative effects on earnings for low-skilled and especially medium-skilled manufacturing workers in Germany (Dauth et al., 2017). Similar negative effects on wages for low-skilled workers across 17 countries are obtained by (Graetz and Michaels, 2017).

Policies to enhance inclusive markets

Stimulate creation of good quality jobs for all in the global and digital era

Making globalisation and digitalisation work for all requires a well-aligned approach. Policies have to go well beyond traditional coping mechanisms to support those who lose out from globalisation and are displaced by the technological change; policies need a strong focus on strengthening the enabling factors to help firms, workers and communities to adjust to rapid changes and thrive. Because of the many critical uncertainties that the simultaneous and rapid unfolding of these mega-trends entail, it is difficult to foresee all the potential changes that might affect the world of work in years to come. If labour markets are unable to adapt quickly and align themselves to the trajectories traced by these mega-trends, countries will struggle to maintain high levels of job quantity and quality, and to ensure labour market inclusiveness. Policy makers should therefore target efforts on making labour markets more flexible, resilient and adaptable, so that workers and firms can manage the transition with the least possible disruption, while maximising the potential benefits. In particular, as set out in the new OECD Jobs Strategy (OECD, 2018a), policy efforts should focus on: investing in skills; facilitating worker redeployment; strengthening social protection; future-proofing labour market regulation; and promoting social dialogue. A special emphasis should be placed on low-income and low-skilled people who may be impacted by mega-trends disproportionally more than high-skilled people. In this regard, policies (e.g. skilling, redeployment, social protection, labour market regulation and social dialogue) need to be targeted and tailored to the most disadvantaged individuals.

Investing in knowledge

An effective education and training system is a precondition to high-quality employment. Individuals with the right skills are more likely to be employed and, when in employment, tend to have better jobs. A skilled workforce makes it easier to innovate and adopt new technologies and work organisation practices, thereby boosting productivity growth. A high-quality initial education and training system will be crucial to give individuals the best possible start in the labour market by providing them with strong basic skills, socio-emotional skills and specific skills required by employers. Life-long learning needs to be encouraged (OECD, 2018a; OECD, 2018b).

Ensuring that everyone has the right mix of skills for an increasingly digital and globalised world is essential to promote inclusive growth. The right mix of skills includes good general cognitive skills, such as literacy and numeracy, that are required in many jobs and needed for life-long learning to meet the skills requirements that keep on changing (OECD 2018a; OECD 2017g; OECD, 2016b). In addition, as routine tasks tend to disappear on the job, and workers need to work in combination with technology, a set of complementarity skills such as solving problems, thinking creatively, and communicating efficiently are increasingly valued by employers as they cannot be easily performed by machines. Finally, most workers need to have some ICT generic skills in addition to technical and professional skills linked to their area of work, with know-how about new technologies such as artificial intelligence and cloud computing (OECD, 2017r, OECD, 2016h; OECD, 2015l).

Not all adults have the skills to face these challenges. The Survey of Adult Skills (PIAAC) shows that on average in the OECD, more than 20% of adults are low performers in literacy and/or numeracy (Figure 2.18). At the time of the PIAAC Survey (2012 or 2015 depending on countries), around 15% of adults had no prior computer experience or did not have basic ICT skills, and around 14% scored at a low level of problem solving skills in technology-rich environments (OECD, 2016b). While young adults have higher cognitive and ICT skills than older ones in most OECD countries, PISA 2015 shows that on average across OECD countries, 28% of students are able to solve only straightforward collaborative problems, if any at all (OECD, 2016b; OECD, 2017a).

Education systems need to take a holistic approach to skills. Empirical evidence shows that social and emotional skills can be developed through strategies that work with students' feelings and relationships, like role-playing, collaborative-based pedagogies, gaming, case-study and social problem-solving pedagogies and through extracurricular activities, such as sports and arts (Le Donné, Fraser and Bousquet, 2016). These strategies can also help to re-engage students with low performance in core domains and increase motivation to attend and complete schooling. As far as ICT and digital skills are concerned, the use of computers at school is not a significant condition to develop students' ICT skills (OECD, 2018a; OECD, 2018b). The way computers and software are used makes a difference. Training policies to foster teachers' knowledge of pedagogical and technological tools are crucial to help them adopt a holistic approach to skills development.

Policies should aim to reduce inequalities of opportunity among schools. In countries where social background has a stronger influence on student performance, differences in performance between schools are larger (OECD, 2016c). One option is to try to lessen the concentration of disadvantaged and low-performing students in particular schools. This can require policies outside the skills domain, such as housing policies. Allocating more resources, including better teachers, to schools with large concentrations of low-performing students and to disadvantaged schools can reduce inequalities between schools. The design of the school funding system is a powerful tool to tackle inequalities and enhance the quality of education (OECD, 2018a; OECD, 2018b; OECD, 2017i).

University is not the only route to pursue further education. In countries with high-quality vocational education and training (VET) such as Austria, Australia, Germany, the Netherlands and Switzerland, the share of youth neither employed nor in education and training (NEET) is relatively small (OECD, 2015a). To ensure equity in learning outcomes, one needs to achieve more uniform quality across VET programmes. These programmes should respond to labour market needs. While building occupation-specific skills, they need to ensure that solid cognitive, and social and emotional skills are enhanced, so that human capital acquired in these schemes is neither too general nor too specific or narrow.

Figure 2.18 The proportion of low performing adults in literacy and/or numeracy

OECD countries, 2015 (or the latest 2012 for most), %

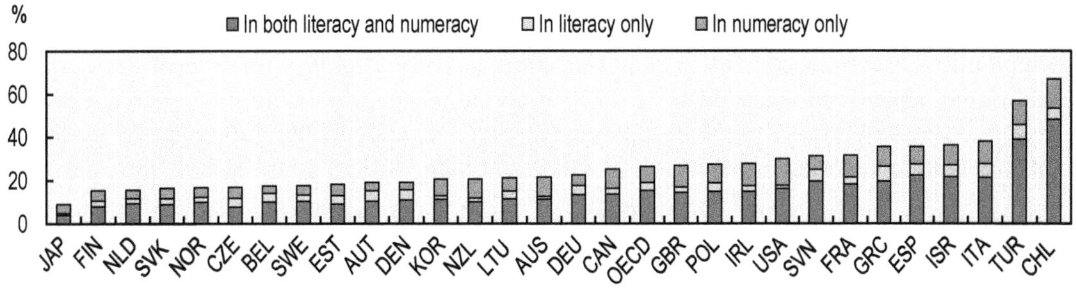

Note: Low performers are defined as those who score at or below Level 1 in either literacy or numeracy according to the Survey of Adult Skills. Chile, Greece, Israel, New Zealand, Slovenia and Turkey: Year of reference 2015. All other countries: Year of reference 2012. Data for Belgium refer only to Flanders and data for the United Kingdom refer to England and Northern Ireland jointly.
Source: OECD calculations based on the Survey of Adult Skills (PIAAC) (2012 and 2015).

StatLink http://dx.doi.org/10.1787/888933725202

Work-based learning is vital to strengthen the links between the education system and the labour market. Work-based learning can be integrated into vocational education and training (VET), but can be encouraged in university programmes. VET programmes that include a work-based learning component at both upper secondary and post-secondary levels offer options to develop skills needed in the labour market. They offer opportunities for employers to engage in the education system and act as quality insurance as employers would be reluctant to provide training places in a programme of poor quality.

Access to tertiary education for youth from low-income families should be supported through specific funding mechanisms. The funding system of tertiary education can play an important role in linking post-secondary education to current and future labour market needs and more generally improving its quality (OECD, 2017f). To achieve these objectives, direct public transfers to higher education institutions can be linked to their performance and need to ensure to guarantee that all students with good performance can enrol in tertiary education. This can be addressed by developing mean-tested student grants and income-contingent loans when tuition fees are introduced or increased. For youth who have dropped out of education and lack the necessary skills, well-designed second-chance programmes can be effective for re-integration. Second-chance programmes promoted by the European Union; or those in Canada, France, Ireland and the US have a strong focus on basic and complementary ICT skills (OECD, 2015a; OECD, 2015b).

Life-long learning

Life-long learning programmes are needed to face some of the digitalisation challenges. As skills requirements keep on changing, adults need learning opportunities beyond initial formal education. Workers in high-technology sectors need to keep pace with rapidly changing techniques. Workers in low-technology industries and those performing low-skilled tasks must learn to be adaptable. Low- and medium-skilled workers are the least-likely to receive training, but may face the greatest risk of job loss.

In general, the existing infrastructures for life-long learning may not be geared up for the significant changes that lie ahead. Significant challenges to reskilling or upskilling over life include: i) the majority of the future workforce has already left initial education; ii) the skills of these workers will become obsolete more quickly as a result of rapid technological change; and iii) they will be required to stay in the labour force for longer. In doing so, countries should fully exploit the opportunities presented by new technologies which allow access to courses to be scaled up massively at only a fraction of the cost of traditional courses, but care must be taken in avoiding marginalising those lacking basic digital skills. Countries should strengthen systems for recognising skills learned through informal and non-formal learning, since this could help workers to relocate to new jobs.

To empower people with productive and employable skills throughout their life, whole-of-government and whole-of-society approaches to skills development and use are needed. Coordination with a range of institutions and actors such as employers, social partners and social institutions can make education and training programmes more responsive to changing needs and help target those with low skills and those who tend to benefit the less from high quality education and training programmes. In many OECD countries, employers and other stakeholders could be more engaged in education and training systems at various stages and through various ways. Good systems and tools for assessing and anticipating skills can also help make the education and training systems more responsive to labour market needs (OECD, 2016d). At the same time, the information on labour market needs should be used to provide career guidance to students and adults to help them make informed education and career choices (OECD 2007f, 2017g).

Policies to create talent pools

Besides developing new competencies, policies that encourage on-the-job training and innovation can improve well-being in the workplace and boost productivity. Good wages and working conditions can promote productivity growth as they enhance motivation, worker effort, skills use and incentives for learning and innovation. Policies supporting learning and innovation in the workplace include adequate regulatory frameworks that promote well-being in the workplace but also a range of labour market policies such as well-functioning collective bargaining institutions. Governments need to put in place well-designed regulatory frameworks that ensure adequate standards for working conditions based on occupational health and safety regulations to reduce physical and mental health risks, working time regulations that limit excessive working hours and frame working schedules as well as balanced employment protection provisions to protect workers against possible abuses.

Well-functioning collective bargaining institutions can be useful, particularly when associated with high coverage. They can foster skills development and use in the workplace and allow for the effective dissemination of good working practices. Governments can promote high-performance management and working practices, which emphasise team work, autonomy, task discretion, mentoring, job rotation and the use of new tools, through information dissemination and advice on best-practices.

Labour market programmes and effective, modern public employment services can ease the transition to new jobs. Rising participation in non-standard working arrangements that are not tied to one's job, like temporary or part-time contracts or gig work, creates the need for training opportunities. In the long term, effective educational and labour market policies can prepare workers for a world in which skills requirements are evolving fast, by facilitating the development of skills at various phases of life. Retraining low-skilled workers is one of the biggest challenges that many countries face. Countries have to find efficient ways to develop skills, while breaking the vicious cycle between being low-skilled and not participating in adult learning. The obstacles to adult education need to be removed by tax systems that provide strong learning incentives, improved access to formal education for adults, recognition of skills acquired after initial education, and cooperation with trade partners to develop on-the-job training opportunities and enhance flexibility in the sharing of time between work and training.

Facilitating worker redeployment

Besides long-life learning, there are a number of policies that can facilitate labour reallocation and adaptation to technological change and other mega-trends. Policies to promote worker re-deployment can be accompanied by targeted policies that help displaced workers to get back to work quickly. Standard activation policies may not be enough. Intervening early has been found to be the most cost-effective way to provide support to displaced workers. In this context, rules requiring advance notice of redundancy allow the affected workers and relevant labour market authorities to start early in preparing for a smooth adjustment. Most displaced workers may not need much additional help apart from being rapidly oriented and motivated towards active jobs search, but some will be at risk of long-term unemployment and benefit exhaustion. Profiling tools help to identify those workers early and target dedicated support at them, while avoiding that unnecessarily intensive and expensive special assistance services are provided to jobseekers that do not need them. Systematic early-needs assessments are particularly helpful, especially when the outcome is formalised in an individual action plan that can lead to early intervention when specific barriers to re-employment have been identified. Services need to be made available to all displaced workers and not only to those affected by collective dismissal in large firms.

In countries with an inadequate housing stock for sales or rentals, housing policies could complement product and labour market reforms to help workers to move to regions with the best jobs available. Depending on specific country contexts, different measures could be explored, such as, improving access to social housing, reducing constraints on the development of private rental markets, reducing transaction costs associated with relocation for renters and home-owners or considering targeted subsidies to cover the costs of relocating that could help workers acquire jobs. Sometimes, occupational licensing can hamper mobility without clear benefits in terms of service quality, consumer health or safety. Such licensing should be used judiciously; with standards harmonised across regions as much as possible.

Strengthening social protection systems

Strong and well-designed social protection systems play a central role in inclusive growth strategies. Social protection must be designed in ways that promote equal opportunities throughout the life-cycle, starting in early childhood and that protect people from income security risks, in particular those due to unemployment, sickness and disability, divorce and separation, as well as retirement. At the same time, social policies need to be designed in ways that provide a launching pad for personal and entrepreneurial development, that empower people to take calculated risks and benefit from economic opportunities. Badly designed social protection can result in benefit and poverty traps, increase informal activity, and distort economic decisions while providing inadequate protection. Well-designed active social policies can help people to invest in their capabilities and provide them with the safety and security they need for economic and social well-being.

Looking at the future, social protection needs to consider digitalisation, globalisation and ageing aspects that are shaping the nature of work. Across OECD countries, 16% of all workers are self-employed, and a further 16% are on temporary employment contracts. Yet, most OECD countries still operate social protection systems tailored to the archetype of full-time and permanent work for a single employer. Self-employed workers are often only covered for the most basic benefits. Those on temporary contracts may not be covered because of insufficient contributions. Only 6 out of 35 European countries studied insure the self-employed in the same way as standard employees (Spasova et al., 2017). Women are at higher risk than men as they take on more part-time work and temporary contracts.

Adjusting to non-standard forms of employment is a key challenge for the future of social protection. Providing social protection coverage to these new forms of employment is key not only for equity reasons, but also to provide the right incentives to ensure the contribution base of social protection systems. As modern technologies lower transaction costs, firms may shift their labour demand to forms of employment that are not subject to social security contributions (OECD, 2016b). Workers who are less likely to have to rely on the social protection system –such as the young, the well-educated and the healthy– may self-select into non-typical employment forms.

Countries could make efforts to incorporate non-standard workers into existing social protection systems. Several countries already incorporate non-standard workers into social protection system. While this is a straightforward solution, it has drawbacks. Traditionally, both the employer and the employee pay contributions, but it is unclear who should pay the employer contribution if the workers cannot afford to pay, if there is no employer, or if the responsible employer is not easily identified. The earnings of self-employed workers often fluctuate and social contributions assessed on the basis of previous income may exceed their current earnings capacity. Finally, moral hazard is an issue, especially for unemployment insurance: voluntary quits are difficult to distinguish from the loss of business, and monitoring whether job search or benefit receipt conditions are met is more challenging for self-employed workers than for employees.

Further efforts are needed to individualise social protection. Tying social protection entitlements to individuals, instead of jobs, may facilitate transitions between jobs and sectors, which may become more frequent in the new era of work. Several OECD countries intend to introduce "individual activity accounts". Under this system, individuals collect entitlements in such accounts, which are not only portable but can be used flexibly according to needs. This raises some challenges. A first question relates to how much redistribution such models should incorporate to ensure that all workers can benefit. A second question relates to funding and the respective roles of employers and the state. A third challenge is to decide how much of the entitlements should be reserved for future retirement benefits versus using the funds to invest in training, start a company, or other assets.

Proposals to make social protection more universal could be explored. Separating social protection from the employment relationship would remove coverage gaps and reduce the need to track entitlements across jobs. Some benefits – such as health insurance and parental leave – are already universal in many OECD countries. Targeting income replacement payments to low-income households through means testing, such as in

Australia and New Zealand, can also close coverage gaps, but tracking self-employment income and dealing with highly fluctuating earnings remains a challenge. Moving towards a universal basic income (UBI) would remove compliance problems and easily incorporate non-standard workers. However, introducing UBI would represent a significant departure from existing policy strategies and would present a major budgetary challenge unless other cash benefits are withdrawn (OECD, 2017b).

Future-proofing labour market regulations

A fresh look at existing labour market regulation is needed to ensure it is fit for purpose. A rise of non-standard work would likely result in a reduction in job security for many workers who would not be protected by the standard rules for hiring and firing that have been defined for open-ended contracts. Often, less strict rules apply (for example, in cases of temporary employment, temporary work agency work or dependent self-employment); in others cases, workers are excluded from employment protection legislation altogether (for example, the self-employed). For some of the emerging new forms of work, it is not even clear what the status of workers is, who the employer is, and what rules should apply to them. The minimum wage policy may need to be reconsidered in the future era of work. Minimum wage legislation may not be applicable to many of the new forms of employment where workers become independent contractors, work for multiple clients and are often paid on a piece-rate basis. It will be critical to re-examine the legal frameworks in light of any updates needed to provide some form of minimum employment protection for all workers. In some cases it may be a question of clarifying the boundaries between different forms of work. Policy coordination across countries will be required.

Policy efforts are needed to address workplace health and safety regulation. New forms of employment, particularly crowd sourcing, tend to transfer responsibilities for occupational health and safety away from the employer and into the hands of individual workers, who often lack the training or resources to take appropriate measures to ensure that working conditions and the working environment are safe. Sometimes, strong competition between workers may result in corners being cut and unnecessary risks being taken while labour inspectorates are often not adequately prepared to deal with these new forms of employment. Regulations may therefore need to be adapted and clarified, while strengthening and improving awareness, monitoring and control mechanisms.

Reinforcing social dialogue

Social dialogue is and will be needed to enhance co-operation and mutual trust. Anticipating future challenges and opportunities, finding solutions, managing change proactively, and shaping the future era of work can be achieved more easily and effectively if employers, workers and their representatives work closely together with governments in a spirit of co-operation and mutual trust. Since the 1980s, the process of collective representation and bargaining has faced many challenges. While the share of workers who are employed by a firm that is a member of an employer organisation has remained relatively stable over the last 15 years at around 51% in OECD countries, small firms are not as well represented as medium and large firms in most countries. The share of employees in OECD countries that are union members has steadily declined, from 30% in 1985 to 17% in 2015. The share of workers covered by collective agreements has declined from 45% to 33% over the same period. In some cases, policy reforms have driven these trends, but technological and organisational changes, globalisation, the decline of the manufacturing sector, the expansion of flexible forms of work (including the emergence of new forms of work) and population ageing have also played their part.

Social dialogue will have to evolve in line with flexible forms of employment. Union membership is usually very low among non-standard workers. The new forms of work add to the challenge of organising worker voice since individuals are increasingly working alone, separated by geography, language and legal status. In some cases there are important regulatory challenges to overcome. For example, in some countries it is illegal for independent workers to unionise since this would be considered forming a cartel and therefore an anti-competitive practice. Some innovative solutions are nevertheless emerging: non-standard workers are setting up new unions and "traditional" unions are trying to improve the coverage of non-standard forms of work. In some cases, companies voluntarily extend the terms set in collective agreements for standard workers to non-standard workers and/or engage in collective bargaining. Private sector initiatives emerge with workers gathering into co-operatives. In addition, new technologies may facilitate organisation of workers through social media and platforms. What is needed from governments to promote such developments in social dialogue and worker representation is a favourable regulatory framework.

Creating quality jobs, tackling informal jobs and preparing for the future of work in developing countries

Skills mismatches as well as brain drain hamper developing countries to integrate into GVCs. Developing countries have a large skill mismatch, regardless of the way skill mismatch is assessed. OECD calculations based on the World Bank Enterprise Survey show that the percentage of firms identifying labour skills level as a major constraint is particularly marked in Latin America and in Middle East and North African countries, even though governments there have invested significant amounts in education, in particular at the tertiary level (OECD, 2012).

Some developing economies have already implemented reforms to improve the skills and reduce the skills mismatches; but the challenge is enormous. Few firms provide training opportunities to their workforce. In developing countries on average, only around 20% of young workers benefit from such an opportunity. Little is known about the quality of such training. Skills policies oriented towards industry upgrading should not only aim at investing in more and better skills, but also at aligning education with labour market and environmental needs, improving the school-to-work transition, encouraging the long-term adaptability of skills and promoting the international mobility of skilled workers.

Fostering high-quality jobs requires reducing informality through a combination of tax policies. Workers employed in the informal sector have limited access to social protection, are typically offered inadequate contracts and earn comparatively lower wages, and are more vulnerable when they lose their job or when they retire. Addressing informality of employment is a complex issue and requires a combination of tax policy and tax administration initiatives to promote firm formalisation, as well as other measures. Such measures can include targeted audits, conditional cash transfers. In countries where the informality of employment requires a practical and sequenced approach.

The efforts to support formal working arrangements should be continued. An important medium-term policy objective is to decrease the costs and increase the benefits of working formally. For entrepreneurs, the benefits of operating formally often relate to eligibility for loans, securing contracts with governments and large corporations, and exporting. The costs of entry into the formal economy include the need to pay taxes and social security contributions, obtain a license or register their accounts. For wage workers, the benefits of formalisation include access to social protection, greater security, and better working conditions. Strengthening the link between contributions and benefits in the social insurance schemes can increase the attractiveness of formal work. Enhancing enforcement mechanisms (for example, by providing labour inspectorates with adequate resources) plays an important role in boosting the incentive to formalise.

The future of work in developing countries will be determined by governments' capacity to address the most pressing inequality issues in the international production. As it may not help to trade without compensating gains linked to production activities and creation of domestic value added, a number of actions are needed to ensure that domestic workers can reap the benefits of GVCs, including:

- Adopting and complying with higher standards for TNCs to re-think corporate governance with equity objectives in mind and redistribute income equally along the global value chain from productive workers to shareholders and executives;
- Supporting formal working arrangements;
- Supporting skills upgrading, both at the level of the individual and the firm; and
- Implementing programs to promote local supply-chain deepening and knowledge transfers.

Making labour markets more inclusive through taxation

Tax policies can help to make labour markets more inclusive. A key priority for many OECD countries should be to reduce structural unemployment. This should include continuing to reduce marginal tax rates for those with low skills and low propensity to work. This could be achieved through an expansion of in-work benefits such as earned-income tax credits (EITCs). A number of OECD countries would also benefit from reductions in payroll taxes, and shifts in the burden of social protection financing away from social security contributions (SSCs) and onto other tax bases. EITCs and SSC reductions that lower the labour tax wedge and therefore raise after-tax earnings are particularly effective for workers that tend to have high labour supply elasticities including young and older workers, women, low-skilled, and single-parent households (Brys et al., 2016) (Box 1.2).

Reducing tax rates for low-income workers can reduce regional inequalities. Apart from raising employment, reductions in effective tax rates at low incomes (Figure 2.19) can reduce regional inequality and provide benefits to firms that employ large numbers of low-skilled workers, benefiting these workers in turn (Saez et al., 2017). When considering this, the design of EITCs and other in-work benefits matters as well their integration with other labour market policies such as minimum wages, and the levels and eligibility conditions of unemployment benefits (Immervoll and Pearson, 2009).

Figure 2.19 Tax wedges on low incomes

Income tax plus employee and employer contributions less cash benefits

By family type, % of labour costs, 2016

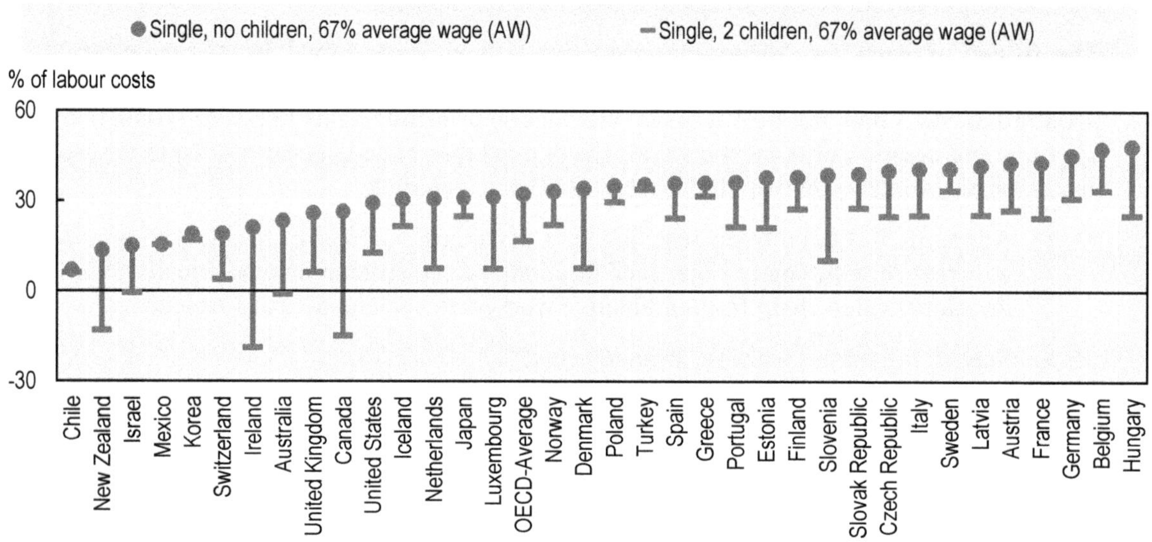

Source: OECD Taxing Wages 2017.

StatLink http://dx.doi.org/10.1787/888933725221

Tax systems can effectively support the labour market participation of second earners. Second earners are often taxed at high marginal rates relative to primary earners, due to family-based-taxation, spousal allowances, and family based benefits (Figure 2.20). Second earners often have particularly strong negative responses to income taxation (OECD, 2011). In most countries, second earners are more likely to be women. The tax system, in concert with other policy approaches, should provide stronger incentives for second earners to work, by removing spousal allowances, targeting tax concessions at second earners and levying personal income taxes on an individual basis. This is especially the case for households with children (Thomas and O'Reilly, 2016).

Creating jobs requires careful attention to the taxation of SMEs. The tax treatment of SMEs and new businesses is crucial to incentivising growth that can deliver jobs, and fostering innovation that can raise wages and productivity therefore also possibly contributing to the quality of these jobs. While not all SMEs are innovative, new and small firms are often the driving force behind innovations that are important for economic growth (OECD, 2010). The tax treatment of SMEs varies across legal forms. The business income of unincorporated SMEs is typically taxed under the personal income tax (PIT); incorporated businesses are taxed under the corporate income tax (CIT) and then again under the PIT when dividends are distributed or capital gains are realised. Some countries have special tax rules for closely-held corporations. Businesses may therefore face tax-induced incentives to incorporate or otherwise alter their legal form, which may create hurdles for SMEs to grow and may undermine the horizontal equity of the tax system.

Figure 2.20 Tax rates are higher on second earners than on single tax payers

Average tax rates, 2015, single and second earner at 67% of the average wage, with 2 children

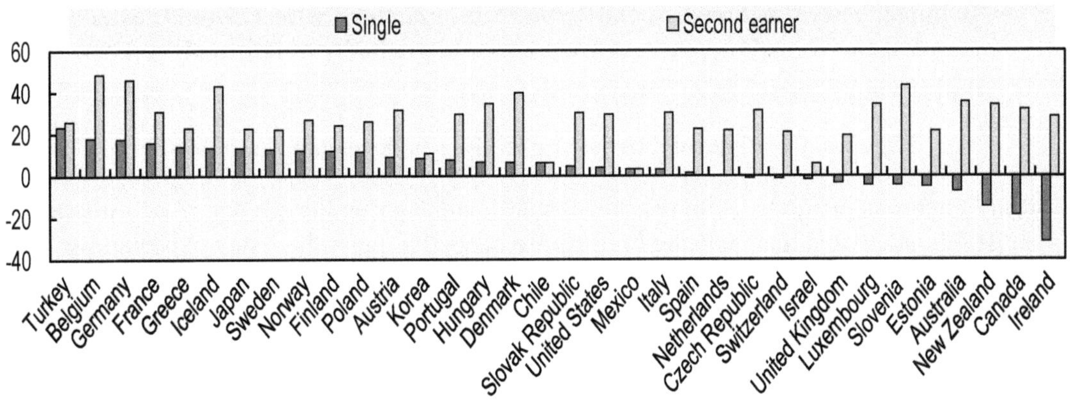

Note: The primary earner is assumed to earn 67% of the average wage. The indicator may differ substantially from measures of who legally has to pay the tax. For example, in Germany spouses can choose between individual and joint income taxation. In the case of joint taxation, Germany treats the family as a taxable unit via an income splitting method. Legally, the splitting effect has to be attributed equally to the primary and second earner.

Source: "The Impact of Tax and Benefit Systems on the Workforce Participation Incentives of Women" (Thomas and O'Reilly, 2016).

StatLink http://dx.doi.org/10.1787/888933725240

As policy makers intend to develop measures to foster the creation of good jobs, greater attention is needed to support the attributes of work that most people value and that contribute to productivity growth and high living standards. A coherent policy framework could be shaped around the national development objectives, particularly in emerging and developing countries (Box 2.4):

- **Make work pay.** Dedicated efforts are needed to increase labour productivity and earning capacity of low-paid workers in developing countries. Governments should continue to invest in the quality of education for all and enshrine equal pay for women and men in the law. Wages need to reflect more closely labour productivity growth. Companies need to be able to pass along the benefits of growth and increase the living standards of workers. Where unions are weak and cannot prevent low wages in the productive sector, minimum wage arrangements need to be carefully reconsidered. In the context of global value chains, the unequal distribution of income from productive workers to shareholders and salaried executives needs to be addressed also in the context of corporate governance.

- **Raise the attractiveness of employment in sectors with poor working conditions and low pays.** Agriculture is currently a major employer in many developing countries and the sector has the space to create more jobs, in particular in high value organic agriculture and processed food. Yet, employment in the agriculture sector must be transformed into high-quality jobs. Governments need to support environmentally-friendly agricultural value chains and help smallholder farmers to capture value added at each stage of the production, marketing and consumption process.

- **Extend social protection to foster creation of good jobs (i.e. in terms of productivity, innovation and working practices).** Social security provision remains biased towards state-sector workers. As a result, many workers in the non-state sector are vulnerable and public employment continues are the preferred form of employment, in particular for young women and vulnerable workers. Creating a modern non-state sector that can be attractive cannot be achieved without comprehensive national social protection systems, which would extend the coverage to formal private sector workers and gradually to informal workers.

Box 2.4. Creating conditions for good jobs in developing countries

Many governments in developing countries are realising that the quality of jobs matters for development and that dedicated efforts are needed to meet the rising expectations of one billion people who will enter the labour force during the coming decades. Policies that stimulate the creation of good jobs recognise altogether the centrality of jobs in the development process and the fact that not all jobs are equal from a sustainable development and societal well-being perspective. Jobs bring private returns to individuals that hold them, but they also have spill-over effects on the rest of society (World Bank, 2013). For instance, the value of maternal and child health services provided by nurses in a developing country is far greater than what they get paid for, so nursing jobs have positive spillovers. Some other jobs may generate negative externalities, for example, air pollution and biodiversity loss due to land use change.

Recent studies have attempted to estimate profession-specific externalities. They suggest that a number of high-paying professions have negative externalities, whereas several low-paying professions have positive externalities. ILO (2017) attempts to identify some of the measures to reduce negative externalities while increasing welfare gains and societal well-being. Using the data from the International Social Survey Programme 2015, ILO (2017) shows for instance that the majority of workers at the global level value their work more than a means for making a living. In developing countries 91% of workers consider as an important or very important job characteristic a job that is interesting and 90% a job that is useful to society; and 92% and 72%, respectively in developed countries. Moreveor, Nathanson and Weyl (2017) find that young workers in emerging and developing countries have high expectations about jobs and value specific job attributes; such as the skill intensity of jobs, having the right skills for the job, training opportunities, job security, and formality in addition to labour earnings.

As policy makers develop measures to foster the creation of good jobs, more attention is needed to support the attributes of work that most people value and that can contribute to sustainable development. The starting point is to promote an integrative framework that creates the enabling conditions for a job-rich growth process that is sustainable and fair, around several development objectives. Dedicated efforts are needed to (i) make work pay, (ii) raise the attractiveness of agriculture employment, where the jobs are tough and the pay is low, (iii) extend social protection by reducing bias towards state-sector workers, (iv) take into account the job security concerns more seriously in the labour market reforms, (v) reduce skills mismatch and prepare workers and firms for a green economy is essential to improve the quality of work and living, and (vi) support formal labour relations as an integral part of a strategy to foster the creation of good jobs.

Sources: World Bank (2013); Nathanson and Weyl (2017); ILO (2017).

- **Consider job security concerns seriously in labour market reforms.** Providing balanced job security through employment protection is often difficult in the context of widespread informality. Investment in effective social protection schemes is key, including through well-designed unemployment insurance schemes. Policy efforts to improve job security can also help firms to attract suitably skilled workers and incentivise investment in skills development. There is a need to protect workers against income loss. In countries that lack unemployment benefits, employment protection provisions (such as severance pay) can sustain dismissed workers as they search for new jobs and improve job matching; but need to be well-designed and enforced.

- **Reduce skills mismatch and prepare workers and firms for a low-carbon, resource-efficient economy.** A package of measures to reduce the skills mismatch and equip workers with the right skills includes providing high-quality career guidance counselling to young people; investing in the quality, relevance and responsiveness of education and initial training; and developing opportunities to learn on the job and to receive continuing training at work. Overall skills development and matching policies need to be an integral part of a national development strategy that can address specific country and environmental constraints. Training of youth needs to be encouraged, particularly in SMEs that provide most of private jobs in developing countries. Governments need to identify delivery modalities that work in the context of high informality and that respond to a large number of out-of-school youth without basic skills.

Agriculture represents an untapped source of productive jobs in developing countries. The growing demand for food and changing consumer preferences, driven by population growth, the emergence of a middle class, urbanisation, and the spread of technology creates new employment opportunities. Rural areas are characterized by a great diversity of economic activities, including processing and marketing of agricultural products, eco-tourism, and services. Tapping on the rural economy potential requires a strategic and youth-sensitive approach to rural development that can create job opportunities outside farms, make regional and domestic agriculture more central in national development strategies, and that closely link food systems to food security and the requirements of a circular economy.

Increasing the diversity of the workplace

Gender equality, diversity and non-discrimination are keystones of prosperous modern economies that provide sustainable inclusive growth. OECD countries have seen a considerable societal change over the past decades. Since 1980 the female employment rate has increased by 10 percentage points to almost 60% in 2016. In the same year, close to 1 out of 10 persons living in the OECD were born abroad; for younger age groups the share is even larger; among the 15-34 year-olds 15% are foreign-born and an additional 12% are native-born with at least one immigrant parent (European Union and OECD, 2015; OECD, 2017j). Also, LGBT persons are generally more likely to be open about their sexual orientation at work than in the past; according to Gallup, the proportion of adults who identify as LGBT in the U.S. is quickly rising, from 3.5% in 2012 to 4.1% in 2016.

It is crucial to ensure that women, migrants and LGBT people are integrated in the labour market, have access to quality jobs and are given the same career opportunities as everybody else. Yet, OECD countries struggle to make the most of diverse societies and provide equal opportunities for these groups. The cost of inaction is high: for example, reducing the gender gap in labour force participation by 25% by 2025 could, through increases in the size of their labour forces, add 1 percentage point to projected baseline GDP growth across the OECD over the period 2013-25, and almost 2.5 percentage points if gender participation gaps were halved by 2025. In the face of sluggish growth, ageing societies and increasing educational attainment of young women, the economic case for gender equality is clear. Diversity of views and experiences in organisations –both private and public– can help expanding the pool of talent available to contribute to organisational performance, and can lead to policies and services that better reflect citizens' needs and promote inclusive growth (OECD, 2013a).

In the past five years countries have made very little progress in reaching gender parity in all areas of social and economic life. Women in OECD countries complete more years of schooling than young men on average, but girls are much less likely to study in the lucrative science, technology, engineering and mathematics (STEM) fields. Women's employment rates have increased, but in every OECD country women are still less likely than men to engage in paid work. Furthermore, when women do work, they are more likely to work part-time, are less likely to advance to management or political leadership positions leadership positions. In 2016, women held only 28.7% of seats in lower houses of Parliament on average across the OECD. While women make up 55% of all judges (according to available national data), their presence decreases when moving up the judicial hierarchy. In the private sector in 2016, women occupied 20% of board seats of publicly listed companies and only 4.8% of chief executive officer positions [C/MIN(2017)7].

Because of these factors and because they are more likely to face discrimination, women continue to earn less than men. The median full-time female worker earns almost 15% less than her male counterpart, on average, across the OECD – a rate that has barely changed since 2010 (Figure 2.21). Many factors drive the gender pay gap, including gender segregation in fields of study and jobs, women's higher likelihood of interrupting their careers for caregiving, and –though harder to identify– discrimination and biases against women. Since 2013, about two-thirds of OECD countries have introduced new *pay equity initiatives* and pay transparency is a key lever in bringing gender pay differentials within companies to light. In six OECD countries gender pay gaps for young workers (25-29) are in favour of women, but gender gaps reverse and widen in favour of men, when children appear in households. It is important to improve access to early childhood education and care (ECEC). Since 2013 several OECD countries have taken steps to address affordability, usually through increases in subsidies or benefits/rebates for public childcare and, occasionally, through the introduction or expansion of free childcare (OECD 2013).

Countries have started to provide incentives to fathers to take parental leave. Fathers' parental leave taking is essential for gender equality in paid and unpaid work. It encourages parents to share caregiving more equally and facilitates mothers' labour market participation. These egalitarian behaviours can improve father's and mother's well-being, set a good example for children, and over time can reduce the prevailing gender stereotypes.

"Gender budgeting", quotas and other measures are helping to increase the number of women in public and private sector leaderships. Women's under-representation in leadership limits the presence of female voices in important decisions, and deprives girls and young women of strong role models. Changing stereotypes requires a broad, societal understanding that women are capable of achieving as much as men in business and in public life. Hiring targets for women in the civil service are in place in 10 OECD countries and 6 OECD countries have promotion targets for women. In many countries, the public sector offers more flexible working conditions compared to the private sector (OECD, 2015c; OECD, 2015d).

Governments and businesses are exploring different policies and strategies to make the most out of a diverse workforce and strengthen the labour market participation of disadvantaged groups. Some tools and policies target a given group specifically –for example, reaching out to ethnic minority candidates during recruitment– others instead are more general, such as providing training courses on unconscious bias. Public policies have used different approaches to increase diversity in the workplace ranging from voluntary commitments for companies, financial incentives and awareness campaigns to mandatory quotas, diversity pre-requisites for public procurement and stricter anti-discrimination legislation. Yet, it is often unclear how effective these approaches are or what the necessary conditions are to enable them to succeed.

Figure 2.21 Median monthly gender pay gap for full-time employees has changed little

Gender gap in median monthly earnings, full-time employees, 2005, 2010 and 2015 or latest available

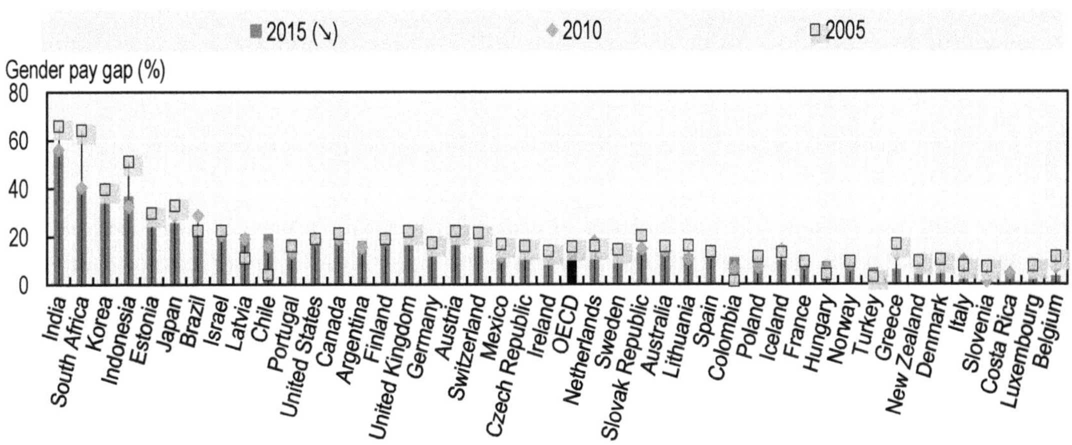

Note: The gender gap in median monthly earnings is defined as the difference between male and female median monthly earnings divided by male median monthly earnings, for full-time employees. Full-time employees are defined as those individuals with usual weekly working hours equal to or greater than 30 hours per week.
Source: OECD (2017k), The Pursuit of gender Equality.

StatLink http://dx.doi.org/10.1787/888933573829

Though policy makers in developing countries are increasingly paying attention to inclusiveness, many factors hold back progress. Inequality, jobless growth, skilled-biased technology and informality are among the main factors that have undermined the ability of some groups of workers to benefit from productivity gains and high-quality jobs. Uncontrolled urbanization and expansion of urban slums has created new opportunities for local communities in terms of remittances, but also spurred security and other challenges for local governments.

Deeply entrenched discrimination in formal and informal laws, social norms or practices poses significant and enduring obstacles for women in developed and developing countries worldwide. OECD estimates show that reducing gender-based discrimination in social institutions through the right policy measures could yield substantial economic benefits, leading to an annual increase in the world GDP growth rate of 0.03 to 0.6 percentage points by 2030, depending on the policy scenario (Ferrant and Kolev, 2016). Looking beyond GDP, other findings reveal that men and women tend to be happier when living in countries where women and men are treated more equally by their social institutions. Eradicating gender-based discrimination in social institutions could reduce the proportion of the world population reporting low levels of life satisfaction from 14% to 5% (Ferrant and Kolev, 2016).

Fostering knowledge creation and technology diffusion in the digital era

Promoting basic research can drive long-run productivity growth by extending the global frontier. Governments play a critical role in providing some of the foundations for innovation (OECD, 2015e; OECD, 2015f; OECD, 2015g). Basic research, in particular, drives long-run productivity growth by helping move the global frontier and by enhancing the ability of economies to learn from innovations at the global frontier (OECD, 2015h). Public funding is needed to address the inherent under-investment in basic research of private firms, linked to the large knowledge spillovers of such research. Long-term funding for curiosity-driven research must be preserved as it has led to significant innovations in the past – including digital innovations, such as the Internet. On the other hand, mission-oriented funding can allow for more direct steering of public research towards major public policy objectives, including innovation and productivity growth. A long-term and stable perspective for public research funding is essential; while public budgets for R&D have held up well since the crisis in most OECD countries, they are now declining in several (OECD, 2015h).

Support for business R&D can help to support innovation, where it is important to focus on high social returns and best international practices. Support for R&D should focus on "expenditure-based" (i.e. input) incentives instead of "income-based" (i.e. output) incentives, such as patent boxes. R&D tax incentives should be designed to meet the needs of young, innovative firms while ensuring they do not create opportunities for base erosion and profit shifting (OECD, 2017k; OECD, 2017l). Good design of tax credits through cash refunds, carry forwards, or other approaches can help ensure that R&D credits not only provide benefits to large incumbents but also to young and smaller firms who might have insufficient profits to claim the tax credits immediately. Governments should also ensure that R&D tax incentives are predictable for firms, and avoid tinkering with them repeatedly to minimise policy uncertainty. It is important to balance indirect support for business R&D (fiscal incentives) with direct support for innovation. Direct support measures –for example, contracts, grants and awards for mission-oriented R&D or support for networks– can be effective for young firms that lack the upfront funds or collateral to finance an innovative project. Non-financial support measures, e.g. training, mentoring and network development, including for SMEs, are an important component of the overall policy mix, since the lack of funding is only one of the barriers that hold back innovation and knowledge diffusion. Across all innovation policies, well-designed public-private partnerships are increasingly important to help lever government funding (OECD, 2017m; OECD, 2017n).

Investing in R&D alone is not enough to promote ICT-induced innovation. Fostering innovation also requires investments in ICTs and in complementary knowledge-based capital (KBC), in particular data, organisation-specific skills and know-how, and in organisational change including new business models and processes (OECD, 2016d; OECD, 2016e). Many businesses, in particular SMEs, but also governments and individuals – in particular those with low or no formal education– lack the necessary skills and know-how, and financial resources to take advantage of ICTs and introduce the changes needed for their productive use in businesses and across society.

Skills are critical to promote ICT-induced innovation, requiring inputs from a wide range of disciplines. Workers in industries that are currently most affected by the digital transformation exhibit higher levels of cognitive, as well as non-cognitive and social skills (OECD, 2017a; OECD, 2017p). As the digital transformation unfolds, and increasingly affects other industries that are at present less impacted, the need for solid cognitive skills combined with a good endowment of social skills will continue to increase and extend to the rest of the economy. In addition, graduates in ICT-related and STEM-related fields (including computer science, information systems, software engineering and artificial intelligence) work in a wide range of sectors beyond computer programming and consultancy, including education, retail trade, financial services and human health activities (Figure 2.22). This highlights the importance of ICT-related skills across the economy (Paunov, Planes-Satorra and Moriguchi, 2017).

Besides building technical skills, "soft" skills should be strengthened as part of formal and vocational education programmes. Skills that most distinguish innovative from non-innovative workers are creativity (i.e. coming up with new ideas and solutions), critical thinking (i.e. the willingness to question ideas) and communication skills (i.e. the ability to present ideas to an audience), followed by alertness to opportunities, analytical thinking, the ability to co-ordinate activities, and the ability to acquire new knowledge rapidly (Avvisati et al. 2013).

Figure 2.22 Skills levels in digital and less digital-intensive industries, 2012 or 2015

Cross-country averages

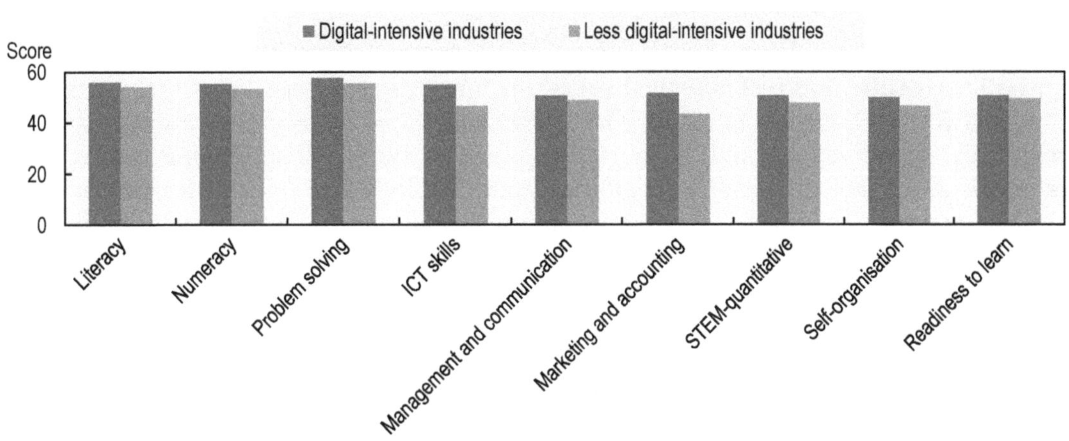

Source: OECD (2017a), Science, Technology and Innovation Scoreboard 2017, calculations based on the Survey of Adult Skills (PIAAC) Database, June 2017.

Note: Some of the presented skills levels have only a very tangential relationship with what is actually measured in PIAAC database. For example, PIAAC does not measure directly marketing and accounting skills or STEM-quantitative skills. Different items have been used to proxy these skills but it is not clear whether they really are good proxies or not.

StatLink http://dx.doi.org/10.1787/888933617453

Specific framework conditions are needed for ICT-induced innovation. Inertia to change in the established businesses can explain why digital innovation is often introduced by start-ups, and puts a premium on framework conditions affecting business dynamics and entrepreneurship. These framework conditions typically include, but are not limited to, regulations related to competition and product market regulation, to employment protection, to bankruptcy, and to access to finance. These framework conditions are crucial for ICT adoption as they influence the incentives to experiment with potentially disruptive innovations, and the ability to scale up successful digital innovations and to scale them down, if they turn out to be a failure. Thereby, they affect the ability of economies to reallocate scarce resources needed for digital innovation (such as ICT-related skills) to more successful firms, and are thus an important determinant of business dynamics. Differences in framework conditions may explain the relative sluggishness of some countries to capitalise on digitalisation.

Governments have started to develop national strategies to stimulate digital innovation. On the one hand, some national digital economy strategies put a strong emphasis on the promotion of ICT-related knowledge diffusion, including between large firms and SMEs or towards disfavoured social groups. On the other hand, some strategies poorly support the complementarities between investments in ICTs and KBCs (in particular organisational change), and the difficulties that established firms face in investing in complementary KBCs. This calls for improved co-ordination between ICT-related policies with policies that affect broader regulatory framework and market conditions.

Developing countries are becoming attractive locations for research and innovation. Investment in R&D is one of the indicators of the commitment towards innovation that is rising in emerging economies. Many companies have opened research labs in emerging markets, including China, Brazil and India, and in growing economies like Costa Rica, Malaysia and Singapore. However, emerging economies still invest significantly less in terms of resources and share of GDP than OECD countries and lag behind, at the aggregate level, in terms of innovation outputs such as patents, trademarks or revenues from innovation (OECD, 2015i).

Some emerging and developing countries are giving priority to innovation policies in specific scientific and technological areas. Such measures include fiscal incentives and targeted financial support to R&D. China, for example, is investing in research in new materials, biotechnology and clean energy vehicles. Brazil is prioritising research in strategic areas, including energy, healthcare, biotechnology and climate change. Sectoral technology funds are increasingly used to channel resources to innovation and to favour collaborative programmes between firms, universities and research centres. They foster technology transfer from research laboratories to firms and offer technological extension services as well as training and business coaching services to develop new business ideas. Public procurement is also increasingly used as a tool to foster domestic industrial capabilities in key sectors and to promote innovation. Brazil, China, India and South Africa include it in their industrial policy mix.

As companies have been pushed to delocalise more knowledge-intensive activities, this has created new opportunities in hosting countries (OECD, 2015h). This type of high-value-added delocalisation has mostly benefited developing countries with some degree of local knowledge capacities, like China and India. Learning and upgrading domestic production from FDI are not automatic, moreover. They require a clear vision of development, empowered institutions and a coherent policy framework encompassing different levels of government and stakeholders (OECD, 2013b).

Inclusive innovation and entrepreneurship

Participation in innovation activities is not evenly distributed across social groups. Women and other under-represented groups of population are not equally participating in research, innovation and entrepreneurship activities in most countries. This is frequently due to: (1) the lack of key capacities or skills (e.g. entrepreneurial and managerial skills, digital literacy, technical skills) in those groups, often linked to insufficient formal education or vocational training; and (2) fewer opportunities for participating in such activities, resulting from discrimination in the labour markets, the persistence of stereotypes, or higher barriers to entrepreneurship faced by certain social groups, among others.

Some governments are developing comprehensive approaches to spur innovation (Figure 2.23). To address these gaps and enhance inclusive innovation and entrepreneurship, many countries have implemented "inclusive innovation policies" in recent years – a specific set of innovation policies that aim to boost the capacities and opportunities of disadvantaged individuals to successfully participate in and benefit from innovation activities, including research and entrepreneurship. South Africa's Thuthuka programme, for instance, provides grants for research projects led by researchers from disadvantaged groups. Other examples include the use of role models and mentoring programmes to tackle stereotypes (e.g. in Sweden and Korea), and the implementation of programmes to popularise science and technology (e.g. in India; Planes-Satorra and Paunov, 2017).

Figure 2.23 Interactions among social, industrial and territorial inclusiveness

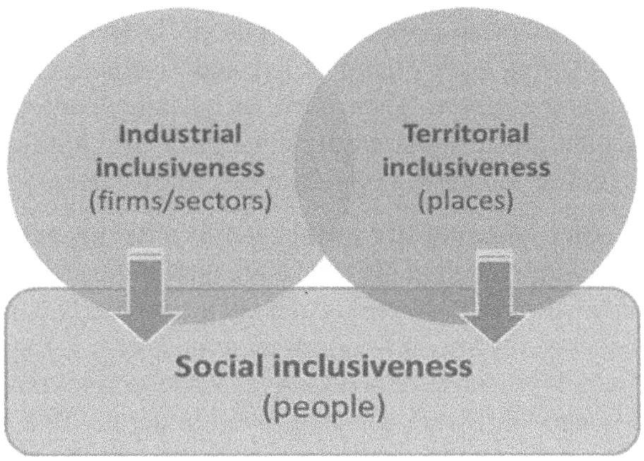

Source: Planes-Satorra and Paunov (2017)

The application of digital technologies and "big data" enables governments to track granular outcomes of policies that were previously imperfectly observable, or only observable at significant cost. The digital transformation can also facilitate the robust and comprehensive enforcement of different regulatory settings as well effective implementation of programs targeted at hard-to-reach populations. Moreover, it can reduce the cost, improve the reliability, and increase the frequency of the evaluation of different types of public policies. Innovation policies that aim to address industrial and territorial inclusiveness should be directed towards shaping the opportunities that individuals in different firms, industries and regions have to participate in innovation. To foster industrial inclusiveness, innovation policies can address the main barriers to entrepreneurship encountered by disadvantaged groups, such as obstacles to access finance (e.g. through the provision of micro-credit in Hungary or equity financing in Ireland), talent (e.g. through grants to SMEs to recruit researchers to implement projects in Horizon 2020 countries) or other support services (e.g. business counselling for Maori businesses in New Zealand). Policies to address territorial inclusiveness challenges may involve facilitating the access of firms and entrepreneurs in lagging regions to existing knowledge and technology (e.g. technology demonstrations in China) and attracting innovative firms to peripheral areas (e.g. technology parks in Korea that locate R&D activities in peripheral regions (Box 2.5).

Innovation policies that aim to address industrial and territorial inclusiveness should be directed towards shaping the opportunities that individuals in different firms, industries and regions have to participate in innovation. To foster industrial inclusiveness, innovation policies can address the main barriers to entrepreneurship encountered by disadvantaged groups, such as obstacles to access finance (e.g. through the provision of micro-credit in Hungary or equity financing in Ireland), talent (e.g. through grants to SMEs to recruit researchers to implement projects in Horizon 2020 countries) or other support services (e.g. business counselling for Maori businesses in New Zealand). Policies to address territorial inclusiveness challenges may involve facilitating the access of firms and entrepreneurs in lagging regions to existing knowledge and technology (e.g. technology demonstrations in China) and attracting innovative firms to peripheral areas (e.g. technology parks in Korea that locate R&D activities in peripheral regions).

Inclusive innovation policies are confronted with a number of specific implementation challenges. These include the low involvement of the disadvantaged group in policy programmes, often due to low awareness of their existence or low trust in governmental intervention; and low capabilities among the group to undertake activities promoted by the programme. The success of these policies depends on how these challenges are being addressed (including by using new digital tools) and requires strong capacity-building efforts matched to funding support. They need to be implemented together with other policies, such as education policies that ensure equal access to high-quality education and labour market policies while supporting opportunities for disadvantaged groups.

Not everyone has an equal opportunity to succeed as entrepreneur. Youth and women are less likely to be self-employed than the rest of the population. In 2016, men were nearly twice as likely as women to be self-employed across most OECD countries (Figure 2.24). Youth are also under-represented in self-employment despite a high proportion indicating a preference for self-employment over working in wage employment. Less than 5% of working youth (15-24 years old) were self-employed in across OECD countries in 2016, approximately one-third of the rate for the adult population. Other social target groups such as seniors and migrants are not under-represented in self-employment in all countries, but people from these groups often face more and greater barriers to entrepreneurship and in the labour market.

Box 2.5. Digitalising the Policy Cycle: Implications for Inclusive Growth

Examples of concrete applications include: the use of advanced sensors to obtain data for environmental outcomes in different spaces and geographies; the use of advanced analytical techniques such as machine learning to identify emerging risks for specific groups of the population; and, the use of blockchain technologies and advanced security markers for goods and contracts whose characteristics may not be readily observable (land titles, product safety), and thus improved consumer protection for the most disadvantaged individuals. It is through the combination of all three elements - digital technologies, new data sources, and advanced analytical techniques – that the digital transformation has the potential to revolutionise policymaking, and help to realise positive outcomes for inclusive growth.

In recent years, there, has been a mushrooming of institutions applying digital methods and technologies commonly used in the hard sciences to identify optimal solutions to public policy objectives. MARS in Toronto, NESTA in London and MindLab in Copenhagen are perhaps the best-known examples, but they are blossoming everywhere. Much of the work has focussed on social policy, education and health, with direct implications for inclusive growth. However, broadly speaking there are implications for IG which cut across all policy domains, namely the implications for:

1. Greater granularity of the data allowing for improved understanding of population characteristics and needs and how different policy settings affect different segments of the population (e.g. age, gender, region).

2. Possibility of linking administrative and surveys data at individual-level and throughout the lifecycle, as well as the various policy programmes that people are recipients of, which opens the way to a finer understanding and evaluation of policy impacts.

3. Enhanced possibilities for broader stakeholder involvement in all stages of the policy cycle, potentially overcoming some of the biases which can favour "insiders" and "incumbents" as well as policy capture dynamics.

However, there are several barriers to with the "digital transformation" of the policy cycle. Firstly, while progress is being made relatively few governments have put in place the infrastructure to link disparate source of data. Secondly, there can be important (and legitimate) barriers to data access at the necessary level of disaggregation. Thirdly, as with any far-reaching change in policymaking there can be bureaucratic resistance.

Source: OECD Secretariat, Friends of Inclusive Growth Seminar, 23 January 2018; adapted from OECD (2018): Going Digital, DSTI/CDEP/GD(2018)2.

Gaps in entrepreneurship are often due to the greater barriers faced in business creation by some women, youth and elderly. One of the most frequently cited barriers to business creation is access to finance, which was cited by 26% of youth and 22% of women in 2012 (OECD/EC, 2013). Other important barriers include the lack of entrepreneurship skills, small and ineffective entrepreneurship networks, and the lack of knowledge about the regulatory and institutional environment, low levels of social capital and language skills (OECD/EC, 2013; 2014; OECD/EU, 2015; 2017).

Specific skills programmes are needed to support inclusive innovation and entrepreneurships. While problem-solving skills are key to succeed in companies or pursue entrepreneurship, some groups of workers like women, young and immigrants have to overcome greater barriers than others (OECD-EU, 2017). For example, while there are gender gaps in the perception of barriers to setting up a business, women feel as confident as men about their business and its future once it is up and running in most OECD countries (Figure 2.25). Improving the quality of business start-ups represents an opportunity to increase participation in the labour market and can boost productivity. Tailored business incubator and business accelerator programmes for innovative entrepreneurs are emerging in OECD countries, to help under-represented and disadvantaged groups with access to venture capital, training, coaching and networking.

Figure 2.24 Self-employment rate

Share in total employment, 2016 or latest available year, %

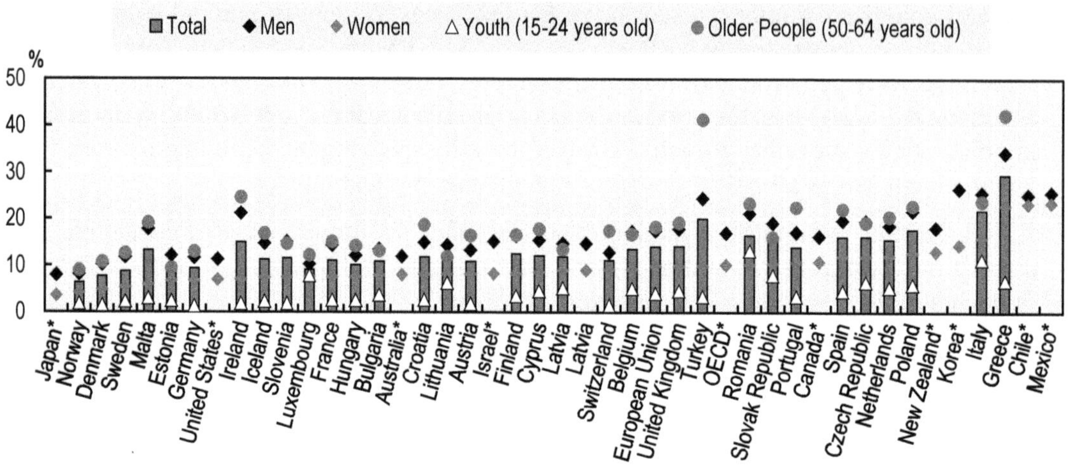

Note: *denotes data from 2015.
Source: Eurostat (2017), Labour Force Survey, available at: http://ec.europa.eu/eurostat/web/lfs/data/database; OECD (2016), "Indicators of gender equality in entrepreneurship", OECD Gender Portal, available at: www.oecd.org/gender/data/.

StatLink http://dx.doi.org/10.1787/888933725259

Inclusive entrepreneurship policies are needed to ensure that everybody has an equal opportunity to start and run their own businesses. These policies seek to support people who come from social groups that are under-represented in entrepreneurship or disadvantaged in the labour market (e.g. women, youth, seniors, the unemployed, ethnic minority and immigrant groups and people with disabilities; OECD/EC, 2013; 2014; OECD/EU, 2015; 2017). Sustainable business start-up is clearly a key outcome sought from inclusive entrepreneurship policies (OECD/EC, 2013). Indeed, inclusive entrepreneurship schemes often increase the skills, motivations, networks and employability of participants.

Figure 2.25 Once in business, women entrepreneurs feel as confident as men about the future

Positive evaluation of current business status, % of survey respondents (average 2016-17)

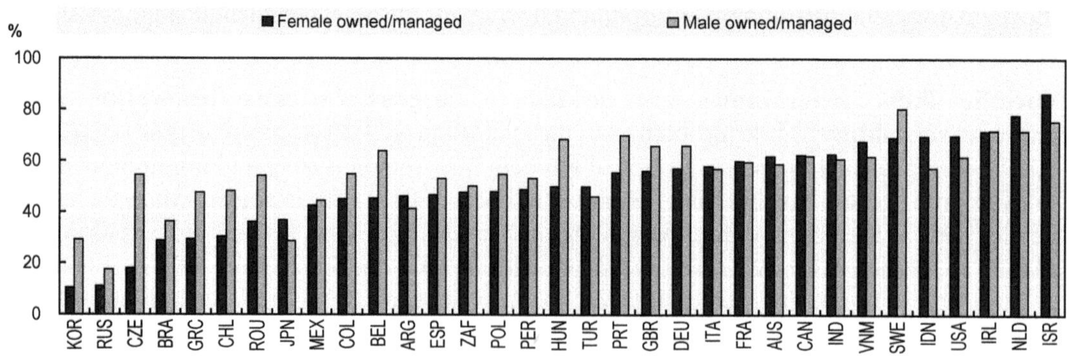

Source: OECD (2017c), based on the Future of Business Survey, conducted by Facebook in collaboration with the OECD and the World Bank.

StatLink http://dx.doi.org/10.1787/888933725278

Key policies to promote and support inclusive entrepreneurship include entrepreneurship training, coaching and mentoring, facilitating access to finance, and building entrepreneurial networks. To be effective, support measures need to be tailored to the unique challenges faced by the different social target groups, and targeted outreach efforts are needed to reach potential entrepreneurs. For example, Going for Growth in Ireland provides coaching and mentoring to growth-oriented women entrepreneurs, as well as helping them build their networks. It is also important for policy makers to consider bundling support measures into packages, since many of the barriers and challenges are inter-related, and to utilise appropriate delivery mechanisms. This approach is taken by the BBZ programme in the Netherlands, which provides entrepreneurship training, coaching and mentoring, and an allowance to support people receiving social welfare assistance in business creation. Support measures are often more effective when specialist agencies or specialist branches of mainstream agencies are used, but client density must be sufficiently high to achieve cost efficiency.

Inclusive innovation programs have also emerged in developing countries. Known as "inclusive innovations", they might appear technically modest, but they can have considerable impacts on people's lives; such as eye care in India, computer-based functional literacy, and solar power utilities and agricultural devices like irrigation pumps (OECD, 2013b). Where low-income groups are the target consumers, one approach is to provide cheaper, simplified and possibly lower quality versions of more sophisticated goods and services. Other initiatives include "grassroots innovations" developed by lower income groups themselves, often using indigenous or traditional knowledge. They are directed towards local development, empowering local communities to find solutions that meet their needs. Various forms of support can be provided for such innovators, such as "business incubators", dedicated technical networks, etc. For example, the Honey Bee Network in India acts as a business incubator, helping innovators by documenting and developing their knowledge, ideas and products, such as the pedal-powered washing machine (Planes-Satorra and Paunov, 2017; Paunov and Rollo, 2016). To date, the impacts of these inclusive and grassroots innovations have not been well evaluated. Irrespectively, facilitating more widespread technology adoption within low-income and middle-income countries will be key response to reduce extreme poverty and prevent global inequality from rising.

Box 2.6. Digitalisation has opened new pathways and markets for entrepreneurial growth

The development of affordable digital tools and platforms has provided new opportunities for micro-enterprises to tap into foreign markets in a way that would previously have been unimaginable. New data from the Future of Business Survey, a joint Facebook-OECD-World Bank collaboration, show that even "just me" entrepreneurs (i.e. self-employed with no employees) can engage in exports as a major activity for their business, by capitalising on digital tools, despite their small scale (Entrepreneurship at a Glance, 2017). While in the past only large multinationals could, effectively, scale globally, small businesses have today a menu of digital tools that allow them to leverage global connections and market directly to potential customers all over the world, overcoming in turn barriers to trade which typically weigh more heavily on smaller firms with lower economies of scale.

The survey findings reveal that among firms that export, exports represent a key element of the business model not only for significant shares of small enterprises (with less than

50 employees), but also for many just-me enterprises. Close to a third (28%) of just-me entrepreneurs who export indicate that more than 25% of their total revenue comes from international trade. Also, two in three exporting SMEs reported that more than 50% of their international sales depend on online tools (Figure 2.26).

Figure 2.26 Exports revenue greater than 25% of total revenue, by enterprise size

Percentage of exporters, March-May 2017

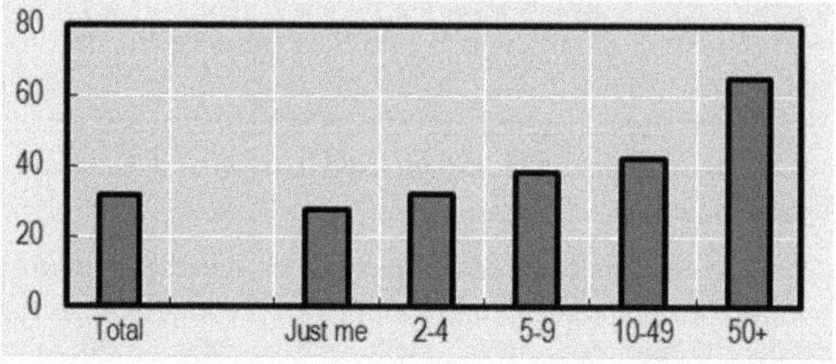

Note: Responses from enterprises with a Facebook Page over the period March-May 2017. Exporters include two-way traders and exporters only.
Source: Facebook-OECD-World Bank Future of Business Survey (database), June 2017; Entrepreneurship at a Glance 2017, OECD Publishing, Paris; and www.futureofbusinesssurvey.org.

Rethinking competition in the global digital era

Effective competition policy is necessary to ensure that competition and innovation are mutually-reinforcing and are not distorted by improper firm conduct. Competitive pressures can spur firms to innovate by improving their products, introducing new products, or reducing costs. At the same time, innovations can allow new firms to enter markets and put pressure on established business models, as is the case with many digital platforms today. These types of innovations may cut out intermediary costs and reduce prices, opening up markets to previously underserved consumers.

There are opportunities to bolster the capacity of competition authorities to address anticompetitive conduct, although a completely new approach may not be necessary. New types of concerns have emerged in the digital economy, but the means to address them are generally already in the toolbox available to competition authorities. Thus, putting emphasis on cooperation and awareness of emerging issues is one of the appropriate responses to the challenges facing competition authorities in innovation-oriented markets.

Reviewing merger notification requirements may be warranted to better assess acquisitions with little or no revenues. One specific challenge of competition policy relates to the acquisition of new, innovative firms by established market players simply to prevent the entry of new competitors. On the one hand, mergers can be beneficial for consumers and competition, and the prospect of being acquired can incentivise efforts to develop disruptive innovation. On the other hand, there is a concern that incumbent firms may seek to suppress the release of disruptive technologies or engage in other anticompetitive conduct to protect their market share. In order to detect these types of transactions, competition authorities may consider targeted to merger notification requirements, since the current thresholds based on firm revenue may not capture acquisitions of new disruptive firms with little or no revenue, but which may have significant competition implications.

The business strategies of superstar firms may require reinforced monitoring by competition authorities. The growing importance of digital technology may lead to network effects and sometimes entry barriers, potentially giving rise to "superstar" firms. If such dominant firms abuse their position in a market, competition authorities must be prepared to step in. For example, if a firm uses the big data assets it has acquired in one market to extend its dominance to another market without appreciable consumer benefits, it may be a competition law infringement. Similarly, possible efforts to impose switching costs on consumers, erect barriers to entry for competitors, exclude competitor's access to markets, or abuse privileged access to consumer data should be monitored carefully by competition authorities.

Increasing transparency of prices and other market data is one emerging challenge for competition authorities. Transparency can benefit the public by facilitating efficient investment, production, and consumption decisions. For example, consumers may benefit because transparency can facilitates product or service comparisons, including via third-party comparison websites. Producers also may benefit because price transparency may provide signals to suppliers about how much to produce. Transparency, however, can facilitate collusion. With the increasing sophistication of machine learning, it has been suggested that pricing algorithms can even reach collusive outcomes without specific instructions, or even awareness, on the part of the firms employing them. Use of an algorithm has already led to competition authority charges for collusion in one case. The detection and enforcement of these types of algorithms may pose challenges for competition authorities, and will require them to increase their awareness of the sophisticated technologies employed by firms.

Competition authorities need to be vigilant and well-informed to swiftly and appropriately react to unexpected market changes driven by the digital transformation. Cooperation between authorities in tackling new challenges associated with the digital transformation can be facilitated by enhancing formal information-sharing arrangements, and participating in international fora such as the OECD's Competition Committee. Further, the use of alternative advocacy tools such as market studies can help authorities better understand how markets are evolving, and the impact of regulation on competition in those markets.

More stringent product market regulation is negatively associated with the net job contribution of firms in more risky and financially-dependent sectors. The effect of regulation on the ability of, as well as incentives for, firms to compete and innovate has been explored in new OECD research. For instance, work on the role of product market regulations for the employment dynamics of entering and incumbent firms suggests that, in sectors that are more risky or financially dependent, more stringent product market regulation is negatively associated with the net job contribution of firms. The strength of this association appears similar for entrants and incumbents (Calvino, Criscuolo and Menon, 2016).

Competition policy enforcement is key to achieve economically efficient and socially beneficial outcomes in developing countries. Strong national competition policy frameworks can boost job creation and make the most out of increasing cross-border mergers and acquisitions. As FDI restrictions are being liberalized worldwide and positive standards of treatment established for transnational corporations, developing countries need to adopt and enforce sound measures to control anti-competitive practices by firms.

Enabling places to achieve a successful transition to digital economy

Access to digital infrastructure is unequally distributed within countries – public policies can help to expand accessibility. Digital infrastructures, including efficient, reliable and widely accessible broadband communication networks and services, data, software, and hardware, are the foundations upon which the digital economy is based. It is essential that governments promote investment in digital infrastructures and competition in the provision of high-speed networks and services, ensuring that key complementary enablers are in place. ICT and broadband infrastructure investments are important to ensure connectivity across regions. This has become a necessary condition to boost productivity and enhance competitiveness as well as to raise quality of life through the provision of public goods and services at high quality or competitive costs (OECD, 2017q; OECD, 2017a). However, access to digital infrastructure is uneven across regions in the OECD (Figure 2.27). While great gains have been made in the expansion of digital infrastructure, some areas, particularly remote rural ones, remain less connected and/or experience much slower connections. The gaps between rural and urban regions in terms of access to broadband access are largest in Greece (21% points), Chile (19% points) and Portugal (15% points) (OECD, 2015j).

Figure 2.27 Households with broadband connections, urban and rural, 2011 and 2016

As percentage of households in each category

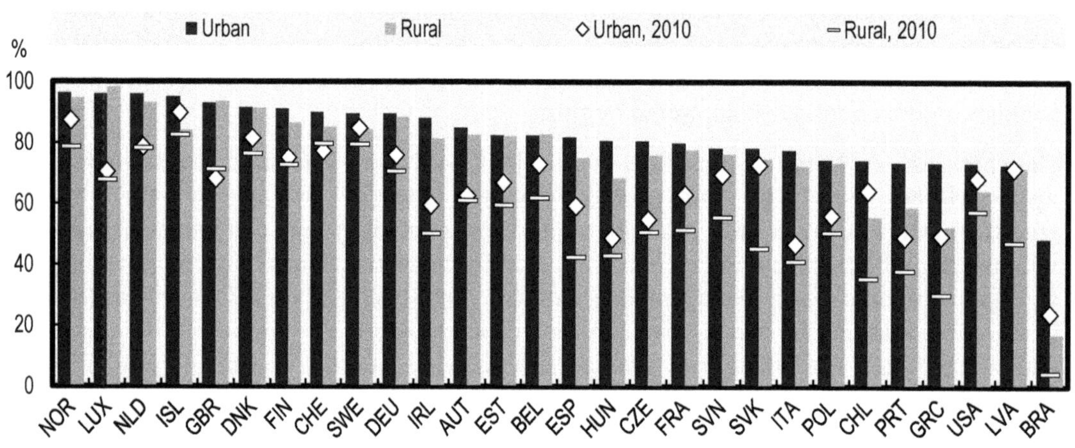

Source: OECD (2017a), Households with broadband connections, urban and rural, 2010 and 2016: As a percentage of households in each category, in OECD Science, Technology and Industry Scoreboard 2017, OECD Publishing, Paris.

StatLink http://dx.doi.org/10.1787/888933619942

The expansion of ICT connectivity in rural regions creates opportunities to deliver a broader array of services to both citizens and businesses. For instance, the use of telemedicine to deliver health care services, including videoconferencing technologies to improve access to health services for patients, families and health care professionals. These technologies reduce the need to travel and reduce costs, meaning that health care professionals can spend more time treating patients. Forward looking and integrated planning solutions help to ensure that digital infrastructure investments are well adapted to the local needs and also take into account future demographic trends. While new technologies are increasing the potential of higher quality digital connections in rural regions, "last mile" connections often remain a challenge and require specific policy supports. This is important because—with the growing importance of new technologies—places that are not connected can be disadvantaged.

Smart city technologies and systems have rapidly evolved as a means to enable cities to become more resilient, liveable and inclusive. The promise of 'smart cities' is their ability to collect, analyse and channel data to make informed decisions at the city level through a greater use of technology. Data and real-time analysis can support decision-making to increase a city's sustainability and economic growth, as well as provide basic services in a way that is cost effective and reinforces government's accountability, citizens' participation and quality of life. Key elements of smart cities include: i) taking advantage of policy complementarities, and ii) making use of local knowledge (grassroots real-time data). This approach has wide applications from helping cities and regions rebuild in the wake of a disaster (OECD, 2013c) to promoting green growth (OECD, 2016f).

Framework policies are critical to business dynamism, scaling up of young and small firms and creation of jobs. Framework policies, including institutional and regulatory settings, as they intend to incentivise risk-taking and entrepreneurial experimentation, are critical to business dynamism and to unleashing the growth potential of young firms and SMEs, especially in high-risk sectors, such as telecommunications, scientific R&D and IT services. Smaller firms, due to internal constraints, are typically more dependent on their business environment and are more vulnerable to market failures, policy inefficiencies and inconsistencies (Calvino, et al., 2016).

Start-ups are particularly exposed to their policy environment which may have been implicitly designed with the needs and conditions of incumbents in mind. The regulations may also be tailored to the prevailing technology adopted by incumbents, rather than to the innovative technology used by the start-ups. Entrants may be less familiar with the policy environment and this may increase their adjustment costs. With growth and risk closely intertwined, policies can help firms to bridge temporary difficulties in growing (e.g. by improving access to finance, skills or assets) and also tackle policy failures that impose an extra cost on the risk (e.g. bankruptcy law, weak contract enforcement).

Financing constraints can be especially severe in the case of start-ups or SMEs whose business model relies on intangible assets. There is a need to broaden the range of financing instruments available to SMEs and entrepreneurs, but alternatives to traditional debt remain underdeveloped in most countries (OECD, 2015k; EU and OECD, 2015). The G20/OECD High-Level Principles on SME Financing advocate a holistic approach to addressing SME financing gaps, recognising a number of demand-side (e.g. lack of financial skills, disadvantageous tax treatment) and supply-side barriers (e.g. opacity of the SME market) to the diffusion of alternative financing options. Consequently, SMEs often operate in thin, illiquid markets, with a low number of market participants. This in turn drives down demand from SMEs and discourages potential suppliers of finance (OECD, 2016g; Nassr and Wehinger, 2016).

End notes

8 Based on a Dynamic Olley-Pakes decomposition, following the methodology outlined in Melitz & Polanec, 2015.
9 In discussing this apparent puzzle, Autor (2015) highlights that wage growth in bottom occupations can be hindered by the fact that these occupations generally do not benefit from significant complementarities with new technologies while also facing a very elastic labour supply, given their low skill requirements, which can be exacerbated by the decline in middle-skill job opportunities if some middle-skill workers have to settle for lower-skilled jobs.

References

Abowd, J.M., F. Kramarz and D.N. Margolis (1999), "High Wage Workers and High Wage Firms", Econometrica, Vol. 67, No. 2, 251-333.

Acemoglu D., Hildebrand N. (2017), "Increasing Concentration and Persistence of Innovation: Facts and Theory ", Working Paper, Massachusetts Institute of Technology.

Acemoglu, D., & Restrepo, P. (2016), "The race between machine and man: Implications of technology for growth, factor shares and employment", No. w22252, National Bureau of Economic Research.

Acemoglu, D., and D. Autor (2011), "Chapter 12 - Skills, Tasks and Technologies: Implications for Employment and Earnings", Handbook of Labor Economics, Vol. 4, Part B, pp. 1043 – 1171.

Adalet McGowan, M., D. Andrews and V. Millot (2017), "The Walking Dead? Zombie Firms and Productivity Performance in OECD Countries", OECD Economics Department Working Papers, No. 1372, OECD Publishing, Paris.

Andrews, D, C Criscuolo, and P Gal (2017), "The Best versus the Rest: The Global Productivity Slowdown Hides an Increasing Performance Gap across Firms", VoxEU.org, 27 March.

Andrews, D. and C. Timiliotis (2018), "Boosting Digital Adoption in Firms: What Role for Structural Policies?", OECD Economics Department Working Paper, OECD Publishing, Paris.

Andrews, D., C. Criscuolo, and P. N. Gal (2016), "The Best versus the Rest: The Global Productivity Slowdown, Divergence across Firms and the Role of Public Policy" OECD Productivity Working Papers 5. Paris: OECD Publishing.

Autor D., Dorn D., Katz L. F., Patterson C., Van Reenen J. (2017), "The Fall of the Labour Share and the Rise of Superstar Firms", NBER Working Papers 23396, National Bureau of Economic Research, Inc.

Autor, D. (2015), "Why are There Still So Many Jobs? The History and Future of Workplace Automation", Journal of Economic Perspectives, Vol. 29/3, pp. 3-30.

Autor, D., D. Dorn and G.H. Hanson (2015), "Untangling Trade and Technology: Evidence from Local Labour Markets", Economic Journal, Vol. 125/584, pp. 621-646.

Avvisati, F., G. Jacotin and S. Vincent-Lancrin (2013), "Educating Higher Education Students for Innovative Economies: What International Data Tell Us", Tuning Journal for Higher Education, Issue No. 1, November, pp. 223-40.

Berlingieri G., Calligaris S., Criscuolo C. (2017b), "Does the Sector Matter? Unbundling the Size-Productivity-Wage Premium", DSTI-CIIE(2017)15.

Berlingieri, G., P. Blanchenay and C. Criscuolo (2017a), "The Great Divergence(s)", OECD STI Policy Paper No. 39.

Bessen, J. (2016), "How Computer Automation Affects Occupations: Technology, Jobs and Skills", Boston University School of Law, Law and Economic Research Papers, No.15-49.

Brynjolfsson, E., McAfee A., Sorell M., Zhu F. (2008), "Scale without Mass: Business Process Replication and Industry Dynamics", Harvard Business School Technology & Operations Mgt. Unit Research Paper, No. 07-016.

Brys, B., Perret, S., Thomas, A., and O'Reilly, P (2016), "Tax Design for Inclusive Economic Growth", OECD Taxation Working Papers, No. 26, OECD Publishing, Paris.

Calvino, F., C. Criscuolo, and C. Menon (2016), "No Country for Young Firms? Start-up Dynamics and National Policies", 29. OECD Science, Technology and Industry Policy Papers, OECD Publishing, Paris.

Card, D, J Heining, and P Kline (2013), "Workplace Heterogeneity and the Rise of West German Wage Inequality", Quarterly Journal of Economics 128(3): 967-1015.

Cazes, S., A. Hijzen and A. Saint-Martin (2015), "Measuring and Assessing Job Quality: The OECD Job Quality Framework", OECD Social, Employment and Migration Working Papers, No. 174, OECD Publishing, Paris.

Cortes, G.M. and A. Salvatori (2016), "Delving into the Demand Side: Changes in Workplace Specialisation and Job Polarisation", IZA Discussion Paper Series, No. 10120.

Criscuolo, C. and J. Timmis (2017), The Relationship between Global Value Chains and Productivity, International Productivity Monitor, Available at: http://www.csls.ca/ipm/32/Criscuolo_Timmis.pdf

Criscuolo, C., P. N. Gal, and C. Menon (2014), "The Dynamics of Employment Growth: New Evidence from 18 Countries", OECD Science, Technology and Industry Policy Papers, OECD Publishing, Paris.

Dauth, W., S. Findeisen, J. Suedekum and N. Woessner (2017), "German Robots: The Impact of Industrial Robots on Workers", CEPR Discussion Papers, No. 12306.

De Backer, K. and D. Flaig (2017), "The Future of Global Value Chains: Business as Usual or "a New Normal"?", OECD Science, Technology and Industry Policy Papers, No. 41, OECD Publishing, Paris.

Dustmann, C., J. Ludsteck, and U. Schönberg (2009), "Revisiting the German Wage Structure", The Quarterly Journal of Economics, Vol. 124/2, pp. 843–881.

European Union and OECD (2015), "Indicators of Immigrant Integration 2015", Settling In, OECD Publishing, Paris.

European Union and OECD (2015), "The Missing Entrepreneurs 2015: Policies for Inclusive Entrepreneurship in Europe", OECD Publishing, Paris.

European Union and OECD (2017), "The Missing Entrepreneurs 2017: Policies for Inclusive Entrepreneurship", OECD Publishing, Paris.

Ferrant, G. and A. Kolev (2016), "Does Gender Discrimination in Social Institutions Matter for Long-term Growth? Cross-country Evidence", OECD Development Centre Working Papers, No. 330, OECD Publishing, Paris.

Gaggle, P. and G.C. Wright (2015), "A Short-run View of What Computers Do: Evidence from a UK Tax Incentive", SKOPE Research Paper, No. 123.

Goldschmidt, D. and J. F. Schmieder (2017), "The Rise of Domestic Outsourcing and the Evolution of the German Wage Structure", NBER Working Paper No. 21366.

Graetz, G. and G. Michaels (2017), "Robots at Work", Available at: http://personal.lse.ac.uk/michaels/Graetz_Michaels_Robots.pdf

ILO (2017), "Future of Work", Inception Report for the Global Commission of the Future of Work.

ILO (2018), "World Employment and Social Outlook", forthcoming.

Immervoll, H. and M. Pearson (2009), "A Good Time for Making Work Pay? Taking Stock of In-Work Benefits and Related Measures across the OECD", OECD Social, Employment and Migration Working Papers, No. 81, OECD Publishing, Paris.

Krueger, A. and L. Summers (1988), "Efficiency Wages and the Inter-industry Wage Structure", Econometrica, Vol. 56, Issue 2, 259-93.

La Porta, R. and Shleifer, A. (2014), "Informality and Development", NBER Working Paper No. 20205.

Le Donné, N., P. Fraser and G. Bousquet (2016), "Teaching Strategies for Instructional Quality: Insights from the TALISPISA Link Data", OECD Education Working Papers, No. 148, OECD Publishing, Paris.

Mann, K. and L. Püttmann (2017), "Benign Effects of Automation: New Evidence from Patent Texts", Available at: https://papers.ssrn.com/sol3/papers.cfm?abstract_id=2959584

Marc J. Melitz & Sašo Polanec (2015), "Dynamic Olley-Pakes Productivity Decomposition with Entry and Exit, RAND Journal of Economics, RAND Corporation, vol. 46(2), pages 362-375.

Marcolin, L., S. Miroudot and M. Squicciarini (2016), "Routine Jobs, Employment and Technological Innovation in Global Value Chains", OECD Science, Technology and Industry Working Papers, 2016/01, OECD Publishing, Paris.

McKinsey (2017), "Global Payments 2017: Amid Rapid Change, an Upward Trajectory", McKinsey Global Institute Report – October 2017.

Mishel, L., H. Shierholz, and J. Schmitt (2013), "Don't Blame the Robots: Assessing the Job Polarization Explanation of Growing Wage Inequality", EPI Working Papers.

Moen, O., Heggeseth, A. G., & Lome, O. (2016), "The Positive Effect of Motivation and International Orientation on SME Growth", Journal of Small Business Management, Vol. 54(2): 659-678.

Nassr, I. K. and G. Wehinger (2016), "Opportunities and Limitations of Public Equity Markets for SMEs", OECD Journal: Financial Market Trends, OECD Publishing, vol. 2015(1), pages 49-84.

Nathanson, C. and E. Glen Weyl (2017), "Taxation and the Allocation of Talent", Journal of Political Economy 125, no. 5: 1635-1682.

Nedelkoska, L. and G. Quintini (2018), "Automation, Skills and Training", OECD Social, Employment and Migration Working Papers, OECD Publishing, Paris.

OECD (2010), "SMEs, Entrepreneurship and Innovation", OECD Publishing, Paris.

OECD (2011), "Divided We Stand: Why Inequality Keeps Rising", OECD Publishing, Paris.

OECD (2012), "Perspectives on Global Development 2012: Social Cohesion in a Shifting World", OECD Publishing, Paris.

OECD (2013a), "Recommendation of the Council on Gender Equality in Education, Employment, and Entrepreneurship", OECD Publishing, Paris.

OECD (2013c), "Policy Making after Disasters: Helping Regions Become Resilient – The Case of Post-Earthquake Abruzzo", OECD Publishing, Paris.

OECD (2014), "All on Board: Making Inclusive Growth Happen", OECD Publishing, Paris.

OECD (2015a), Employment Outlook 2015, Paris Publishing.

OECD (2015b), "Skills and Learning Strategies for Innovation in SMEs", Available as: CFE/SME(2014)3/REV2.

OECD (2015c), "New Approaches to SME and Entrepreneurship Financing: Broadening the Range of Instruments", OECD Publishing, Paris.

OECD (2015d), "OECD 2015 Recommendation of the Council on Gender Equality in Public Life", OECD Publishing, Paris.

OECD (2015f), "OECD Skills Outlook 2015: Youth, Skills and Employability", OECD Publishing, Paris.

OECD (2015g), "The Innovation Imperative: Contributing to Productivity, Growth and Wellbeing", OECD Publishing, Paris.

OECD (2015h), "The Future of Productivity", OECD Publishing, Paris.

OECD (2015i), "In It Together: Why Less Inequality Benefits All", OECD Publishing, Paris.

OECD (2015j), "Cities as hubs for data-driven innovation", in Data-Driven Innovation: Big Data for Growth and Well-Being, OECD Publishing, Paris.

OECD (2015k), "Taxation of SMEs in OECD and G20 Countries", OECD Tax Policy Studies, No. 23, OECD Publishing, Paris.

OECD (2015l), "Students, Computers and Learning: Making the Connection", PISA, OECD Publishing, Paris.

OECD (2016a), "Skills for a Digital World: 2016 Ministerial Meeting on the Digital Economy Background Report", OECD Digital Economy Papers, No. 250, OECD Publishing, Paris.

OECD (2016a), "Indicators of gender equality in entrepreneurship", OECD Gender Portal.

OECD (2016b), "New Markets and New Jobs", Background Report for the 2016 Ministerial Meeting on the Digital Economy, OECD Publishing, Paris.

OECD (2016c), "Stimulating Digital Innovation for Growth and Inclusiveness: The Role of Policies for the Successful Diffusion of ICT", Digital Economy Papers No. 256, OECD Publishing, Paris.

OECD (2016d), "Skills Matter: Further Results from the Survey of Adult Skills", OECD Skills Studies, OECD Publishing, Paris.

OECD (2016e), "Getting Skills Right: Anticipating and Responding to Changing Skill Needs", OECD Publishing, Paris.

OECD (2016f), "Green Growth in Bandung, Indonesia", OECD Publishing, Paris.

OECD (2016g), "Fostering Markets for SME Finance: Matching Business and Investor Needs", Working Party on SMEs and Entrepreneurship, CFE/SME(2016)4/FINAL.

OECD (2016h), "PISA 2015 Results (Volume I): Excellence and Equity in Education", PISA, OECD Publishing, Paris.

OECD (2017a), "OECD Science, Technology and Industry Scoreboard 2017: The Digital Transformation", OECD Publishing, Paris.

OECD (2017b), "OECD Economic Outlook 2017", Issue 1, OECD Publishing, Paris.

OECD (2017c), "OECD Employment Outlook 2017", OECD Publishing, Paris.

OECD (2017e), "Unlocking the Potential of Youth Entrepreneurship in Developing Countries", OECD Publishing, Paris.

OECD (2017f), "Investing in Climate, Investing in Growth", OECD Publishing, Paris.

OECD (2017g), "Going Digital: Making the Transformation Work for Growth and Well-Being", Meeting of the OECD Council at Ministerial Level, Paris 7-8 June 2017.

OECD (2017i), "Inclusive Innovation Policy Toolkit", Available at the Innovation Policy Platform: https://www.innovationpolicyplatform.org/inclusivetoolkit
OECD (2017j), "International Migration Outlook 2017", OECD Publishing, Paris.
OECD (2017k), "The Pursuit of Gender Equality, an Uphill Battle", OECD Publishing, Paris.
OECD (2017l), "Small, Medium, Strong. Trends in SME Performance and Business Conditions", OECD Publishing, Paris.
OECD (2017m), "Enhancing Productivity in SMEs: Interim Report", Available as: CFE/SME(2017)14.
OECD (2017n), "Towards an OECD Strategy for SMEs", available on OLIS, CFE/SME(2017)2.
OECD (2017p), "Making Innovation Benefit All: Policies for Inclusive Growth", OECD Publishing, Paris.
OECD (2017q), OECD Digital Economy Outlook 2017, OECD Publishing, Paris.
OECD (2017r), PISA 2015 Results (Volume V): Collaborative Problem Solving, PISA, OECD Publishing, Paris.
OECD (2018a), New OECD Jobs Strategy, forthcoming.
OECD (2018b), OECD Employment Outlook 2018, forthcoming.
OECD (2018c), "Automation, skills use and training", OECD Social, Employment and Migration Working Papers Series, OECD Publishing, Paris (forthcoming).
OECD (2013b), "The role of FDI in Costa Rica's economic development", in OECD Investment Policy Reviews: Costa Rica 2013, OECD Publishing, Paris.
OECD (2017d), "Entrepreneurship at a Glance 2017", OECD Publishing, Paris.
Paunov, C. and V. Rollo (2016), "Has the Internet Fostered Inclusive Innovation in the Developing World?", World Development, Vol. 78, pp. 587-609.
Paunov, C., S. Planes-Satorra et T. Moriguchi (2017), "What Role for Social Sciences in Innovation? Re-assessing How Scientific Disciplines Contribute to Different Industries", OECD Science, Technology and Industry Policy Papers, No. 45, OECD Publications, Paris.
Piketty, T. (2013), "Capital in the Twenty-First Century", Harvard University Press.
Planes-Satorra, S. and C. Paunov (2017), "Inclusive Innovation Policies: Lessons from International Case Studies", OECD Science, Technology and Industry Working Papers, 2017/02, OECD Publishing, Paris.
Richbell, S., Watts, H., & Wardle, P. (2006), "Owner-managers and Business Planning in the Small Firm", International Small Business Journal, Vol. 24(5): 496-514.
Sabadish, N. and L. Mishel (2012), "How Executive Compensation and Financial-sector Pay Have Fuelled Income Inequality", Economic Policy Institute, Issue Brief No. 331.
Saez, E., B. Schoefer and D. Seim (2017), "Payroll Taxes, Firm Behavior, and Rent Sharing: Evidence from a Young Workers' Tax Cut in Sweden", NBER Working Paper 23976.
Salvatori, A. (2015), "The Anatomy of Job Polarisation in the UK", IZA Discussion Papers, No. 9193.
Schaefer, Daniel & Singleton, Carl (2017), "Recent Changes in British Wage Inequality: Evidence from Firms and Occupations," MPRA Paper 76744, University Library of Munich, Germany.
Song, J. et al. (2015), "Firming Up Inequality", NBER Working Papers, No. 21199.
Spasova, S. et al. (2017), "Access to Social Protection for People Working on Non-standard Contracts and as Self-employed in Europe", European Social Policy Network.
Thomas, A. and P. O'Reilly (2016), "The Impact of Tax and Benefit Systems on the Workforce Participation Incentives of Women," OECD Taxation Working Papers, No. 29, OECD Publishing, Paris.
Torres, S., Portugal, P., Addison, J. T. and Guimaraes, P. (2013), "The Sources of Wage Variation: A Three-Way High-Dimensional Fixed Effects Regression Model", IZA Discussion Papers 7276, Institute for the Study of Labor (IZA).
World Bank (2013), "World Development Report 2013: Jobs". Washington, DC: World Bank.
World Bank (2015), "The State of Social Safety Nets 2015", Washington, DC: World Bank.
World Inequality Report (2018), "World Inequality Report", Available at: http://wir2018.wid.world/files/download/wir2018-full-report-english.pdf.

Chapter 3. Invest in people and places left behind, providing equal opportunities

This chapter is structured in two main parts. First, it outlines trends in key opportunity and future prosperity outcomes. This includes trends in children's well-being, and particularly its evolution over the past decade, educational outcomes and opportunities as they relate socioeconomic background, health outcomes, social mobility, and trends in regional disparities and inclusive communities. Second, the chapter discusses key dynamics and policies to enhance opportunities and foundations for future prosperity.

This chapter emphasises the importance of inclusive education systems that provide people with the skills and opportunities to flourish throughout life, and the importance of early childhood education and intervention to mitigate the accumulation of inequalities later in life. It also highlights the centrality of reducing regional disparities and place-based policies in the inclusive growth agenda: enhancing innovation and knowledge diffusion across regions, providing affordable housing and enhancing mobility and connectivity are key components of this regional approach. It concludes by discussing policies that create vibrant communities that can foster people's well-being.

The Inclusive Growth Framework for Policy Action on Inclusive Growth consolidates some of the key policy recommendations to sustain and more equitably share the gains of economic growth from related OECD work, around broad principles to invest in people and places left behind through:

(i) targeted quality childcare, early education and life-long acquisition of skills;

(ii) effective access to quality healthcare, education, justice, housing, infrastructures; and

(iii) optimal natural resource management for sustainable growth.

Trends in key opportunity and future prosperity outcomes

Trends in child well-being

Child poverty is on the rise in most OECD countries. Children are paying a high price for the large and often rising inequalities in different dimensions of well-being. The proportion of children in poverty has grown in almost two-thirds of OECD countries (Figure 3.1) due to the great recession and despite measures that were often taken to mitigate the effects on families' standard of living (Adema et al., 2014; Ali et al., 2014).

Figure 3.1 Child income poverty rates on the rise in most OECD countries since 2007

Share (%) of children (0-17) with an equivalised post-tax-and-transfer income of less than 50% of the national annual median equivalised post-tax-and-transfer income, 2007a, and 2014-15b or nearest available year

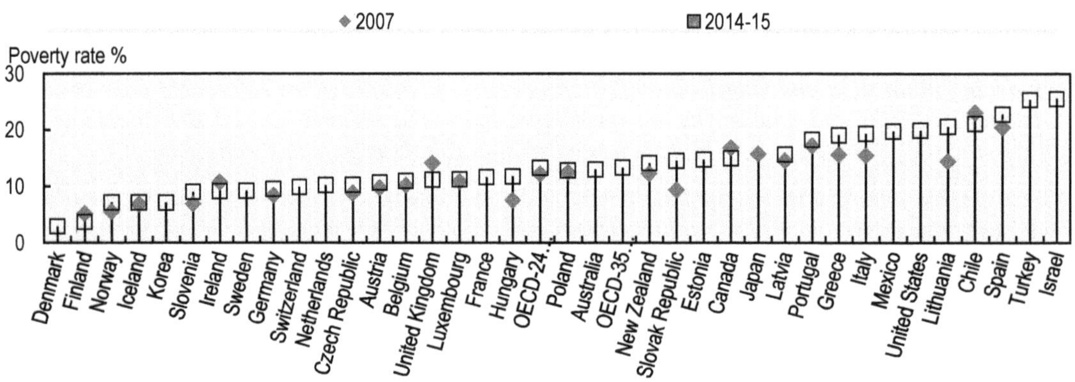

Note: a) 2008 for Germany, Israel, New Zealand; Norway; 2009 for Chile, Japan; b) 2013 for Brazil, China; 2015 for Chile, Finland, Israel, the Netherlands, the United Kingdom. c) The OECD-24 average is the unweighted mean average for the 24 OECD countries with data available for 2007.
Source: OECD Income Distribution Database.

StatLink http://dx.doi.org/10.1787/888933725297

Family living arrangements influence the risk of child poverty. On average, one in three single-parent families live in relative poverty; which is three times higher than the poverty rate among two-parent families. A growing proportion of children experience a period of poverty because the share of single-parent families is increasing: 15.8% of children were living with a single-parent in 2007 and 17.2% in 2016 (OECD, 2017a).

Continued parental employment is the most durable protection against the risk of poverty. On average across the OECD, 66% of jobless single-parent families are income poor and this rate is divided by three when the parent has a job; also on average 62% of families with two parents are income poor when none of the parents work, but the proportion drops to 4% when the two parents work. However, about one in ten children live in a jobless family, and this proportion increased sharply in countries hard hit by the economic recession, including France (+3%), Ireland (+4.1%), Greece (+7%), Italy (+5%), Portugal (+3%), Slovenia (+3%), and Spain (+8%) (OECD, 2017a; OECD, 2017i).

Child well-being goes beyond material conditions. Raising children out of income poverty is just one aspect of ensuring that children can lead happy, healthy and productive lives. Housing conditions, the neighbourhood and environment in which children live, their health, safety, education, leisure time and personal relationships, as well as their subjective well-being and mental health, are all essential factors that contribute to the quality children's lives (OECD 2009, 2015, 2017a; Richardson and Ali, 2014). For instance, almost one third of children (32%) in low-income families live in overcrowded households while less than 18% of them are in this situation in higher-income families (OECD, 2017a).

Poorer children are unhappier. While strongly conditioning children's aspirations and educational outcomes (section below), the economic and social background of families affects the general level of satisfaction that children experience with their lives. Indeed, 15 year-olds adolescents from the most socio-economically disadvantaged families are both less likely to report high life satisfaction (32% compared to 37% for children from more privileged families) and more likely to report low levels of satisfaction (14% compared to 9% for adolescents from more favoured families). Data for selected OECD countries suggest that 20-40% of children aged 11 to 15 have multiple recurrent psychosomatic health complaints, which are more prevalent in girls than boys and increase with age (OECD, 2015a; OECD, 2015b).

Figure 3.2 Change in self-reported overweight (including obesity) among 15-year-olds

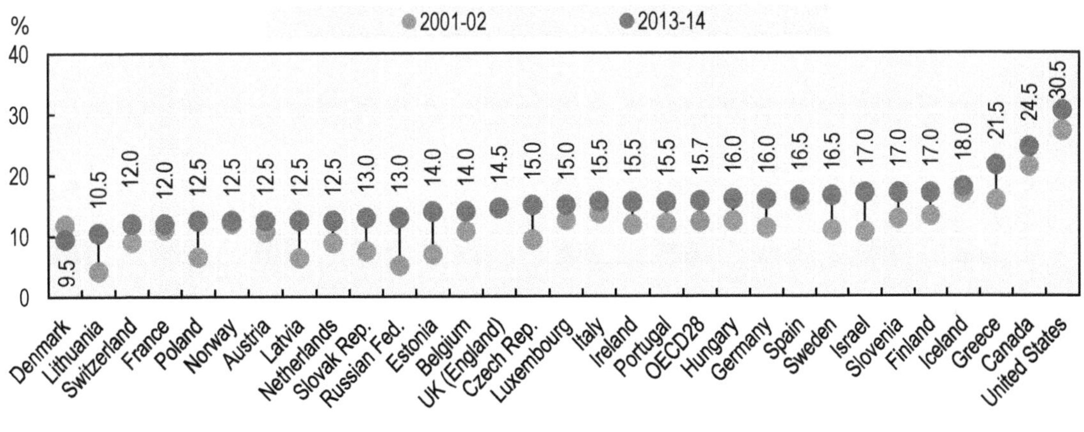

Source: OECD (2017b), Health at a Glance 2017.

StatLink http://dx.doi.org/10.1787/888933603051

Income poverty affects children's nutritional practices and health outcomes, giving rise to child obesity. In Europe, around 16% of income poor children do not have either fruits and vegetables at least once a day or one meal with meat, chicken or fish (or vegetarian equivalent) at least once a day, while the proportion is four times lower in higher-income families (OECD, 2017a). Equally significant is the risk of "overweight" and "obesity" that is markedly dependent on family affluence: 22% of adolescents aged 11 to 15 in low family affluence are being classified as 'overweight' or 'obese' while the proportion is only 15% among children in high family affluence (Inchley et al, 2016; OECD, 2017a; OECD, 2017b). In addition, the prevalence of child overweight (including obesity) has increased by 28% in the last decade, from 12% in 2001-02 to 16% in 2013-14 (Figure 3.2). Such rise in the childhood obesity is a great concern for OECD countries because it is a strong predictor of adult obesity (WHO, 2016a) and therefore is associated with a higher risk of experiencing later in life cardiovascular, endocrine, or pulmonary diseases. At a shorter horizon, child obesity often affects mental health through the development of poor self-esteem, eating disorders, and depression (Inchley et al., 2016). Obesity is associated with poorer educational attainment (Devaux et al, 2011).

Childhood and adolescence are crucial periods for good mental health. A large number of children suffer from mental health diseases, especially among low-income households. Many mental illnesses have an onset in childhood or adolescence, and around one in four young people have a mental disorder (Figure 3.3). Data for selected OECD countries suggest that 20-40% of children aged 11 to 15 have multiple recurrent psychosomatic health complaints, which are more prevalent in girls than boys and increase with age (OECD, 2015a). Good mental health in early childhood and even infancy has also been associated with better long-term mental, physical and social outcomes (McDaid, Hewlett and Park, 2017). Mental well-being is generally lower among children in poorer families than among children in richer families (McDaid, Hewlett and Park, 2017). Children and adolescents experiencing mental ill-health are more likely to leave school early, have poorer education outcomes, and consequently have greater difficulty accessing the labour market.

Figure 3.3 People aged 15-24 with a mental disorder

OECD countries, % of the total youth population, late 2000s and mid-1990s

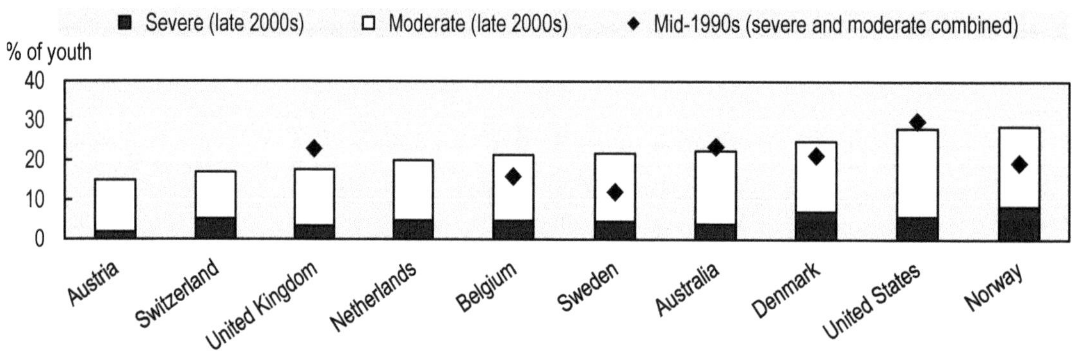

Note: National health surveys. Australia: National Health Survey 2001 and 2007/08; Austria: Health Interview Survey 2006/07; Belgium: Health Interview Survey 1997, 2001 and 2008; Denmark: National Health Interview Survey 1994, 2000 and 2005; Netherlands: POLS Health Survey 2001-03 and 2007-09; Norway: Level of Living and Health Survey 1998, 2002 and 2008; Sweden: Survey on Living Conditions 1994/95, 1999/2000 and 2004/05; Switzerland: Health Survey 2002 and 2007; United Kingdom: Health Survey of England 1995, 2001 and 2006; United States: National Health Interview Survey 1997, 2002 and 2008.
Source: OECD (2012), Sick on the Job? Myths and Realities about Mental Health and Work.

StatLink http://dx.doi.org/10.1787/888932534292

Trends in educational outcomes and opportunities

Home background influences success in education and schooling can either reinforce or mitigate that influence. In 2006, on average across OECD countries, 14% of the variation in students' science performance could be explained by students' socio-economic status. A one-unit change in the PISA index of economic, social and cultural status (ESCS) – which corresponds to the difference between students with average socio-economic status and disadvantaged students – was associated with a difference in science performance of 39 score points.

In the last decade, educational opportunities have not increased much (as measured through the strength of socio-economic gradient). By 2015, the degree to which students' socio-economic status predicted performance in science decreased to 13 score points, while the difference in performance between students who were one unit apart on the ESCS index decreased to 38 score points (OECD, 2016a, 2016b, 2016c; OECD, 2015c). Over the period 2006-15, the strength of the gradient decreased by more than 3% points in eight countries that also managed to maintain their average performance: Brazil, Bulgaria, Chile, Denmark, Germany, Slovenia, Thailand and the United States. In these countries, students' socio-economic status became a less reliable predictor of achievement as there was no significant change in performance (Figure 3.4).

Figure 3.4 Change between 2006 and 2015 in the strength of the socio-economic gradient

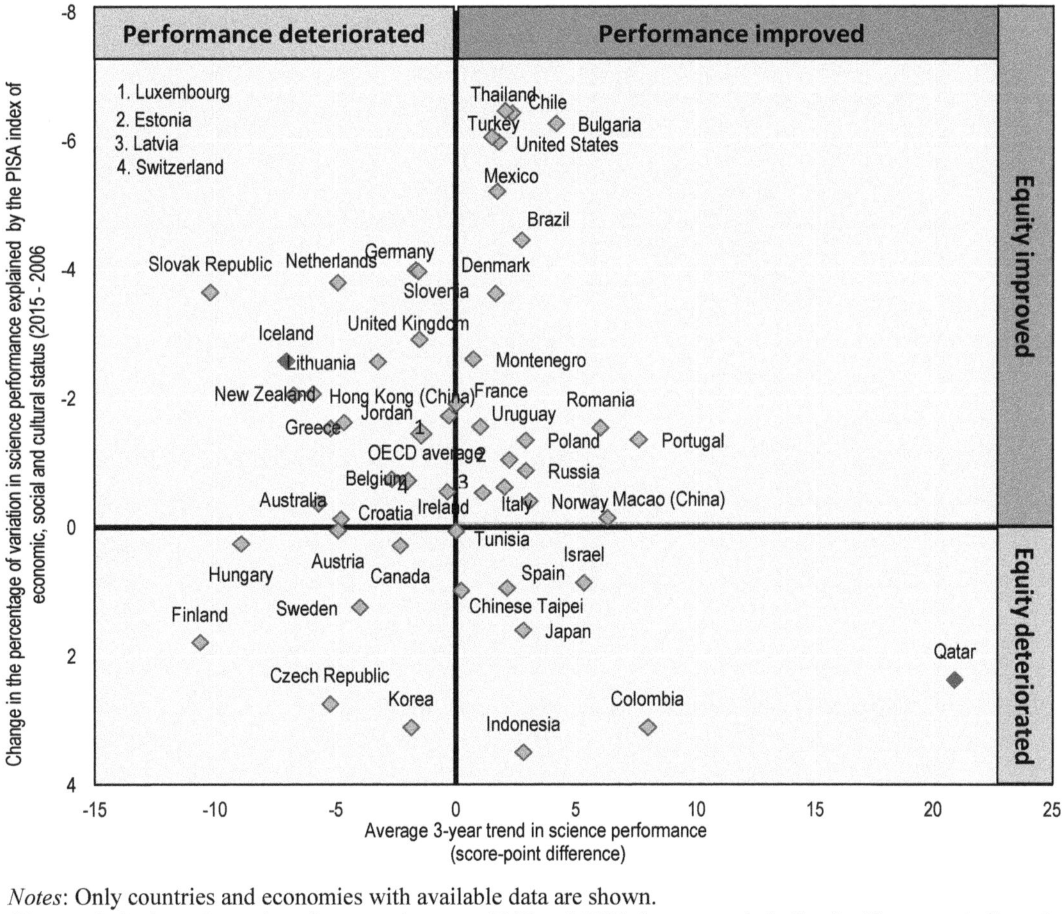

Notes: Only countries and economies with available data are shown.
Changes in both equity and performance between 2006 and 2015 that are statistically significant are indicated in a darker tone (see AnnexA3).
The average three-year trend is the average rate of change, per three-year period, between the earliest vailable measurement in PISA and PISA 2015. For countries and economies with more than one available measurement, the average three-year trend is calculated with a linear regression model. This model takes into account that Costa Rica, Georgia, Malta and Moldova conducted the PISA 2009 assessment in 2010 as part of PISA 2009+.
Source: OECD, PISA 2015 Database, Table I.6.17

StatLink http://dx.doi.org/10.1787/888933725316

Improving performance and equity of the school system at the same time is possible. In some OECD countries where educational opportunities have increased without offsetting improvements: between PISA 2006 and PISA 2015, in Chile, Denmark, Mexico,

Slovenia, Turkey, the United Kingdom and the United States, the average impact of students' socio-economic status on performance weakened by more than 4 score points while mean science achievement did not decline (Figure 3.5).

Figure 3.5 Change between 2006 and 2015 in the slope of the socio-economic gradient

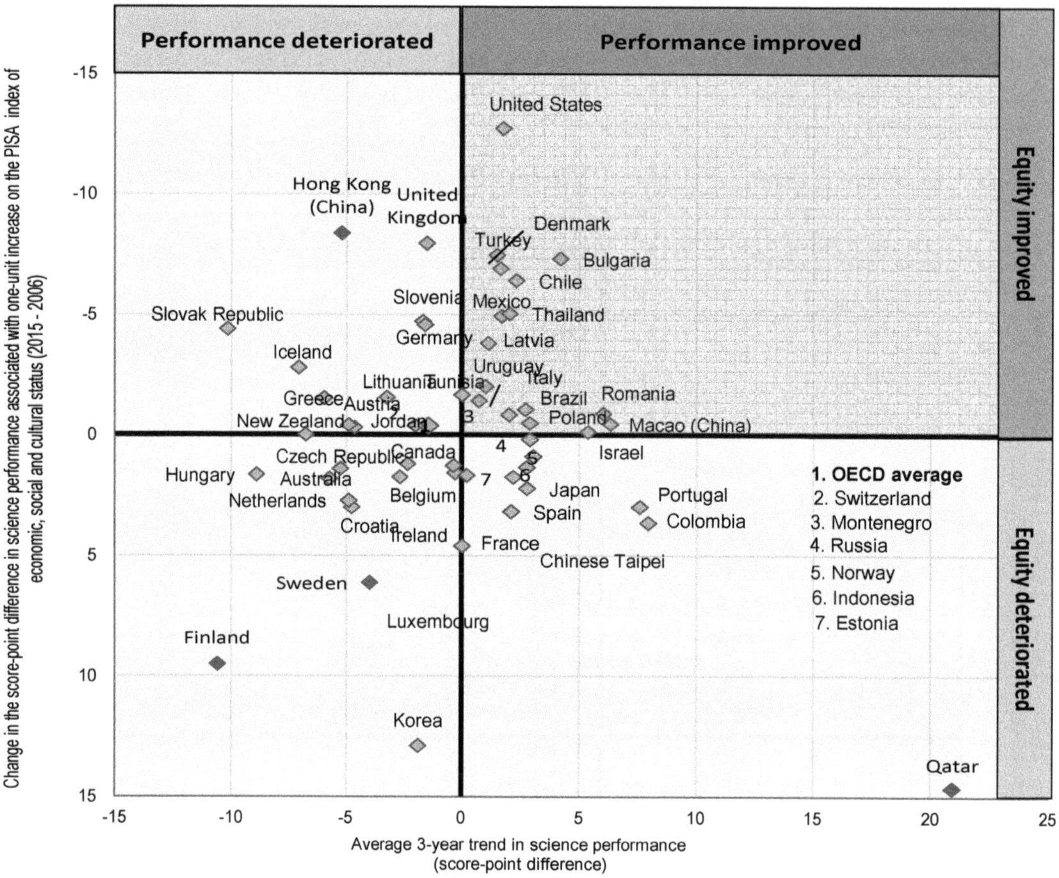

Notes: Only countries and economies with available data are shown.
Changes in both equity and performance between 2006 and 2015 that are statistically significant are indicated in a darker tone (see AnnexA3).
The average three-year trend is the average rate of change, per three-year period, between the earliest available measurement in PISA and PISA 2015. For countries and economies with more than one available measurement, the average three-year trend is calculated with a linear regression model. This model takes into account that Costa Rica, Georgia, Malta and Moldova conducted the PISA 2009 assessment in 2010 as part of PISA 2009+
Source: OECD, PISA 2015 Database, Table I.6.17.

StatLink http://dx.doi.org/10.1787/888933725335

Trends in health outcomes disparities

While longevity differences between countries have narrowed, within countries, inequalities in longevity remain large. Inequality in life expectancy between countries has narrowed over the last decade, although gains in longevity have been mediocre (i.e. less than one year) in Mexico, the United States and Germany, as compared to an average of 2 years gained among OECD and key partner countries, and 1.8 years among OECD countries. Within OECD countries, inequalities in longevity remain large however. Across

25 OECD countries with available data, in 2001, the gap in life expectancy at the age of 30 between high and low-educated people was around 7 years for men and 4 years for women (Murtin et al., 2017; OECD, 2017a).

Longevity gaps differ markedly across countries. High-educated men aged 30 can expect to live more than 10 years longer than their low-educated counterparts in the Slovak Republic, Estonia, Poland, Hungary, Latvia and the Czech Republic, while the gap is less than 5 years in Turkey, Sweden, Canada, the United Kingdom, Italy, Netherlands and Norway. In the case of women, inequalities in life expectancy are relatively small in Turkey, Greece, Canada, France and Sweden but exceed 8 years in Latvia and Estonia. Inequalities in longevity by education persist even at older ages. At 65 years, the gap in life expectancy between the high and low-educated was, on average across the 23 countries with available data, 3.6 years for men and 2.5 for women (Figure 3.6Figure 3.6). In relative terms, i.e. expressed as a share of the remaining lifespan, gaps in longevity are even larger at 65 than at 25. While differences in average life span (i.e. life expectancy) between education and gender groups are large, they are even wider within groups.

Figure 3.6 Gap in life expectancy at age 30 between highest and lowest education level

OECD countries, by gender, 2015 or latest available year

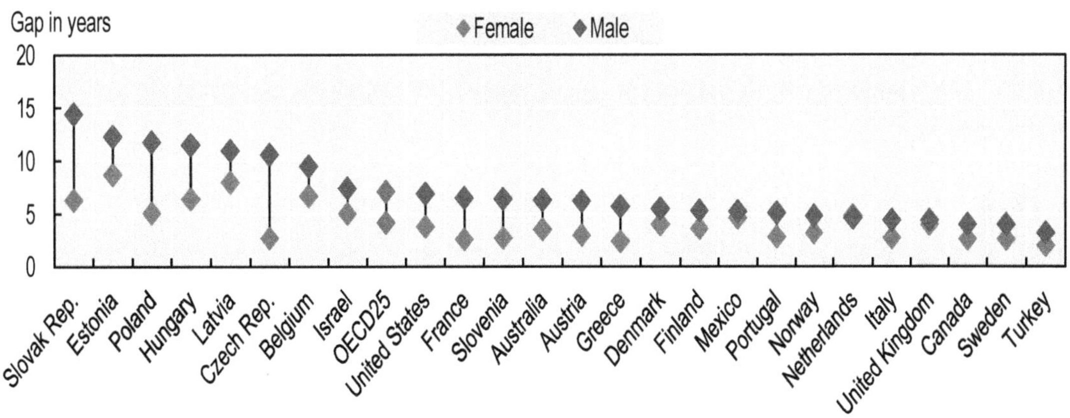

Source: Murtin et al. (2017) and OECD (2017).

StatLink http://dx.doi.org/10.1787/888933725354

Circulatory problems are the main factor explaining the mortality gap between education groups at older age. For older people, circulatory diseases contribute to 41% of the difference in mortality rates between low and high-educated men, and to around 50% of the gap between low and high educated women. Addressing the risk factors underlying circulatory diseases, in particular smoking, would go a long way towards reducing both average mortality rates and inequalities in longevity across education groups (Figure 3.7). Smoking accounts for up to half of the inequalities in mortality rates in some European countries (OECD, 2017b); also, while its contribution to inequalities in longevity has declined in most countries for men, it has increased for women.

Figure 3.7 Mortality rates by gender, education and cause of death

Population aged 65-89 years around 2011

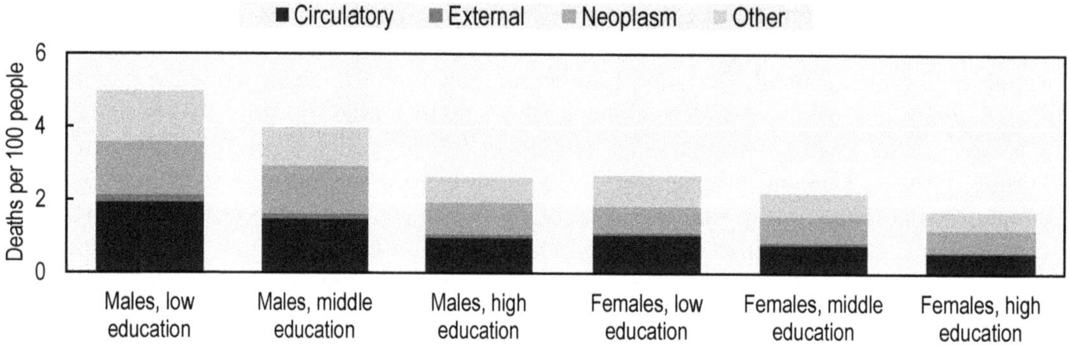

Source: Murtin et al. (2017).

StatLink http://dx.doi.org/10.1787/888933725373

Figure 3.8 Change of the regional gap in life expectancy

OECD countries, 2000-15

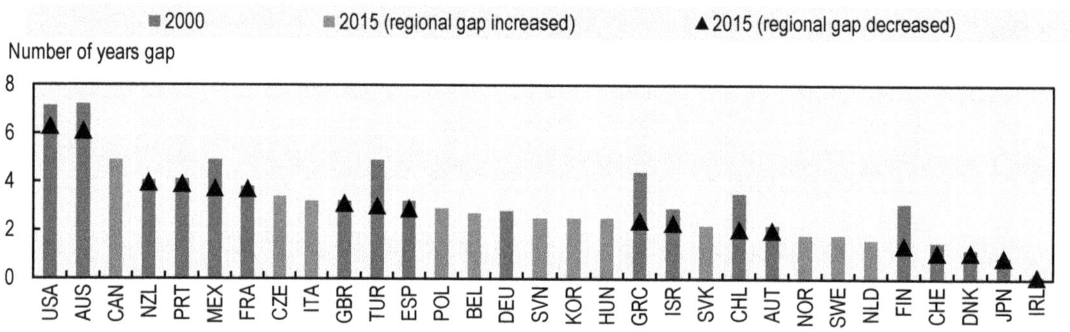

Note: The figure shows the difference between the TL2 regions with the highest and the lowest life expectancy at birth in OECD countries, and the evolution of this difference in 2000-15. Since life expectancy has improved in all regions during this period, the reduction of the regional gap is due to a relative better performance of the region with the lowest value. Conversely, an increase of the regional gap is due to faster improvement of life expectancy in the healthiest region. Nunavut (Canada), Ceuta (Spain) and Melilla (Spain) are not included.
Source: Calculations based on OECD Regional Statistics (database).

StatLink http://dx.doi.org/10.1787/888933725392

The regional gap in life expectancy is striking across OECD countries. On average, citizens in regions with the highest life expectancy live two and a half years longer than citizens in regions with the lowest life expectancy (Figure 3.8). In some countries such as Finland, Japan or Switzerland, regional gaps in life expectancy are very low, and these gaps remained stable or even decreased between 2000 and 2015. In contrast, within country differences in the US or Australia are approximately as large as the difference in national average life expectancy between those countries and Mexico, the OECD country with the lowest life expectancy. Although regional discrepancies in life expectancy have, on average, declined only slightly from 2000 to 2015, some countries have experienced a significant drop in the regional gap in terms of life expectancy. For instance, Finland managed to halve its life expectancy gap; Turkey, Greece and Chile also reduced it by 30%.

Figure 3.9 Health worsens with age

Share of people reporting bad health by age, gender, and education in 24 OECD countries

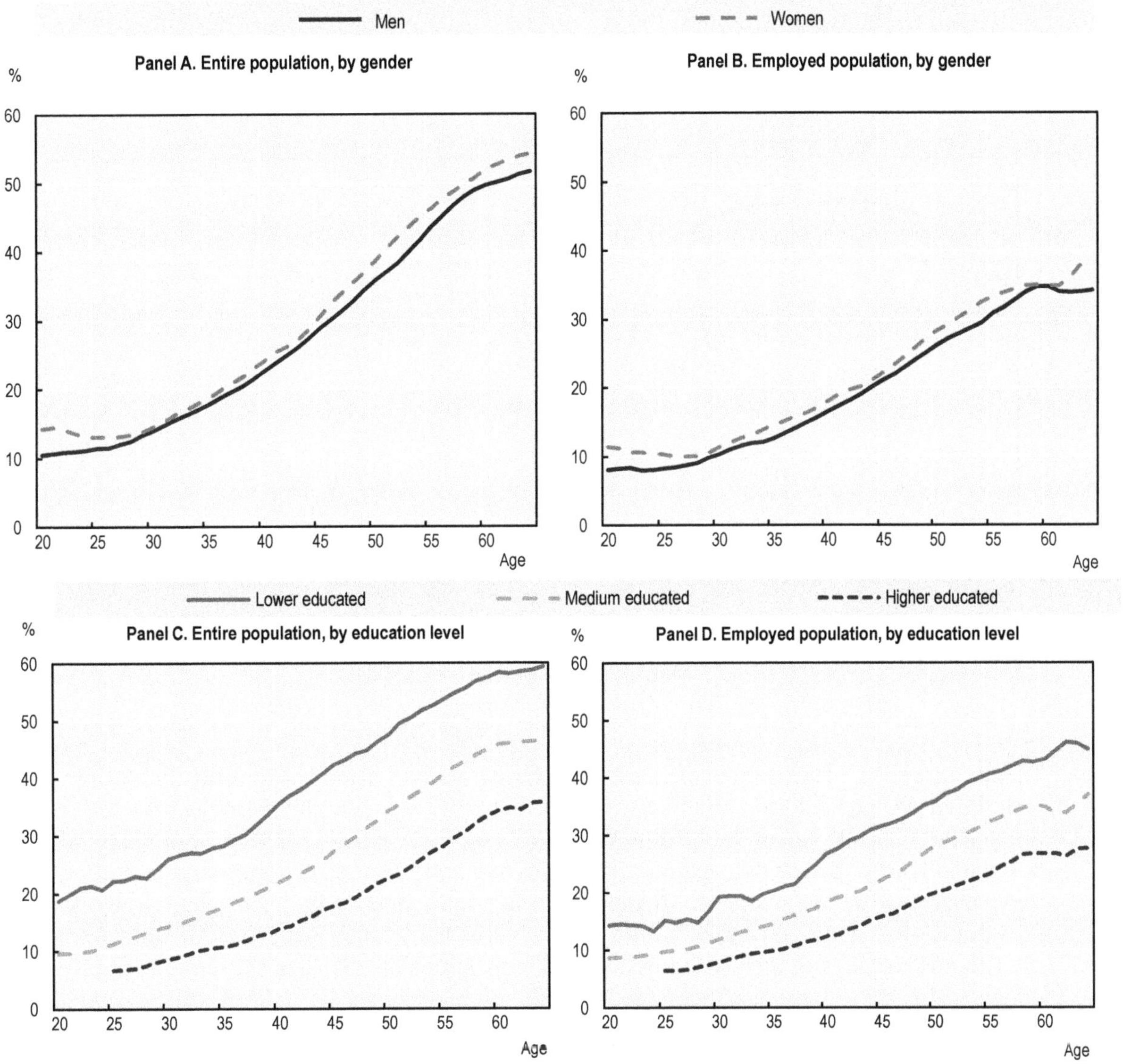

Note: "Low", "medium" and "high" levels of education correspond to International Standard Classification of Education (ISCED) codes 0-2, 3-4, and 5-6, respectively.
Source: Figure 2.1 in OECD (2017d), Preventing Ageing Unequally.

StatLink http://dx.doi.org/10.1787/888933566514

Health inequalities widen with age. The proportion of people reporting bad health rises with age: from about one-tenth of the entire population at the age of 20 to more than half at 64 years old (Figure 3.9A); and from about one-tenth of the employed to slightly over one-third, respectively (Figure 3.9B). While there are no significant differences between men and women, there are substantial disparities between education levels (Figure 3.9C;

Figure 3.9D). Among the highly educated, less than 10% are in bad health at the age of 25 and about 35% at the age of 64. The figures are close to 20% and 60%, respectively, among people with low levels of education.

Figure 3.10 Employment rates at all ages are lower for individuals in bad health

Employment rate by gender, age and self-reported health in 24 OECD countries

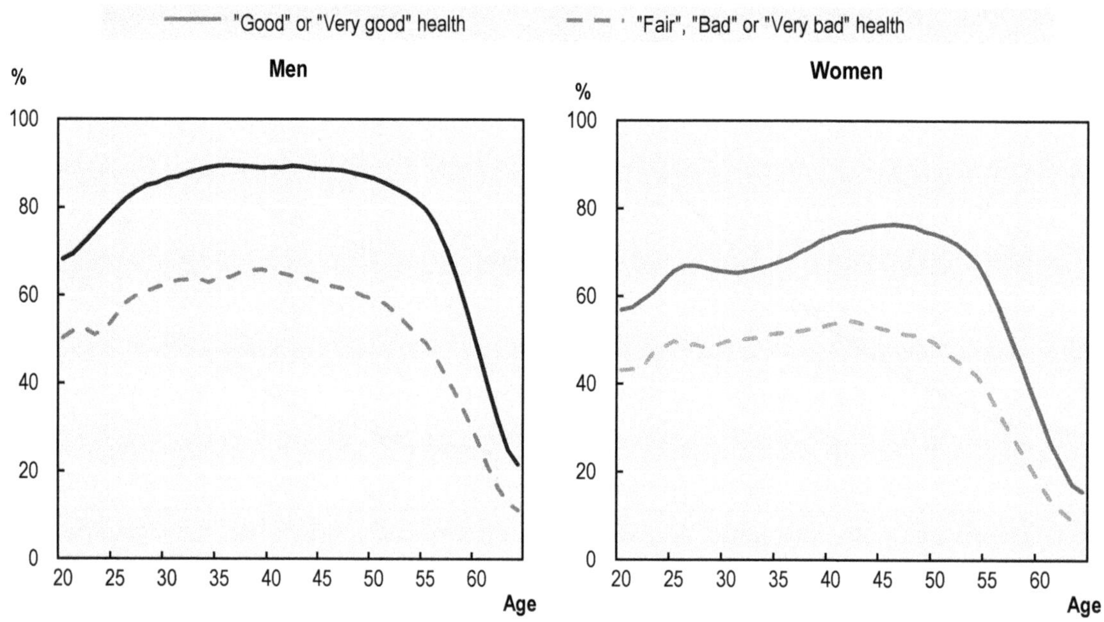

Source: Figure 2.2. (Panel A) in OECD (2017d), Preventing Ageing Unequally.

StatLink http://dx.doi.org/10.1787/888933566533

Disadvantage in education, health and the labour market often compound each other. Individuals in bad health are less likely to work and, at all ages, employment rates are lower among the unhealthy than the healthy (Figure 3.10). For example, among both men and women in good or bad health, age-related employment rate curves are hump-shaped, falling away sharply after the age of 55. In addition, when individuals with poor health do work, they earn lower wages than their healthy peers. Over the whole career, bad health lowers the lifetime earnings of men with low levels of educations by 33% and those of the highly educated by 17%. Earnings trajectory patterns among women are a little different and health effects are less pronounced (at 18 and 13%, respectively) as the risk of health-related non-employment is lower (OECD 2017a; OECD, 2017b; OECD, 2017d).

Improving education, for instance, could have positive knock-on effects on the labour market and health. Inequality-reducing policies in education, labour market or health will generate greater total returns in terms of welfare as they spill over into other areas. Interventions at an early age are also important because, in most aspects of human capital (e.g. education and health), inequalities emerge very early in life and interventions that reduce inequality will complement each other over the life course.

Trends in environmental quality of life

Inter-country inequalities raise equity concerns that are linked to countries' approaches to mitigate environmental degradation, while intra-country inequalities can inform about parts of population exposed to and responsible for environmental pressures and risks. Distributional questions cut to the heart of both environmental quality of life and resource consumption. The extraction and use of energy and non-energy materials has continued to rise at the global level in recent years, while changing trade patterns and the displacement of resource-intensive production to other countries have contributed to production-based productivity gains in OECD countries accompanied with higher emissions (OECD, 2017f; Figure 3.11). There is a potentially larger negative impact of emissions on some countries (e.g. low-lying islands) and negative health effects (not just CO_2 emissions) on those countries/regions where activities have relocated.

Natural resource consumption and its by-products, raise concerns about how the appropriation of rents, access to resources and exposure to potential contamination and pollution are being shared among the population. Demand-based CO2 emission patterns hide behavioural traits linked to the inter-country and intra-country dynamics of inequality. Globally, about half of the CO2 emissions associated with individual lifestyles are estimated to be generated by the top 10% of the global income distribution, who disproportionately live in the least egalitarian OECD countries (Chancel and Piketty, 2015). Related work (Levinson and O'Brien, 2015; Oxfam, 2015) has also suggested that the lifestyles and consumption patterns driven by economic inequality typically imply that the top few earners use more energy and create more waste.

Figure 3.11 CO_2 emissions from energy use are still growing worldwide

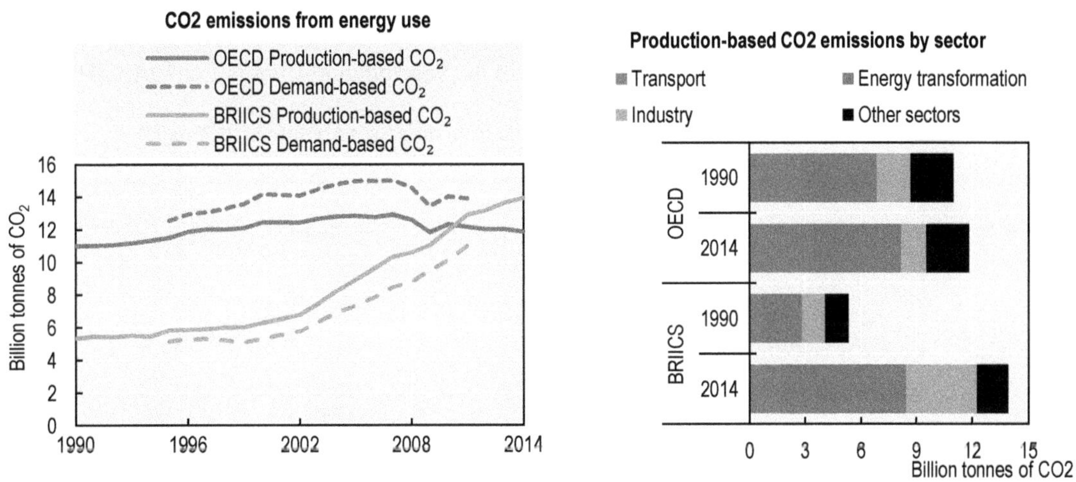

Source: IEA (2016), "CO2 emissions by product and flow (Edition 2016)", IEA CO2 Emissions from Fuel Combustion Statistics; OECD (2015d), "Carbon dioxide embodied in international trade", OECD Structural Analysis Statistics: Input-Output.

StatLink http://dx.doi.org/10.1787/888933725411

Uneven consumption of resources is matched by an unequal distribution of its environmental effects. The effects of environmental degradation are unevenly distributed between and within countries, with those least prepared and able to cope suffering the greatest socio-economic consequences. In terms of climate change, the World Bank estimated that unmitigated climate change could push 100 million people in developing countries into extreme poverty by 2030 (World Bank, 2016). Likewise, the economic risk of climate change is shown to be unequally geographically distributed in the US; implying that temperature rises could induce a transfer of value from the poorer south towards wealthier parts of the US, thereby increasing economic inequality (Hsiang, Solomon et al 2017). Poorer communities are ill-prepared to meet the challenges of climate change, being less able to invest in ex-ante preventative measures or ex-post mitigation (OECD, 2017e).

Taking decisive action on climate change provides an opportunity to generate new jobs and spark economic growth, but it will also result in job losses with specific distributional impacts. According to the IEA's 66% 2°C scenario, putting the planet on a trajectory that would see a 66% chance of limiting temperature rises to 2°C would lead to around 1 million jobs being lost in the energy sector (against a total of 30 million in the sector) due to the premature closure of assets (IEA, 2017). Though modest at the aggregate level relative to the total number of jobs in the energy sector, associated job losses could be unevenly spread and concentrated in specific localities, leading to geographical dislocations (OECD, 2017b).

Acting on climate change will allow reduce exposure of people to air pollution, which is the single greatest environmental health risk worldwide with specific consequences for some segments of the population. Globally, exposure to outdoor fine particles (PM2.5) and ozone can be attributed to an estimated 4.4 million deaths annually. OECD countries account for an estimated 500 000 of these (GBD, 2015). The annual welfare cost is estimated to be USD 1.7 trillion, equivalent to 3.6% of GDP for the OECD area (Figure 3.12Figure 3.12). Without stronger policy efforts, the cost is projected to reach USD 3.5 trillion in 2060 (equivalent to 5% of GDP in 2060). In non-OECD economies, the costs are projected to increase tenfold and could reach USD 15-22 trillion in 2060 (equivalent to 7-10% of their GDP in 2060; OECD, 2016b).

Figure 3.12 The OECD annual welfare cost of outdoor air pollution is 3.6% of GDP

OECD and BRIICS, the cost of premature deaths from outdoor air pollution, trillion USD

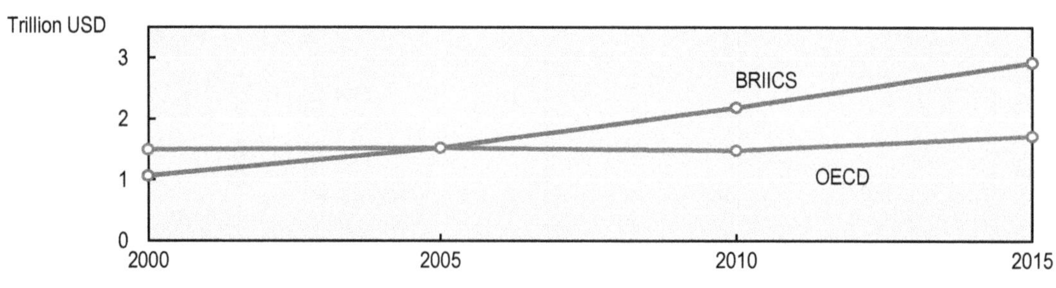

Note: OECD calculations using methodology adapted from OECD (2014). A standard value-of-statistical-life (VSL) estimate is used to calculate the costs of premature mortalities. The country-specific costs presented here account for differences in income levels and income elasticities across countries (elasticity of 0.8 for high-, 0.9 for middle- and 1 for low-income countries). Nevertheless, the underlying VSL estimate might be less reliable when applied to countries with different standards of living or extrapolated over time. VSL also captures non-market values that are unrelated to expenditures and therefore not an integral part of the calculation of GDP. Consequently the cost estimates are compared with GDP only for illustration.
Source: OECD (2014), The Cost of Air Pollution: Health Impacts of Road Transport.

StatLink http://dx.doi.org/10.1787/888933725430

Exposure to air pollution is not uniform across income groups and varies across countries. A recent meta-analysis of existing work on global air pollution and inequalities showed that generally air pollution is higher in poorer communities – with 8 of the 10 studies analysed illustrating this relationship (Hajat A, et al, 2015). The relationship between exposure to ambient air pollution and low income status was most consistent in North America, Asia and Africa (though data are extremely limited). In Europe, by contrast, there was no clear relationship. This indicates the extent to which the distribution of environmental outcomes may depend on numerous other factors, such as: geography, urban planning, infrastructure design, technology and the level of intra-country inequality.

Access to safe water supply and sanitation is widespread across the OECD, but further progress is needed in emerging economies especially for the most vulnerable households. At the global level, inadequate access to safe water supply and sanitation acts as a large drag on economic growth and well-being, increasing mortality and morbidity, reducing labour productivity and undermining freshwater ecosystems. These effects are typically concentrated in the lower parts of the income distribution in emerging economies and developing countries (OECD, 2017e and OECD, 2012b). Across the OECD area, the share of population whose wastewater is connected to a municipal sewage treatment plant rose from about 60% in the early 1990s to almost 80% today. About 72% benefit from at least secondary treatment (OECD, 2017f). Reductions in health impacts, in terms of disability-adjusted life years (DALYs) due to insufficient access to safe water and sanitation, have been substantial, falling by 90% in Mexico and Turkey since 1990 and by 70% or more in the BRIICS (OECD, 2017a). However, further progress is needed in Indonesia, India and South Africa to increase access to improved sanitation and drinking water facilities (OECD, 2017f). This will become increasingly difficult as increased water demand exacerbates water stress in many river basins in densely populated areas in rapidly developing economies. More river basins are projected to come under severe water stress by 2050, mainly as a result of growing water demands and the number of people living in these stressed river basins is expected to increase sharply, from 1.6 billion in 2000 to 3.9 billion by 2050 (OECD, 2012b). By then, around three-quarters of all people facing severe water stress will live in the BRIICS (OECD, 2012b).

Trends in inclusive places and communities

Across a range of dimensions, well-being outcomes can also vary considerably within and across metropolitan regions, with higher income inequality in cities. Educational attainment can vary by more than 15 percentage points across cities in Canada, France, the Netherlands and the United States (OECD, 2016 Making Cities Work for All). Life expectancy can vary by a staggering 20 years across neighbourhoods in Baltimore (United States) or London (United Kingdom) (OECD, 2016 Making Cities Work for All).

Residential segregation has increased in many OECD countries. Residential segregation in which individuals with shared characteristics, such as income level, race or ethnicity, are spatially concentrated– has been increasing in many OECD countries over the past decades, although the trends, challenges and drivers differ across countries (OECD, 2016f). For instance, the most income-segregated cities in the Netherlands and France are at comparable levels to the least income-segregated cities in the United States (OECD, 2016f). Even within the same country, income segregation can vary across cities depending on place-specific factors, such as urban size and productivity, the degree of concentration of population in a single centre, and demographic profile (OECD, 2017h). By extension, these disadvantages can weigh on future generations and limit social mobility. Evidence suggests that transport plays a crucial role in this regard: a lack of, or poor access to, transport options is central to limitations on access to jobs, educational institutions, health facilities and social networks, which in turn can generate a "poverty trap" (ITF, 2017).

Healthy communities and their connectedness are strong foundations of future prosperity. At the individual level, social support among friends and family, and time spent socialising as core elements of community relationships. At the next level up, factors such as volunteering, trust in others, housing conditions, environmental quality, and personal safety are all highly relevant for community well-being and social capital. Meanwhile, at the wider societal level, acts of civic engagement (e.g. such as voting) and the functioning of public institutions (e.g. trust in government; having a say in government, and government stakeholder engagement) become important factors to consider.

Social ties have weakened since 2005. Mirroring the increasing distance between people and the public institutions, most of OECD countries saw a weakening of social ties among people. This is shown by the fall in the share of people across OECD countries who feel they have friends or family members to count on in times of need (Figure 3.13).

Social divisions threaten community inclusiveness. Like most well-being outcomes, there are large societal divides in terms of who feels safe in their neighbourhood, who feels supported by friends and family, who has time to spend socialising, who trusts in others, who volunteers, and who votes (OECD, 2015e; 2017j). Younger people are worse-off in terms of voter turnout, while older people are heavily disadvantaged (relative to the middle-aged) in terms of social support, feelings of safety and having a say in government – despite being more likely to vote (Figure 3.14). Relative to the native-born, migrants and low-educated feel less safe and less supported.

Trust is also fragmented among different groups of population. Recent data from the European Union's Statistics on Income and Living Conditions (Eurostat, 2015), and from the OECD's Trustlab (Box 3.1) both indicate that trust in others increases with income and education, and is lowest among the unemployed.

Figure 3.13 Social support, voter turnout and trust in government have fallen since 2005

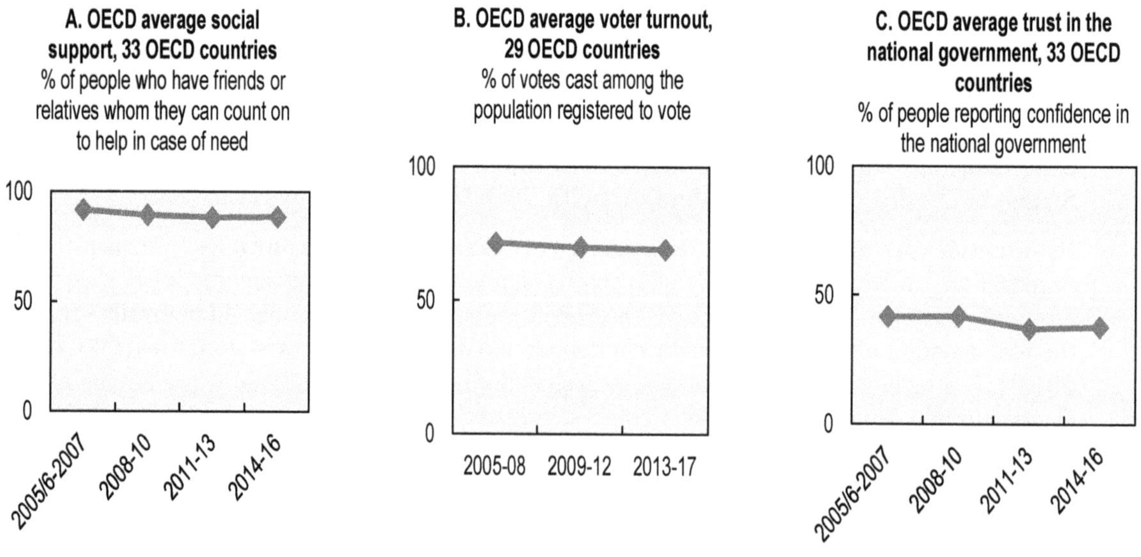

Source: OECD (2017j), How's Life? 2017; Figures 1.13 and 1.29.

StatLink http://dx.doi.org/10.1787/888933725449

Box 3.1. Using experimental methods to measuring trust and other social preferences

Trust is indispensable for social and economic relations (Arrow, 1972, Putnam, 2000, Guiso et al., 2008). At the same time, citizen's trust in public institutions is a crucial component for policy reform and the legitimacy and sustainability of any political system (OECD, 2015). However, available measurement instruments of trust so far have mostly been narrowly focused and survey-based, with limited evidence on their validity. The OECD's Trustlab project is the first internationally comparable instrument that combines behavioural measures of trust and other social preferences with an extensive survey of attitudinal, institutional and social determinants of trust in other people and trust in institutions. The database currently contains data from six countries: France, Korea, Slovenia, the United States, Germany and Italy and is supported by a network of affiliated research institutions and government agencies.

The main determinants of trust in others include beliefs about others' trustworthiness and other-regarding preferences such as altruism, trustworthiness and willingness-to-cooperate, as well as the quality of institutions and proxies of social capital such as neighbourhood connectedness and volunteering. For trust in institutions, perceived government integrity, government reliability and government responsiveness, as well as neighbourhood connectedness and positive attitudes towards immigrants appear as main drivers.

Source: Murtin et al. (2018).

Figure 3.14 Divided communities in terms of social support, feelings of safety, civic engagement

OECD countries, by gender, education, age and migrant status

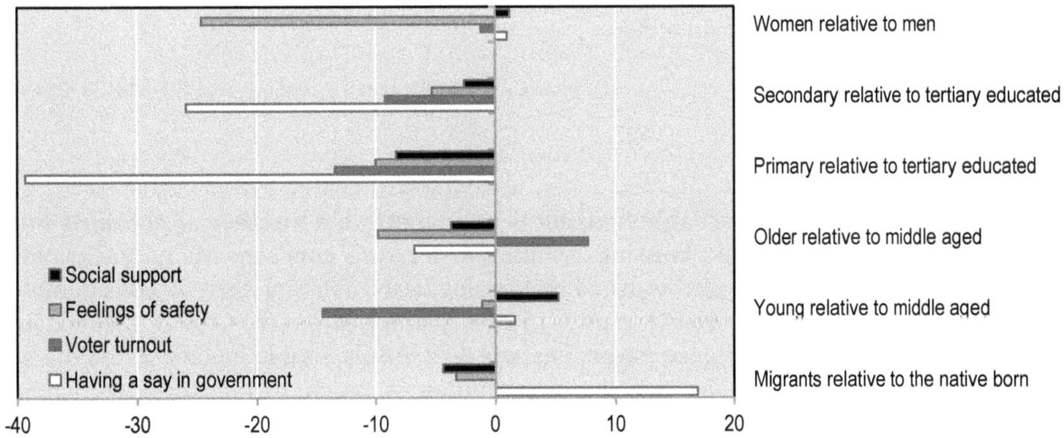

Note: The figure shows the percentage difference between groups, relative to the reference group indicated. Social support and feelings of safety are captured on a simple yes/no scale; voter turnout concerns the percentage of votes cast among the population registered to vote in the most recent national elections, while having a say in government refers to the share of people who disagree or strongly disagree with the statement: "people like me don't have any say in what the government does".
Source: OECD (2017j), How's Life? 2017.

StatLink http://dx.doi.org/10.1787/888933725468

Figure 3.15 Trust in others increases with income and education

Mean average, on a scale from 0 (you do not trust any other person) to 10 (most people can be trusted) by socio-demographic characteristics, 2016-17

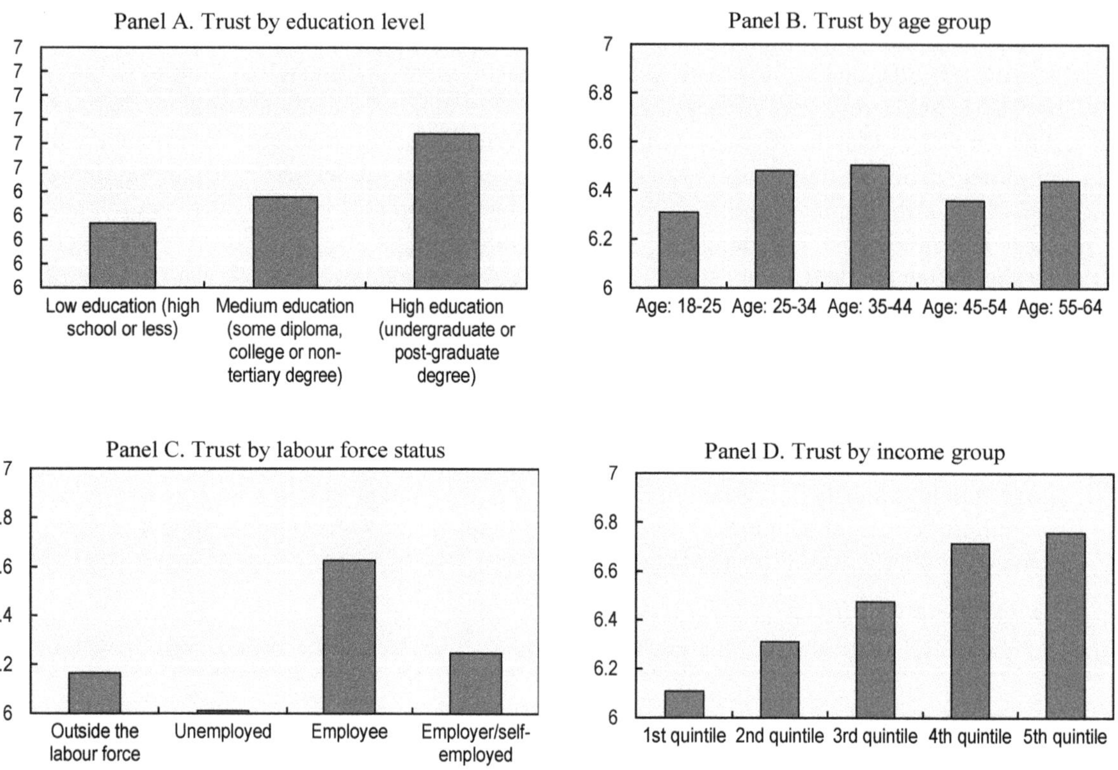

Note: Data is pooled from four countries that participated in the OECD Trustlab project (Germany, Italy, Slovenia, United States). Sample size is N=1000 per country.
Source: OECD Trustlab, Murtin et al. (2018).

StatLink http://dx.doi.org/10.1787/888933725487

Housing and land use

Access to good-quality affordable housing is important on a number of accounts but good-quality and affordable housing remains a pressing concern. Many households across OECD countries are overburdened by housing costs, although there is considerable variation across OECD countries (Figure 3.16). On average across the OECD, the median housing cost burden for mortgage payers is about 18% of disposable income while this is 23% for tenants. The median housing cost burden is much higher for low-income household, at more than one-third of disposable income across the OECD on average (OECD, 2017h). In addition, significant numbers of people are homeless: while statistics are difficult to compare, OECD countries report that 1 to 10 people in every thousand lack regular access to housing. In addition, many households live in low-quality dwellings: 18% of low-income households live in overcrowded dwellings. Neighbourhood crime and pollution are also problematic for many households throughout the OECD.

Housing affordability is a significant issue especially for low-income residents of metropolitan areas. Across the OECD, housing affordability varies considerably. While households in Australian regions only spend around 15% of their disposable income on housing, residents in Scandinavian countries, Belgium or Israel can spend more than a third of their disposable income on housing (Figure 3.17). In Oslo and Akershus (Norway) or Brussels Capital Region (Belgium), housing expenditure accounts for around 40% and 35% of disposable household income, respectively. Overall, competition for housing is significantly stronger in capital city regions. Residents in such metropolitan areas need to spend relatively more on housing, even when higher income levels in capital regions are taken into account. As a consequence, lower income groups risk getting priced out of capital city regions.

Housing policies need to be carefully designed to avoid adverse distributional impacts. OECD countries use a range of policies to promote access to good quality and affordable housing (Figure 3.18). One common type of policy consists of subsidies to homeowners, who receive considerable public support. In many OECD countries home-buyers can benefit from grants, financial assistance and public guarantees often reserved to young and low-income first-time buyers. Homeowners often benefit from favourable tax treatment of housing, which tends to favour better-off households; in addition, they distort incentives to invest in other tenures and/or assets and actually often put pressure on housing prices.

Figure 3.16 Regional differences in housing costs

Housing expenditure as a share of household disposable income, 2014 or latest available year

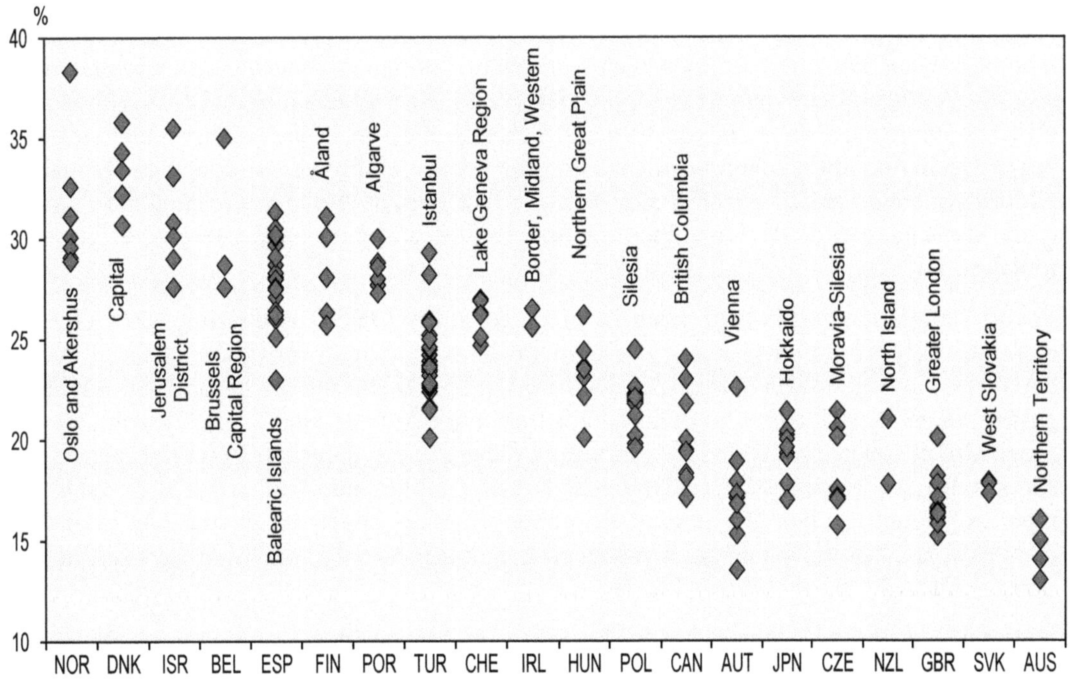

Note: Each diamond in the figure represents the value in a large region (TL2). The graph presents the data sorted by range of regional disparity within country from the larger to the smaller.
Source: OECD Regional Statistics (database).

StatLink http://dx.doi.org/10.1787/888933725506

Figure 3.17 Households' housing cost burden (mortgage and rent cost)

Share of disposable income, 2014 or latest year available

Median of the mortgage burden (principal repayment and interest payments) or rent burden (private market and subsidized rent) as a share of disposable income, in percent

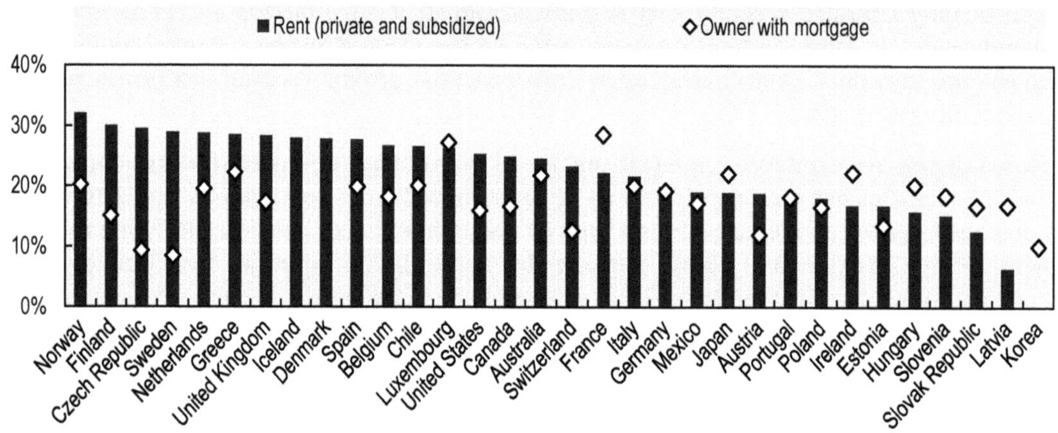

Note: For detailed notes and national sources, see the OECD (2017) Affordable Housing Database.
Source: OECD (2017h), Affordable Housing Database.

StatLink http://dx.doi.org/10.1787/888933725525

Housing allowances may distort rental prices. Housing support is also delivered through income-related housing-cost subsidies, generally known as housing allowances, and reporting countries spent up to 1.4% of GDP on housing allowances in 2015. Almost all OECD countries use this policy instrument. Housing allowances are usually means-tested, but eligibility conditions and payment rates vary considerably across countries. Housing allowances have weaknesses: they may be less effective in providing access to good-quality rental housing, especially for vulnerable households, and may have perverse effects on rental prices.

Social rental housing is also often in place in many OECD countries. Most OECD countries support the provision of social rental housing. Direct provision exists in many countries – mostly delivered by local authorities or NGOs and funded in part by the central governments. Low-income households are the majority of tenants in many countries – especially in countries affected by shortages of social rental housing. Central government support for the provision of social rental housing ranges goes up to 0.5% of GDP in reporting countries but the amount of public funding has been decreasing in many countries. In 2015 social housing constituted less than 5% of the total housing stock in the average OECD country (OECD, 2017h).

National housing policies need to be flexible and cities need to be given more freedom and resources to respond to their particular circumstances. Regions, cities, and villages have particular housing needs that require a flexible and localised response. Local governments can integrate housing policy objectives within their urban planning responsibilities to support sustainable urban development. Local governments influence public and private housing markets through their planning and development control decisions, have strong connections to the local community, and are well positioned to facilitate a whole of government approach to housing outcomes. Local authorities can formulate 'local housing strategies' incorporating an analysis of local housing supply, expected demand, socio-demographic and market trends as well as recommendations for planning processes, land use plans and development regulations.

Figure 3.18 Housing allowances, social housing and support for home-ownership

Overview of housing policy instruments, by number of reporting countries adopting each policy type 1, 2

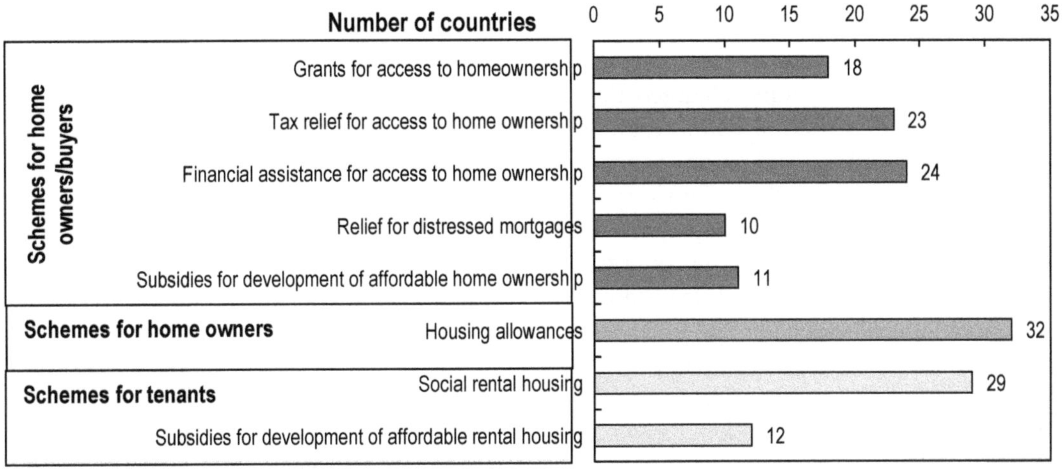

Note: The list of policy types refers to those surveyed through the 2016 Questionnaire on Affordable and Social Housing, which gathered information from 35 countries. No information is available for Belgium, Denmark, Iceland, Israel, Italy and Turkey.
Source: OECD Questionnaire on Social and Affordable Housing, 2016.

StatLink http://dx.doi.org/10.1787/888933725544

Local governments play an essential role in ensuring equitable access to an adequate supply of affordable and good quality housing as well as for reducing segregation of communities. In many OECD countries local governments build and manage public rental housing, either directly or through municipal public housing companies. Furthermore, local governments can require from developers that a share of newly built housing is made available to low-income residents at below market rents. Decisions on where to locate public and social housing can also contribute to inclusion by promoting mixed-income neighbourhoods and preventing the risks linked with spatial segregation by income. Local governments can use land use regulations and the building approval process. If land use regulations prevent housing supply from adjusting to growing demand, house prices will rise. Recent evidence suggests that this mechanism is responsible for rising house prices in many large and growing cities in OECD countries (e.g., Glaeser and Gyourko, 2017, and Hilber and Vermeulen, 2016). In cities and regions with fast-growing populations, land use regulations need to permit sufficient housing construction to meet growing demand for housing while preventing the negative externalities of urban sprawl, for example, by encouraging the densification of the existing housing stock (OECD, 2017h).

One challenge for housing policy is to address residential segregation, which reflects and contributes to socioeconomic and racial inequalities. Poor people living in areas with highly concentrated poverty experience inadequate schools, limited job prospects, and disadvantaged peer groups, all of which contribute to social exclusion. Although people have the legal right to live wherever they want, segregation has continued through discrimination (e.g., in the private housing market), historical housing policies (e.g., governments' placement of social housing in undesirable locations, zoning and planning restrictions), and economic factors (e.g., the affordability of quality housing). National and local policies to address spatial segregation have been put in place in many countries. Some European countries, the US and Chile used tenure diversification, sometimes combined with demolition programmes, as part of wider urban renewal policies integrating economic and social elements. The effectiveness and unintended consequences of these programmes, as well as their integration with social elements, should be further explored (Salvi et al, 2017).

Policies that ease geographic mobility and improve regional connectivity can help individuals to connect to jobs, services and opportunities. In the 29 OECD countries studied, 24 million people changed their region of residence each year during 2011-13. There is a lot of variation within regional migration rates – with the highest rates seen in Gümüshane (Turkey) and North Aegean (Greece) and la Plama (Spain) the lowest rates in Agri (Turkey), the Northern Territory-Outback (Australia) and the Northwest Territories (Canada) (Figure 3.19). In aggregate terms, the net migration rate in the predominantly urban regions of 26 OECD countries is much higher than in intermediate and predominantly rural ones. While predominantly urban areas grew by 6 persons per year (10 000 population in total) in 2011-13, intermediate and predominantly rural areas declined by 2 and 10 persons per year, respectively (Figure 3.20). Distance to labour markets and services seems to explain migration within OECD countries; with the exception of Turkey, the United States, and Sweden, remote rural regions – i.e. regions which are far in driving distance from urban agglomerations – show higher net negative flows than the rural average. Adopting a territorial development strategy based on the functional linkages between urban and rural areas helps to foster better integration between them.

Transport systems help reduce social exclusion by improving individuals' access to jobs, educational institutions, health facilities and social networks. Extensive public transport coverage is a prerequisite for good accessibility, but in reality, coverage and access are not necessarily related due to low frequencies, low station density and inadequate networks (Figure 3.21). Accessibility to opportunities by public transport varies greatly by cities of different sizes, with European cities generally offering higher accessibility than North American and developing cities. Reducing the accessibility gap in regions and cities requires significant investment in infrastructure and improved services. It is particularly important to identify accessibility limitations faced by vulnerable groups. Lower-income populations tend to suffer more from restricted transport options, have lower quality transport services available to them and travel under worse conditions (safety, security, reliability, and comfort). This in turn generates a "poverty trap". Other factors, such as age, and disability can also limit peoples' access to activities and services. Within functional urban areas, more effective and reliable public transport infrastructure can contribute to improve labour market outcomes of minority groups residing in poorly connected areas of cities.

Improved data and analysis can help to develop transport that focuses on creating access, while land-use policies can foster urban accessibility. Coherent pricing policies for each transport mode can support sustainable mobility and social inclusion goals; for example, by ensuring that externalities created by private vehicles are reflected in the pricing framework. Transport-oriented development (TOD) refers to the principle of building high density housing and office space primarily along public-transport corridors and hubs. In cities that are planned along this principle, residents without private cars can access a much larger share of the available jobs than in cities where housing and office space is built without considering public transport. Likewise, TOD proposes mixed-use policies which improve the accessibility of cities. They encourage the construction of residential buildings and commercial facilities, such as office and retail space, within the same neighbourhood. This reduces the average distances residents need to travel for commuting and activities of daily life, such as shopping. Transport-oriented development reduces the need for driving, contributing to lower congestion and decreasing air pollution and carbon emissions, which benefits all residents of a city. Urban renewal and transit-oriented development strategies can be readjusted by measuring their performance in terms of equity and social inclusion and can be used to mobilize increases in land value to deliver objectives for social inclusion

Figure 3.19 Maximum and minimum annual regional migration rate, average 2011-13 (left)

Figure 3.20 Annual regional migration rate per typology of region, average 2011-13 (right)

Net flows across TL3 regions, % of total population   Net flows across TL3 regions per 10 000 population

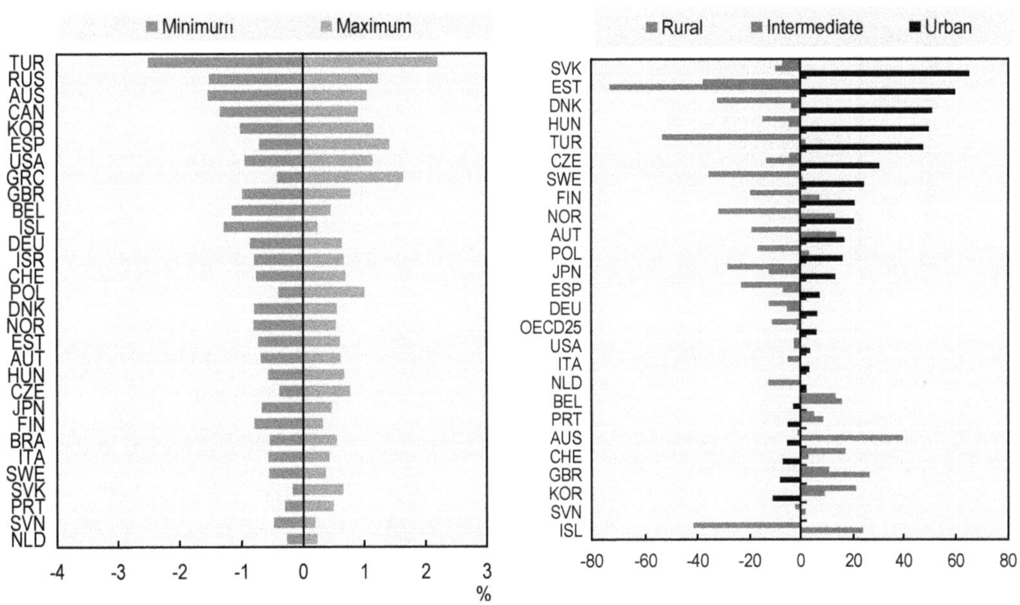

Source: OECD Regional Statistics and Indicators (Database).

StatLink http://dx.doi.org/10.1787/888933725563; StatLink http://dx.doi.org/10.1787/888933725582

The impact of urban planning policies that intend to counter segregation has been mixed so far, suggesting that interventions will have to be carefully designed to increase social capital. While several evaluations found no improvements in social cohesion after changes in the housing stock increased the social mix (Van Bergeijk, 2008, Van Kempen and Bolt, 2009), other authors have found that community connectedness and interactions were stronger in walkable rather than in car-dependent suburban neighbourhoods, as well as in communities that feature good public transport connections and vibrant public spaces (Leyden, 2003; Schreiber and Carius, 2016). Furthermore, the recent relocation of refugees from the Calais "Jungle" in France to temporary refugee-centres has been found to significantly reduce the vote share increase for the far-right in recipient municipalities, suggesting that actual contact with people from another background can improve attitudes towards diversity (Vertier, 2017).

Figure 3.21 Public transport accessibility in cities

Public transport coverage and average accessibility by public transport

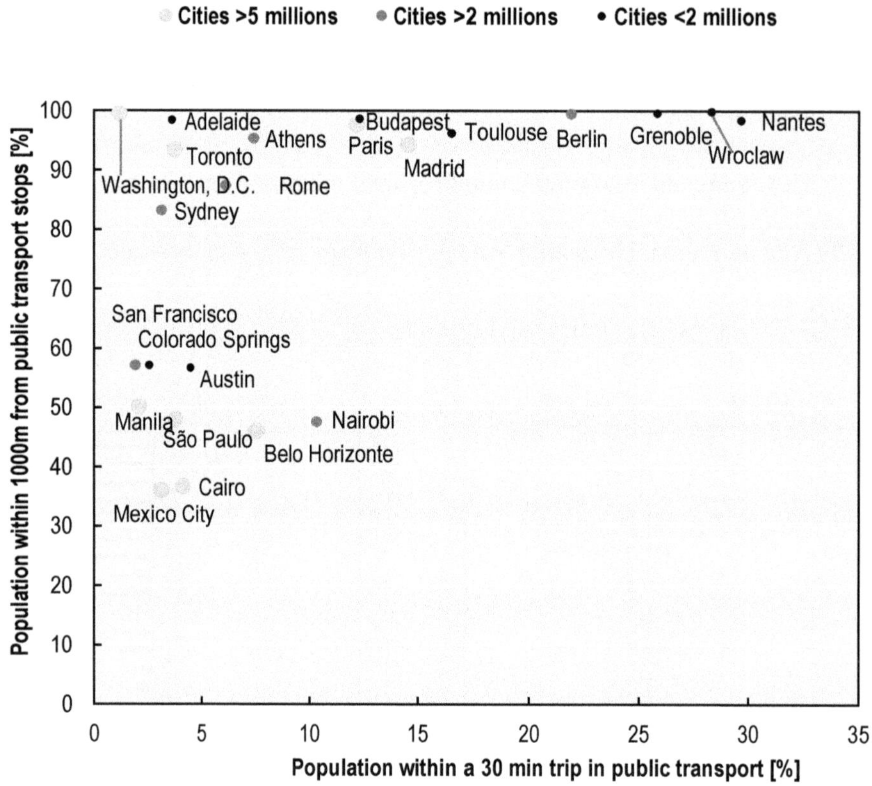

Source: International Transport Forum (2017).

StatLink http://dx.doi.org/10.1787/888933725601

Policies to enhance opportunities and foundations for future prosperity

Improving the life of every child

Effective interventions can protect children's mental wellbeing, or mitigate the impact of mental illness during childhood and adolescence. Infant, child and adolescent mental health promotion and disorder prevention are amongst the areas that have received the most attention from OECD countries in recent years (McDaid, Hewlett and Park, 2017). Education systems can also play a key role in identifying and supporting children with mental health issues at an early stage, including through investments in preventive mental health programmes in schools to develop resilience, and mental health competence training in the teacher-training curriculum (OECD, 2017i; OECD, 2012; OECD, 2009). Timely access to support for young people with mental ill-health is also critical. Although in-school mental health services are common in OECD countries, they lack the capacity to provide timely support to all students in need. The availability of psychological support in schools, and high-quality and easily accessible children's and adolescents' mental health services could stand to be improved in most if not all OECD countries.

Social policies can help foster equal opportunities for children by:

- **Addressing family poverty and its effects on child material deprivation and family climate.** Poverty can affect child outcomes through different channels. Inadequate economic resources first reduce households' ability to purchase or produce important "inputs" for child development, such as nutritious meals, educational resources, leisure activities, or high-quality formal childcare. Low-income families also often live in neighbourhoods with a lower provision of transportation or care services, more difficult access to good schools, and sometimes a greater exposure to crime. Financial strain also damages the family climate and affects family relationships, including interactions between parents and children, which in turn can affect children's outcomes. Better policies helping low-income families to reconcile work and family are also crucial to improve the quality of parental time and of child-parent interactions.
- **Addressing the multiple needs of disadvantaged children**. Integrated service delivery has the potential to improve service-use outcomes for families with multiple needs (OECD, 2015e). Successful initiatives share common traits, such as case management and a community-based single-entry point to services, although existing programmes vary greatly across countries in scope and design. Another strategy is home-based services (e.g. mobile family support teams), which help reach families that have difficulties in receiving services or are unable to access co-located services (e.g. in rural areas). Integrated home services also enable providers to assess and treat the full range of problems adults and children face. Programme effectiveness depends crucially on how different services work together and how well local, regional and national authorities facilitate the integration of service delivery.
- **Adapting social protection systems to changes in family living arrangements.** The growing heterogeneity of family living arrangements creates inequities between children, as the policy support they receive often depends on the legal recognition of their parents' partnership status. Many countries should consider increasing support for children with non-married parents in the event that their parents separate or die. Tax and benefit systems, as well as child support regimes, also need to ensure that all children have access to the same supports regardless of their parents' legal partnership status.
- **Investing in children early on**. Early interventions, in response to emerging signals of need, must be delivered before disadvantages become entrenched. This can also limit future costs to individuals, society and the state. Policies supporting the early development of cognitive (e.g. language and numeracy) skills, social (e.g. self-confidence, self-control, pro-social behaviour) skills, and physical health can have long-lasting positive effects on educational attainment, employment and income.

Providing strong educational opportunities

Inclusive education systems that provide people with the life-time skills and opportunities are the main foundations of future prosperity. By focusing on early childhood education and targeting disadvantaged children and schools, such systems can foster inclusive growth and social cohesion by focusing on mitigating inequalities early on in people's lives. Evidence shows that intervening early on in children's lives is one of the most effective ways to prevent the accumulation of inequalities later on in life (OECD,

2017a). Inclusive education systems must also provide continuous learning and skill development opportunities for adults throughout their lifecycle and remove barriers to adult education by targeting financial assistance to those most in need.

Public investment in education, especially for disadvantaged children and young individuals, need to be prioritised to build equitable and inclusive societies. In 2016, public social spending was 21% of GDP on average across OECD countries. In recent years, public social spending-to-GDP ratios have been highest in France, at 32% of GDP, followed by Finland (over 30%). Social spending-to-GDP ratios have fallen in a few OECD countries, including Hungary, Luxembourg, Latvia and Ireland, but have only slightly increased or have remained stable in most. Most OECD countries spend far less on education as a percentage of GDP, especially post-secondary education, than on pensions or healthcare. On average, public expenditure on primary, secondary and post-secondary education as a percentage of GDP was 3.4%. Given the substantial returns to education countries should consider increase their spending on education focusing on programmes targeted on disadvantaged children and youth (Box 3.2).

Box 3.2. Financing Tertiary Education

The returns to tertiary education are significant (OECD, 2015b). In general terms, countries can provide direct support for tertiary education (e.g. tuition reductions, increases in scholarship, grants, subsidised loans) or through the tax system. Non-tax approaches to providing support for skills investments (e.g. tertiary education, including scholarships, reduced tuition, and income-contingent loans) may be more beneficial for low-income students. Higher tuition levels reduce enrolment, and tuition reductions or increases in scholarship and grant spending has positive distributional and efficiency consequences (Kane, 2006). Fee reductions or scholarship and grant provision is more effective at raising enrolment and completion rates compared to tax-based subsidies. It is also better targeted towards those on lower incomes, and finally it is more likely to raise the enrolment rates of those on lower incomes compared to skills tax expenditures (STEs), which are often less beneficial to those on lower incomes due to a lack of taxable income or to the administrative burden of applying for STEs.

Income contingent loans can be another attractive option. While on average, a skills investment will pay for itself, many students make skills investments that may just break even or may not breakeven at all. This can be the case even if the investment did have positive expected returns. Loans that feature income contingent repayment offer insurance for the student against these risks. Support to students through income-contingent loans has been found to be particularly effective, in terms of ensuring access to education for low-income students, sharing the financial burden between government and students, distributing the risk of human capital investments, and balancing equity and efficiency considerations.

Access to quality early childhood education, to schools with highly qualified teachers and to adult education and training must be warranted to all individuals. The cognitive, social and emotional skills developed during the first years of life set the stage for future potential (OECD, 2015f). Early learning deficiencies can be overcome, but inadequate learning environments and lack of support can hamper educational development and have lasting impacts on individuals later in life (OECD, 2015f). Children from less privileged socio-economic backgrounds are far less likely to benefit from high-quality home learning environments and early childhood education and care services (ECEC) than their more affluent peers. As a consequence, targeted policies need to be considered to ensure high quality learning opportunities for children from disadvantaged backgrounds. These include remove barriers to ECEC, ensure provision of quality of ECEC, and support family and community-based interventions.

Disadvantaged schools should be further supported. Disadvantaged schools are typically most in need of high-quality resources and support, but in most countries, they are more likely to suffer from financial constraints and a lack of staff. Disadvantaged schools also tend to have a disproportionately high number of students considered to be low performers and at risk of dropping out (OECD, 2016c). Allocation of adequate resources to disadvantaged schools is essential in ensuring that all students receive the high-quality education and training they need to fully participate in society (OECD, 2016c). Providing such schools with additional financial and human resources is essential. School budgets should prioritise spending, as well as investing in high-quality human resources such as school leaders and teachers, who play a critical role in reducing educational inequality in their schools. Monetary or professional-level incentives can also be used to attract effective school leaders and teachers to disadvantaged schools. Targeted support should be given to school leaders and teachers in disadvantaged schools, and efforts need to be made to connect them to other school leaders and teachers, which can help them share knowledge and provide assistance to each other (OECD, 2012c; OECD, 2016c).

Young people need support to move on with education and employment. Fifteen percent of the OECD youth population were not in employment, education or training (NEET) in 2015 – about 40 million young people. More than two-thirds of them were not actively looking for work. Job and income uncertainty can keep young people from reaching other traditional markers of adulthood, leaving them disenchanted and discouraged. NEET youth have lower levels of life satisfaction and trust in others compared to non-NEET youth. They also show less interest in politics and are more likely to feel that it is the government's responsibility to provide for citizens, with rising inequalities when regions fail to catch up (Figure 3.22). Being NEET can also have serious long-term effects on health, fertility and crime, and eventually endanger social cohesion.

Poor health and poor school performance have strong bearings on the risk of joblessness in young adulthood: 15-29 year-olds suffering from poor health are four times more likely than their peers to be not in employment, education or training (NEET), while not having completed upper secondary education more than doubles the risk of becoming NEET later (OECD, 2016c; OECD, 2016f).

School leavers and young people with patchy employment records often fail to qualify for insurance-based income support. Only around 30% of all unemployed young people receive unemployment benefits, while over 40% of all jobseekers aged 30 and over are covered. Consequently, social safety nets are less effective in fighting poverty among young people: 40% of young people who would have incomes below the poverty line are kept out of poverty by public transfers, compared to 50% of adults aged 30 and over. Roughly every eighth young person lives in poverty, and youth poverty rates are higher than those of the elderly (OECD, 2016c; OECD, 2016f).

Comprehensive support is needed to ensure that all young people complete their upper-secondary schooling. Because low educational attainment is such an important risk factor for NEETs, fighting early school leaving is essential. This typically involves actions such as monitoring school attendance to spot warning signs of drop-out; addressing pupils' social or health problems; and offering after-school programmes to engage pupils and strengthen their motivation.

Figure 3.22 NEET rates are substantially higher among young people with low education

NEET rates as percentages, 25 to 29 year-olds, by level of education, 2013-14

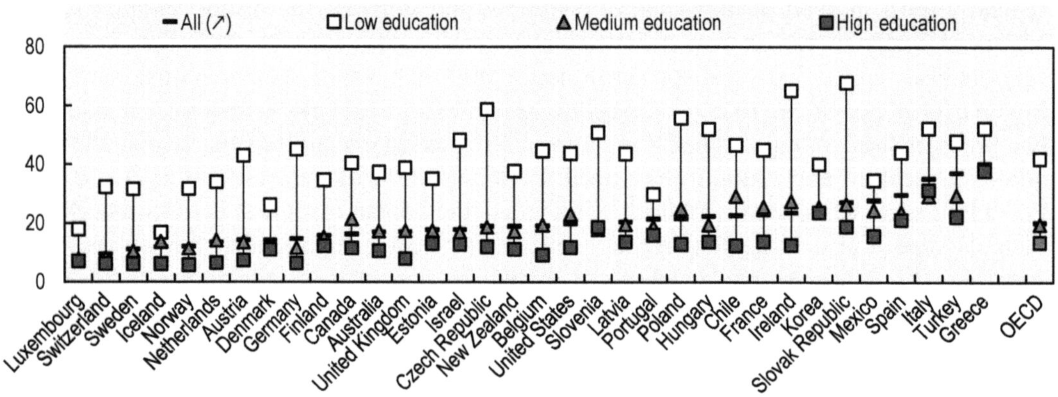

Note: Data refer to 2014, except for Australia, Chile, Germany, Israel, Korea, Mexico, New Zealand and Turkey (2013). No data were available for Japan "Low-education" denotes lower-secondary school and lower (Levels 0-2 in the International Standard Classification of Education [ISCED]); "medium education" refers to upper- or post-secondary education (ISCED Levels 3-4); and "high education" means higher, or tertiary, education (ISCED Levels 5-6).
Source: OECD (2016f), Society at a Glance.

StatLink http://dx.doi.org/10.1787//888933404887

An effective school-to-work transition also requires specific policy interventions. Those who experience a period of unemployment early in their careers are more prone to become unemployed later in life (Schmillen and Umkehrer, 2013; Möller and Umkehrer, 2014) and have been shown to earn less (Umkehrer, 2015). To prevent unemployment at young ages a number of measures have proved particularly effective:

- **Provide work experience early.** Working a moderate number of hours (below 15 a week) has been shown to lower the risk of early school leaving, possibly because it helps develop important life skills such as conscientiousness and motivation, and can steer students towards a career path. There are also benefits for university students, especially if they work moderate hours (less than half-time) in a job related to their field of study (Quintini and Martin, 2014). For example, many Swedish municipalities and county councils, as well as the city of New York, run summer internship programmes for 16-18 year-olds. These programmes have been shown to help young people to accumulate more work experience later and increase earnings in young adulthood, especially for the most disadvantaged young people. They also seem to protect young people against adverse outcomes such as incarceration lower mortality (Alam et al., 2013, Gelber et al., 2016).
- **Offer career guidance to help ensure that students make the right choices.** Quality career guidance can boost education and training completion rates by improving the match between young people and their chosen path. It can strengthen social mobility by informing young people of career paths that their family and social networks may not suggest, and encouraging them to choose paths more likely to lead to stable employment. Career guidance is of special importance to young

people who consider VET programmes –including apprenticeships– as they affect students' career prospects more directly than general secondary programmes. Young people's participation in career guidance is easiest to ensure in the case of school-based career counselling. The involvement of employers or outside specialists helps make information more comprehensive and truer to the realities of the labour market.

- **Supply good-quality practical training.** Good-quality practical training can help smooth school-to-work transitions by making educational programmes attractive to young people while providing them with skills that are valued in the labour market. To ensure quality and relevance, training should be partly company-based, ideally in the form of apprenticeships. But succeeding in vocational programmes can be challenging for the most disadvantaged, who may lack foundation skills or motivation. Pre-apprenticeship programmes can help prepare young people with skills gaps for participation in standard vocational education programmes by helping them to brush up on patchy literacy or numeracy skills, build motivation, familiarise them with the work routine, and even give them short spells of work experience.
- **Support jobless young people with targeted interventions.** While many young NEETs need only some support to find a job, those without upper secondary education and those with health problems or disabilities need more intensive help. The most promising programmes combine schooling and practical training with counselling, psychological support, and housing assistance to build cognitive, vocational and social skills simultaneously. Social skills have been shown to be malleable through adolescence and early adulthood, and to hugely impact a wide range of life outcomes including delinquency, labour market attachment and earnings, as well as family stability (e.g. Kautz etl., 2014). And indeed, intensive programmes that combine training with accommodation, mentoring and social support have been shown to have positive long-term effects on labour market participation, earnings, and reduced criminal activity (Schochet et al, 2008).

It is essential to reduce barriers to participation in adult education. Removing financial, situational and time-related barriers to participation in learning programmes is absolutely essential, especially for the socio-economically disadvantaged. Co-financing and tax incentives are particularly effective. A variety of co-financing arrangements policymakers are one option to consider, including Individual Learning Accounts (ILA), accounts set up exclusively for adult-learning purposes, vouchers and training allowances and training leave. In addition, tax-based mechanisms such as tax allowances and tax credits that reduce the tax liability on at least part of an individual's spending directly related to skills training costs can remove cost barriers and act as an incentive for participating in adult learning (OECD, 2017k). Such tax incentives can increase the returns to skills by making the costs of skills acquisition deductible for personal tax purposes. To remove time and situational barriers, innovative and effective adult learning programmes, such as online, distance and family-based learning programmes can be used. In addition, providing courses on a part-time basis, on evenings and weekends, can help increase flexibility and encourage participation in adult education (OECD, 2016c).

Invest in health outcomes for all groups in the population

Within the health service delivery system, universal access to quality healthcare services is encouraged. Policies could address the needs of socially disadvantaged and vulnerable population groups (e.g. poor, elderly and pregnant women, among others).

Despite significant governments' efforts to protect vulnerable populations from excessive cost-sharing, unmet needs across these groups are still large. In New Zealand, for example, very low cost access (VLCA) practices serving disadvantaged populations receive government subsidies if they remove patient fees (Paris et al., 2010). In Canada and France, subsidies are provided for the poor to obtain complementary or supplementary private health insurance. Further, whilst patients from OECD countries often have to pay out-of-pocket for pharmaceuticals, dental care and eye care, the poor, children and elderly populations are commonly exempted from such charges. Nevertheless, unmet care needs are still higher among the poor, with 14% of low income adults reporting unmet care needs due to cost compared with 25% amongst other adults, amongst the 10 OECD countries with comparable data (OECD 2017b).

Ensuring access requires an adequate distribution of health professionals throughout a country as well as harnessing new technologies. Concentration of doctors and other health professionals in one region and shortages in others can lead to inequities in access such as longer travel or waiting times. In many OECD countries, remote and sparsely populated areas, as well as deprived rural and urban regions, have insufficient health professionals. This often reflects the difficulty in recruiting and retaining doctors in such localities. A range of policy levers can be used to influence the choice of practice location of doctors. For example, Japan established in 1973 the Jichi Medical University specifically to educate physicians for service in rural communities, which has contributed to improving access in underserved rural regions (Ikegami, 2014). More broadly, key policy options include: (1) using financial incentives for doctors to work in underserved areas; (2) increasing enrolments in medical education programmes of students coming from specific social or geographic backgrounds; (3) regulating the choice of practice location of doctors (e.g. for new medical graduates or foreign-trained doctors); and (4) re-organising service delivery to improve working conditions in underserved areas (OECD 2017b). Better exploiting information and communication technologies can also improve access in remote areas, for example through greater use of telemedicine and other innovative models of service delivery.

Alongside policies to improve access to health services, a priority is to address the major causes of ill-health and premature deaths amongst disadvantaged populations. This includes tackling preventable major risk factors, such as obesity and smoking. The prevalence of these risk factors varies across socioeconomic categories and may be disproportionately prevalent amongst poorer and less educated populations. For example, less-educated women are two to three times more likely to be overweight than those with a higher level of education in about half of the eight countries for which data are available (Figure 3.23). Disparities are smaller for men, although they are growing. Greater efforts targeting modifiable behavioural risk factors among disadvantaged groups can play an important role in promoting healthier lifestyles, offering individuals better choices, and reducing health inequalities.

Figure 3.23 Less educated women are more likely to be overweight

Education-related inequality in being overweight for women, 2014 or latest year available

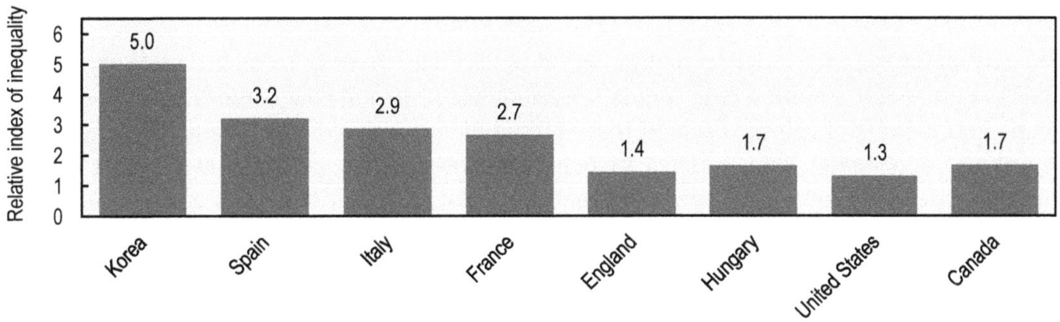

Note: Overweight defined as BMI≥25kg/m². Education level is categorised into three groups (primary, secondary, tertiary education). On the Y-axis, the relative index of inequality measures the inequality of being overweight by education level.
Source: OECD analysis of national health survey data.

StatLink http://dx.doi.org/10.1787/888933725620

A comprehensive policy package, tailored to local contexts and engaging across all stakeholders and across all sectors is suggested to tackle obesity, especially among disadvantaged individuals and households. New health care initiatives implemented in some OECD countries over the last few years include interventions in the primary care setting (e.g. prescribing physical activity) and communication policies which promote healthy diets (OECD, 2017c). For instance, informative food labelling can help people make healthier choices. Policies outside the health sector include pricing and fiscal measures, school-based and worksite interventions, reformulation of products, changes in portion sizes, and transport policies (e.g. subsidies for active commuting as an alternative to cars).

Design of health policies must specifically take into account low-income groups. For example, communication policies that promote healthy diets by improving health literacy and empowering consumers (e.g. mass media campaigns to increase awareness of healthier food consumption) designed to target specific disadvantaged population groups. A number of OECD countries (e.g. Belgium, Chile, Finland, France, Hungary, and Mexico) increasingly implemented taxation policies in the past few years to increase the price of potentially unhealthy products such as foods high in salt, sugar or fat, or sugary drinks. Taxation policies financially affect low-income people disproportionally more than high-income people. But at the same time, these low-income individuals also are more likely to be obese. Additional evidence is however needed to establish the efficacy of these policies in reaching specific health outcomes.

Reducing alcohol consumption requires a range of policy interventions. Policies aiming to reduce alcohol consumption include fiscal measures (e.g. taxation and minimum unit pricing for alcohol), regulatory measures (e.g. regulation about point of sales, location and hours, age limits, drink-driving enforcement, advertising regulation), and health promotion and health care policies (e.g. treatment of alcohol dependence) (OECD, 2015a). Regulations of alcohol advertising have been implemented in many OECD countries but the forms of media included in these regulations (e.g. printed newspapers, billboard, and internet) and law enforcement vary considerably across countries. Norway may have the strictest regulation of alcohol marketing in the OECD. Among recent policy initiatives to limit harmful drinking, minimum unit pricing was implemented in Scotland in 2012. Minimum unit pricing, devised to increase the price of cheap alcohol, is likely to change the consumption among low-income heavy drinkers whereas high-income heavy drinkers may continue to afford to maintain harmful drinking patterns (OECD, 2015a).

A variety of policies exist to tackle smoking. Policies aiming to tackle smoking range from taxation to regulation (e.g. regulation about age limit, smoking-free areas, advertising bans and plain packaging), through mass media campaigns to warn about the dangers of smoking, and health care policies to help smokers to quit. All OECD countries have implemented anti-tobacco programmes and policies, although the types and the intensity of policies vary by country (OECD, 2015b). New anti-tobacco initiatives have been recently implemented in some countries. Australia and France have adopted plain cigarette packaging. Regarding tobacco taxation –a highly cost-effective policy to reduce smoking rates– 26 OECD countries applied taxation rates at 70% in 2014 (WHO, 2016a). France announced a gradual price increase to EUR 10 per cigarette pack by 2020.

Box 3.3. Employment conditions matter for health

Long working hours and limited choice over working hours are harmful to health (Bassanini and Caroli 2014). A review of workplace interventions spanning Canada, Japan, the Netherlands, Sweden, the United Kingdom and the United States found that policies which improved employee control had positive mental health effects (Egan et al 2007). Better educated individuals and their offspring are healthier, independent of income and employment-related effects. A large part of this difference has been attributed to healthier lifestyles. Poor housing conditions (e.g. cold and damp, inadequate safety) and certain neighbourhood characteristics such as the risk of crime have frequently been shown to adversely affect health (Gibson et al 2011). Households with low-incomes and many ethnic minorities are more likely to experience these inadequate living conditions. Air pollution also varies greatly across different neighbourhoods. Across a number of OECD countries, policies targeting better housing infrastructure (home visits, removal of hazards) and rental assistance policies, have had positive health effects (Bambra et al 2010).

Reducing health inequalities also requires developing policies that address the wider social determinants of health. Income, unemployment, education and other socioeconomic factors, as well as lifestyle choices and a person's living environment can all affect an individual's health (James et al, 2017). Low income and poverty, particularly when persistent, have clear detrimental effects on health by, for example, causing people to have unhealthy diets. Progressive policies on taxation, benefits and minimum wages are therefore likely to contribute to improved health outcomes. Policies providing more targeted material support can be complementary. For example, studies of the Supplemental Nutrition Assistance Program, which provides food vouchers to low-income families in the United States, find evidence of positive impacts on birth outcomes and child health (US Executive Office of the President 2015). Being unemployed also adversely affects health. For example a meta-analysis of studies using individual data found that unemployment is associated with a 63% higher risk of mortality after controlling for age and other control factors (Roelfs et al 2011).

Policies enhancing environmental justice

Policies aimed at reducing environmental inequalities need to take a holistic perspective to address the social drivers of environmental footprints. Meeting the targets set out in the Paris Agreement will call for a rapid acceleration of the phase out and reform of inefficient fossil fuel subsidies and efforts to broaden the carbon pricing base. Targeted measures can compensate for any potentially regressive impacts of climate policy or removal of fossil fuel subsidies on poor households. There remains a risk that though the effects of new environmental levies (or the removal of subsidies) would affect those higher up the income distribution harder in absolute terms, the poorest groups in society may feel the reduction in spending power more. In that light, it is key to ensure that a portion of the revenue raised from environmental taxation or the removal of subsidies is recycled to support those same groups. Recent OECD work has provided evidence of the need for revenue recycling with respect to addressing inequality. It found that between 1995-2011, in those OECD countries without an explicit mechanism to redistribute environmentally related tax revenues, energy tax revenues (% of GDP) were shown to have a positive, although modest, relationship with income inequality. In contrast, in countries where energy tax revenues are, at least partially, used to reduce tax burden on income and labour, there is a negative relationship between energy taxes and inequality in income sources (OECD, 2016d).

Governments ought to seek out potential policy complementarities between promoting greater resource efficiency and equity. To improve resource efficiency, policies need to target the entire life-cycle of any given material resource (OECD, 2016e). To date, policy instruments have generally been applied further downstream in the product lifecycle rather than upstream (OECD, 2016e). For example, the number of countries reporting the use of economic instruments such as landfill taxes increased significantly in the past 15 years, which has led to a move away from landfill towards energy recovery. Despite this and other downstream successes, further efforts are needed upstream to encourage waste prevention in the first place. Such efforts could include policies that encourage greener product designs and measures to change consumer behaviour. These prevention efforts would naturally have socio-economic distributional implications, as their focus would be on those consuming the greatest quantities of material resources, who typically come from the upper end of the income distribution (in the wealthiest countries). Ultimately, efforts to improve resource efficiency will only be successful if governments can embed the objective into key existing policies areas from innovation, to investment, trade, education and skill development. Notably, several of these policy areas are also crucial for determining the shape and extent of socio-economic inequalities, suggesting that cross-cutting actions could be undertaken to address both issues. For instance, efforts to foster 'green' skills and entrepreneurship to promote resource efficiency could also be targeted at population groups lower down the income distribution.

There are several barriers to a just transition to a low-carbon economy but past industrial transitions can help policy makers chart a course. At present there are several barriers to the transition to a low-carbon economy that need to be overcome. For firms, these barriers include the administrative costs of closure, severance payments for workers and the irretrievability of sunk costs in capital intensive industries. There are also barriers which impact government action, such as the geographical concentration of industries and the role of state owned enterprises – particularly in emerging economies and developing countries (OECD, 2017e). For guidance in overcoming these barriers, lessons can be learnt from previous industrial transitions, where governments have deployed all manner of measures to support both workers and companies. From the perspective of workers, past experience indicates the value of a combination of: public support to promote job creation in depressed areas; active labour market policies (in terms of training and counselling); and closure aid to help with severance pay (OECD, 2017e). For businesses, several measures can help, including: investment aid; loan guarantees coupled with commitments to reduce capacity; and financing instruments and other measures to promote diversification and modernisation (OECD, 2017e).

Policies tailored to combat the deterioration of environmental quality of life should be designed with their social impact in mind. Whilst everyone in our societies stands to benefit from a reduction in air pollution, reductions are likely to be particularly beneficial to low income groups (i.e. North America, Asia and Africa) where exposure is characterised by the distribution of income (Hajat A., et al, 2015). First and foremost, prevention measures are key. These can include strategies to reduce harmful emissions by replacing dirty fuels with cleaner ones and encourage the development of cleaner industries (OECD, 2017e). OECD work has found that policies that provide incentives across a broad spectrum of firms and consumers, such as emission or energy taxes tend to be more cost-efficient than those that target a specific product, fuel or technology, such as subsidies for electric cars. Such policies are particularly cost-efficient when they are spatially heterogeneous, allowing for more stringent measures in densely populated areas or for emission sources located upwind from urban areas (OECD, 2017e). Mitigation measures also have a key role to play in addressing residual pollution. For instance education about the risks of air pollution, and the provision of up-to-date information on pollution levels, can significantly reduce health impacts, particularly amongst populations at higher risk. More broadly, the effectiveness of the healthcare system can play an important role in reducing the negative effects of illness on individual well-being and limit the impact on labour productivity (OECD 2016d).

Access to water remains a policy priority in developing countries and emerging economies, whilst financing is a key concern in the OECD area. In developing and emerging economies, promoting wider access to crucial water supply and sanitation services, particularly in rural areas and to the poorest communities, remains key. Much can be gleaned from the advance of OECD countries like Mexico in increasing population coverage in recent years. In Mexico, efforts by initiatives such as the Social Infrastructure Fund, which supports local and state governments in developing basic social infrastructure (including drinking water and sanitation), have seen access to drinking water increase from covering less the 80% of the population in the early 1990s to around 95% today. From 2000, coverage of water treatment has grown from just over 20% to approaching 60% (INEGI and CONAGUA). In OECD countries, the main challenge is often to renew and upgrade existing infrastructure. This is particularly vital in light of climate change, which makes water demand and availability more uncertain, and, in some instances, also increases rainwater run-off in urban environments. The financing of water services remains an important challenge. An important first step towards addressing this challenge is to combine revenues from water tariffs, transfers from public budgets and transfers from the international community (i.e. the 3Ts). Well-designed tariffs for water supply and sanitation services should cover the operation, maintenance and renewal costs of infrastructure and a progressive proportion of capital costs (OECD, 2017e). Sometimes it may raise affordability issues for lower-income groups, but these are best addressed through targeted social measures outside the water bill.

Reducing disparities in regional opportunities and urban segregation

Regional catching up in productivity is associated with the presence or the proximity to a well-governed city and to a dynamic tradable sector. Two characteristics stand out in distinguishing regions that narrowed the gap to their country's most productive regions and those falling further behind (OECD, 2016c). First, well-functioning cities are important, not only through economic activity in the city itself but also for rural areas in the city's proximity. Second, regions catching up in terms of productivity have a larger share and growth rate of the tradable sector in their economies.

Strategically diversifying regional economies supports productivity growth. For traded goods and services, sector-clustered firms are an important source for productivity growth and innovative activity. In some regions, firms specialising in sectors related to a single category of goods or services can play an important economic role. In Europe, the largest specialisation in such a traded clusters accounts for more than 40% of the workforce in the region (OECD, forthcoming). Other regions are more diversified with the largest concentration of traded sectoral clusters that employ less than 5% of the workforce, whereas others employ more than 40% of the workforce. Highly specialised regions have higher per capita GDP levels than regions where economic activity is distributed more diversified across many clusters. In contrast, per capita GDP growth is higher in more diversified regions. This implies that specialisation is increasing when regions become richer, but this effect can limit the future growth potential of regions.

Strategic investments are key to unlock the growth potential of regions. Public investment, as a percentage of government spending, has, however, dropped from 9.5% to 7.7% over the past two decades (OECD, 2016b). Subnational governments remain responsible for the majority of public investment (59%), but boosting their capacity to implement projects is often not a high priority. Investments that facilitate the diffusion of innovation and good practices across sectors and firms within and beyond a region are an opportunity to increase productivity, as the frontier keeps pulling further away from other firms (Andrews et al., 2015). While in many countries policies seek to reduce gaps across regions, they should avoid stifling growth in the highest-productivity regions.

Enabling regional catching up and promoting regional development policies that build economic potential in lagging regions is vital for future prosperity. Such regional development policies should focus on innovation and knowledge diffusion to boost productivity growth, and focus on developing the tradeable sector, whilst enacting policies to mitigate the adjustment costs of trade shocks. Providing affordable housing is a major part of the inclusive growth agenda and should be central to regional development strategies. Finally, encouraging geographical mobility and connectivity across regions is important for social inclusion and productivity growth.

Support for innovation and knowledge diffusion can narrow regional gaps and boost aggregate productivity growth. Knowledge diffusion requires working with different types of actors in the region. Industry associations can help firms to learn from each other's experiences and can coordinate joint research activities of businesses. Governments should aim to set framework conditions that support coordinated efforts by businesses, but avoid room for collusion among competing firms. Effectively links between universities and private businesses can foster and spread innovation, particularly when universities research activities are linked to areas that are of importance for the local economy. These links are mutually beneficial as they can provide grants to universities. Technology centres that aim to connect university research with firm R&D can be catalyst that helps translate abstract research into innovative new products.

Regions need to focus on tradable activities. Regions with the largest expansion in non-tradable sectors, suffered most since the 2007-08 global financial crisis. On average, employment grew by about 0.7% annually since 2008 in regions that experienced only small shifts in employment to the non-tradable sector before the 2007-08 crisis (Figure 3.24). In contrast, regions where employment shifted strongly towards non-tradable sectors saw employment decline by nearly 1% annually between 2008 and 2014. The lack of resilience is most pronounced for the 10% of regions with the largest shifts towards non-tradable sectors before the crisis. In these regions employment dropped after the crisis with an average decline in employment of 2.9% annually. The result might seem counterintuitive as local sectors can appear less dependent on global trends. But non-tradable activities are not truly disconnected from global shocks. Local sectors are tied to tradable sectors through demand and supply links.

Trade is beneficial at the national level and most regions benefit from it, but in a few regions the downsides dominate. Greater trade integration creates benefits for firms that make use of larger markets for their goods and sources and the ability to source inputs at lower costs. But firms that originally provided these inputs locally can be priced out of the market. Often these shocks are regionally concentrated. Manufacturing in Portugal's Norte region is highly specialised in textiles and shoe manufacturing. Following accession of the People's Republic of China to the World Trade Organization and adoption (and subsequent appreciation) of the Euro, Norte lost nearly 170 000 jobs in manufacturing, a decline of 30% in employment in the sector between 2000 and 2015.

Figure 3.24 Regions with strong pre-crisis increases in non-tradable sectors lost more jobs

Annual average employment growth (2008-13) and change in the share of non-tradable workers in total employment in 2007 compared to 2000

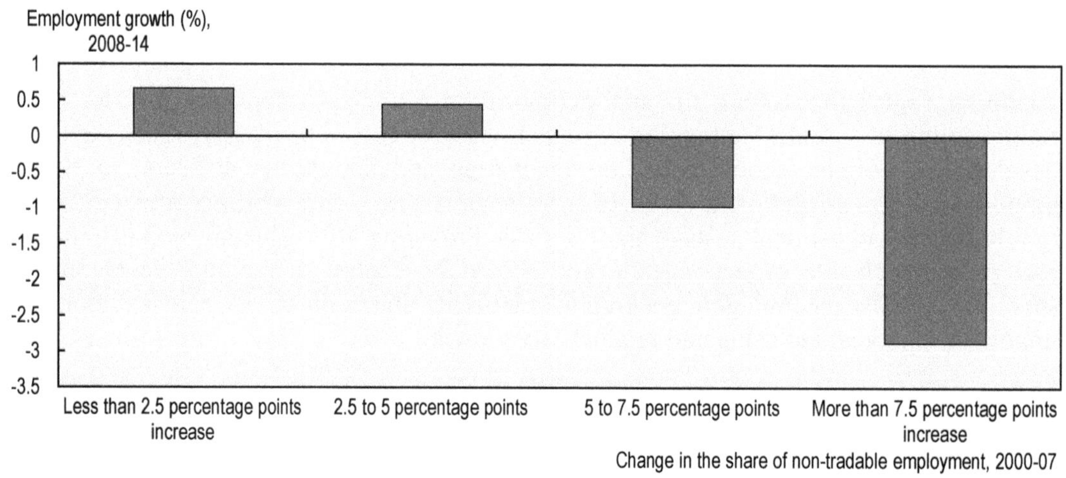

Note: Data for 203 territorial level 2 (TL2) regions in 19 OECD countries: Austria, Australia, Belgium, Bulgaria, Czech Republic, Denmark, Finland, Greece, Ireland, Italy, the Netherlands, Portugal, Romania, Slovenia, Slovak Republic, Spain, Sweden, the United Kingdom and the United States. Categories from left to right include 81, 84, 19 and 19 regions.
Source: OECD Regional Statistics [Database].

StatLink http://dx.doi.org/10.1787/888933725639

No single policy can address the concentrated losses following trade shocks. Policy packages need to include training and education programmes to reduce the impact on workers. The changing demand for skills requires workers to adapt to find new opportunities when economic sectors disappear. However, it is unlikely that skill and education policies alone will be enough. Since trade can lead to a decline in the number of firms in a region, it is important to target not only workers but also consider local labour demand. Policies should therefore consider incentives for firm creation or those to attract foreign direct investment into a region. Furthermore, workers should be supported to find jobs in other regions were unemployment rates are lower. Economic and social constraints may prevent workers from seeking jobs in other regions. Providing support and information on how to overcome these constraints helps workers to find jobs elsewhere. Such policies can also benefit workers who remain in the region by reducing the number of people competing for limited job openings.

Good governance arrangements are necessary for cities to pay a double dividend in terms of productivity and inclusiveness. A doubling in the number of municipalities in a (functional) urban area is associated with a productivity penalty of 6%. That penalty is halved when there is a governance body for the metropolitan area (Ahrend et al., 2017). This is one of the reasons why many countries in reforms of their metropolitan governance arrangement (OECD, 2015a). A given level of municipal fragmentation has a greater negative impact on growth in urban regions due to the higher density of interactions than in rural areas (Bartolini, 2015). Fragmentation is also associated with greater levels of segregation by income in metropolitan areas, which in turn influences access to opportunities (Boulant et al., 2016).

Creating vibrant, inclusive communities

Governments should stimulate investment in social capital, civic engagement and other more intangible goods, such as social support networks and trust and cooperative norms. Creating vibrant, inclusive communities goes beyond good quality jobs, productivity growth, affordable housing and well-connected transportation systems. At their heart, vibrant and inclusive communities are also founded on positive social relationships, one of the main pillars of social capital (Scrivens and Smith, 2013). These are not traditionally areas that have garnered close attention in public policy. Yet this presents a vital missed opportunity – both because of their role in supporting higher individual and community well-being, but also because of how these factors influence the effective functioning of both the economy and governments. This ranges from the health impacts of social isolation; to the educational, employment and mental health advantages of having good social support; the improved institutional performance that comes from greater civic engagement; and the benefits to business of operating in a high-trust society where economic interactions run smoothly (Scrivens and Smith, 2013; OECD, 2017l).

Institutional quality and neighbourhood connectedness can increase social capital. Social capital can be strengthened by policies that focus on improving institutional quality (e.g. by reducing corruption) or that increase neighbourhood connectedness (Box 3.4). Most of research on the latter has focused on the role of community diversity in building trust - in terms of inequality and ethnic fractionalization (Rothstein and Uslaner 2005; Algan and Cahuc, 2013). For instance, in the United States, people that live in a racially mixed community or in one with a high degree of income disparity trust other people less (Alesina and La Ferrara, 2002). Similar patterns have been found in other countries (Bjørnskov, 2006; Helliwell and Wang, 2010). There is increasing evidence that residential segregation lowers trust, rather than diversity (de Souza Briggs, 2002; Rothwell, 2011; Uslaner, 2012; Laurence, 2017). OECD countries with large immigrant populations (e.g. Australia, Canada, Luxembourg, New Zealand and Switzerland) are high-trust countries, suggesting that the interplay between diversity and trust may be complex.

Box 3.4. What is social capital and how can it be strengthened?

While there is no single interpretation of 'social capital' and the term has been applied to a vast range of situations, four main ways of conceptualising and measuring the concept have been identified: (i) Personal relationships; referring to people's relationships and the actions taken to create/maintain those relationships (such as spending time with others); (ii) Social network support, referring to the resources – emotional, material, practical, financial, intellectual or professional – available to individuals through their personal networks; (iii) Civic engagement, referring to activities that contribute to civic and community life such as volunteering, political participation, group membership and other forms of community action; and (iv) Trust and cooperative norms, referring to the trust, social norms and shared values that underpin societal functioning and enable mutually beneficial cooperation.

Figure 3.25. Interpersonal trust is associated with a variety of community and institutional factors

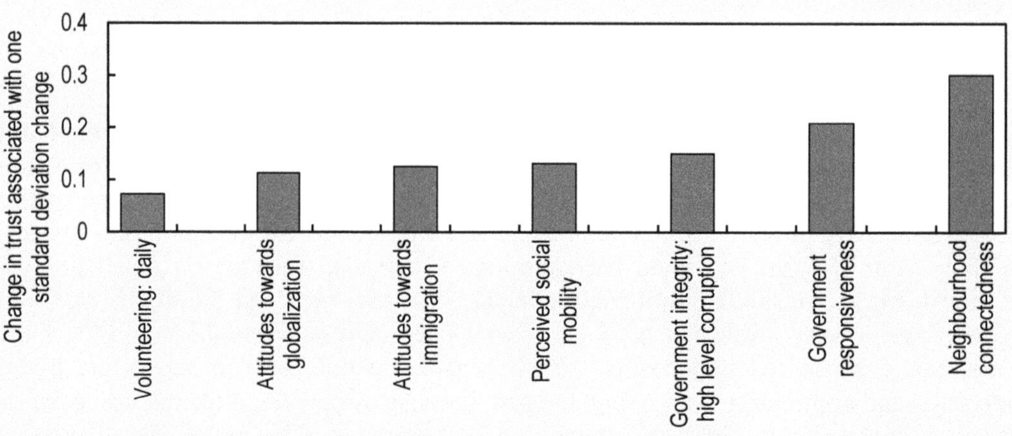

Note: This graph reports the simulated change in generalised trust, which is measured on a 0-10 scale, following the increase in selected drivers. Regression coefficients are based on a multivariate analysis of trust in others, controlling for a range of individual, societal and institutional variables. Data is pooled from four countries that participated in the OECD Trustlab project (Germany, Italy, Slovenia, the US). Sample size is N=1000 per country and the sample is representative by age, gender, income and location.
Source: Murtin et al. (2018).

StatLink http://dx.doi.org/10.1787/888933725658

Evidence from OECD's Trustlab project shows that trust in others, one of the proxies of social capital, goes hand in hand with neighbourhood connectedness, institutional quality (in terms of government responsiveness and integrity), perceived social mobility, attitudes towards immigration and globalization, and a high frequency of volunteering.

This mirrors previous research: for instance, frequent interactions with other people in the neighbourhood foster the development of trust in people in general because such trust is inferred from ongoing social experiences, which in turn allow inferences about shared social norms in society at large (Offe, 1999; Glanville and Paxton, 2007).

The link between a person's community relations and interpersonal trust has been established both in correlational and causal designs (Putnam 2000; Delhey and Newton 2003; Li, Pickles, and Savage 2005; Glanville and Paxton, 2013). Meanwhile, quality of government matters for interpersonal trust since fair and effective institutions enable a person to extend trust to strangers without putting themselves at risk (Gambetta, 1993; Tabellini, 2008; Herrmann et al, 2008; OECD, 2017b)

Governments need to actively promote volunteering and look for collaborative ways for engaging with the society and citizens on volunteer activities. One in three people of working age volunteer through an organisation at least once a year in OECD countries, ranging from 18% in Spain and the Czech Republic, to more than 55% in the United States and Norway. Employed people, and those with a higher level of education and income are more likely to volunteer than those without. When adding up the value of the time people spend on volunteering, it amounts to around 2% of GDP on average in OECD countries (OECD, 2015e). Volunteering also creates a "virtuous circle", whereby those who help others in the community also gain in terms of their own well-being – including their subjective well-being, skills and earnings potential (Box 3.5).

Box 3.5. Volunteer services are attractive schemes as concerns youth inclusion

Governments have increasingly focused supporting volunteers in their commitment - be it through a validation of the skills acquired in order to unleash potential career benefits, involvement of citizens in political processes, or in providing support to volunteers when they want to solve a social problem. Some of these policies include:

The French "service civique" (volunteer service), which was statutorily institutionalised at the beginning of 2010 as a special form of volunteering. The programme has two objectives: to reinforce "civism" and national cohesion, and also allow young people to participate in a collective project. The government supports volunteers engaged in the "service civique" by paying them a small stipend and their insurance contributions, and by providing advanced trainings. Between 2010 and 2016 around 182,000 young people have done their "service civique". Over time, this programme has gain in popularity amongst the unemployed and those from disadvantaged background.

Mirroring, in some ways, the French volunteer service, the United Kingdom Government introduced the National Citizen Service as a flagship initiative to support building a "bigger, stronger society" (UK Cabinet Office, 2013). A summer programme for 16 year olds that includes both residential and at-home components, it offers an opportunity for young people to work in teams to design and implement a social action project in their local area. An evaluation published in 2011 indicated that participation in the Citizen Service yielded significant gains to young people's well-being, when compared to a control group.

The Danish Social Service Act imposes on municipalities the duty to support economically and cooperate with voluntary organisations. They have to develop a policy to support volunteering and review their activity. In effect, about 60-80% of all municipalities in Denmark have a voluntary policy and 55% of all municipalities have established a voluntary council, which functions as a bridge between the municipality and the local voluntary organisations. Voluntary organisations are represented at the voluntary council, which recommends to the municipality what type of activity should be supported (Principi, Jensen and Lamura, 2014).

In order to strengthen the cohesion and foster the solidarity in European society, a European Solidarity Corps has been set up by the European Commission to create a community of young people willing to engage in a wide range of solidarity activities, either by volunteering or gaining occupational experience in helping to resolve challenging situations across the European Union and beyond.

References

Adema, W., N. Ali and O. Thévenon (2014), "Changes in Family Policies and Outcomes: Is there Convergence?", OECD Social, Employment and Migration Working Papers, No. 157, OECD Publishing, Paris.

Alam, M., K. Carling and O. Nääs (2013), "The Effect of Summer Jobs on Post-schooling Incomes", IFAU Working Paper No. 2013:24.

Alesina, A. and E. La Ferrara (2002), "Who Trusts Others?", Journal of Public Economics 85: 207-34.

Algan, Y. and P. Cahuc (2013), "Trust, Growth and Well-being: New Evidence and Policy Implications", IZA Discussion Paper, No. 7464.

Ali, N. and D. Richardson (2014), "An Evaluation of International Surveys of Children", OECD Social, Employment and Migration Working Papers, No. 146, OECD Publishing, Paris.

Arrow, K. (1972), "Gifts and exchanges", Philosophy & Public Affairs, Vol. 1, No. 4, pp. 343 362.

Bjørnskov, C. (2006), "Determinants of Generalized Trust: A Cross-country Comparison", Public Choice, Vol. 130, pp. 1- 21.

Brauer, M. et al. (2016), "Ambient Air Pollution Exposure Estimation for the Global Burden of Disease 2013", Environmental Science and Technology, Vol. 50/1, pp. 79-88.

Burnett, R.T. et al. (2014), "An Integrated Risk Function for Estimating the Global Burden of Disease Attributable to Ambient Fine Particulate Matter Exposure", Environmental Health Perspectives, 122: 397-403.

Caiazzo, F. et al. (2013), "Air Pollution and Early Deaths in the US; Part I: Quantifying the Impact of Major Sectors in 2005", Atmospheric Environment, 79: 198-208.

Chancel L and Piketty T (2015), "Carbon and Inequality: from Kyoto to Paris Trends in the Global Inequality of Carbon Emissions (1998-2013) & Prospects for an Equitable Adaptation Fund, Paris School of Economics.

D'Costa, S., E. Garcilazo and J. Oliveira Martins (2013), "The Impact of Structural and Macroeconomic Factors on Regional Growth", OECD Regional Development Working Papers, No. 2013/11, OECD Publishing, Paris.

D'Costa, S., E. Garcilazo and J. Oliveira Martins (2016), "Impact of Structural Reforms on Regional Growth: Distance to the Frontier Matters", SERC Discussion Paper 203.

de Souza Briggs, X. (2002), "Social Capital and Segregation: Race, Connections, and Inequality in America", KSG Working Paper No. RWP02-011.

Delhey, J. and K. Newton (2003), "Who Trusts? The Origins of Social Trust in Seven Societies", European Societies, Vol. 5, No. 2, pp. 93-137.

Devaux, M , et al. (2011), "Exploring the Relationship Between Education and Obesity", OECD Journal: Economic Studies, Vol.2011/1

Dorling D (2017), "The Equality Effect", New Internationalist Publishing

Downey, D.B. and D.J. Condron (2016), "Fifty Years since the Coleman Report: Rethinking the Relationship between Schools and Inequality", Sociology of Education, Vol. 89/3, pp. 207-220.

EEA (2016), "Air Quality in Europe: 2016 Report", Available at: www.eea.europa.eu/publications/air-quality-in-europe-2016

Gambetta, D. (1993), "The Sicilian Mafia: The Business of Private Protection", Harvard University Press.

GBD (2015), "Global Burden of Disease Study 2015 Results", Institute for Health Metrics and Evaluation, Seattle, United States.

Gelber, A., A. Isen and J.B. Kessler (2016), "The Effects of Youth Employment: Evidence from New York City Lotteries", Quarterly Journal of Economics, Vol. 131, No. 1, pp. 423-460.

Glaeser, E., & Gyourko, J. (2017), "The Economic Implications of Housing Supply", No. w23833, National Bureau of Economic Research.

Glanville, J. L., P. Paxtion (2007), "How Do We Learn to Trust? A Confirmatory Tetrad Analysis of the Sources of Generalized Trust", Social Psychology Quarterly, Vol. 70, pp. 230–242.

Glanville, J.L. and P. Paxton (2013), "Do Social Connections Create Trust? An Examination Using New Longitudinal Data", Social Forces, Vol. 92, No. 2, pp. 545-562.

Grotlüschen, A. et al. (2016), "Adults with Low Proficiency in Literacy or Numeracy", OECD Education Working Papers, No. 131, OECD Publishing, Paris.

Guiso L., P. Sapienza, and L. Zingales (2004), "The Role of Social Capital in Financial Development", American Economic Review, Vol. 94 (3). pp. 526-56.

Hajat A., Hsia C., O'Neill M.S. (2015), "Socioeconomic Disparities and Air Pollution Exposure: A Global Review", Curr Environ Health Rep 2(4):440–450.

Helliwell, J.F. and R.D. Putnam (2007), "Education and Social Capital", Eastern Economic Journal, Vol. 63(1), pp. 1-19.

Helliwell, J.F. and S. Wang (2010), "Trust and Well-being", National Bureau of Economic Research, Working Paper No. 15911.

Herrmann, B., C. Thöni and S. Gachter (2008), "Antisocial Punishment across Societies", Science, Vol. 319.

Hilber, C. A., & Vermeulen, W. (2016), "The Impact of Supply Constraints on House Prices in England", The Economic Journal, 126(591), 358-405.

Hsiang, Solomon et al. (2017), Estimating Economic Damage from Climate Change in the United States", Science 30 Jun 2017: Vol. 356, Issue 6345, pp. 1362-1369.

IEA (2016), "CO_2 Emissions by Product and Flow (Edition 2016)", IEA CO2 Emissions from Fuel Combustion Statistics.

IEA (2017), "Investment Needs for a Low-Carbon Energy System", "Chapter 2 in Perspectives for the Energy Transition, IEA/OECD Publishing, Paris, and IRENA, Abu Dhabi.

Inchley, J. et al. (eds.) (2016), "Growing up Unequal: Gender and Socioeconomic Differences in Young People's Health and Well-being", Health Behaviour in School-aged Children (HBSC) Study: International Report from the 2013/2014 Survey, WHO Regional Office for Europe, Copenhagen.

International Transport Forum (2017), "Public Transport Accessibility in Cities: Public Transport Coverage and Average Accessibility by Public Transport", in ITF Transport Outlook 2017, OECD Publishing, Paris.

Kane, T.J. (2006), "Public Intervention in Post-Secondary Education", in Hanushek, E.A. and Welch, F. (Eds.), Handbook of the Economics of Education, Vol. 2, Elsevier.

Kautz, T., et al. (2014), "Fostering and Measuring Skills: Improving Cognitive and Non-cognitive Skills to Promote Lifetime Success", OECD Education Working Papers, No. 110, OECD Publishing, Paris.

Laurence, J. (2017), "Wider-community Segregation and the Effect of Neighbourhood Ethnic Diversity on Social Capital: An Investigation into Intra-Neighbourhood Trust in Great Britain and London", Sociology, 51(5), 1011–1033.

Levinson, A. and J. O'Brien (2015), "Environmental Engel Curves", NBER Working Paper No. 20914.

Leyden, K.M. (2003), "Social Capital and the Built Environment: The Importance of Walkable Neighbourhoods", American Journal of Public Health, Vol. 93, No. 9, pp. 1546-1551.

Li, Y., A. Pickles, and M. Savage (2005), "Social Capital and Social Trust in Britain", European Sociological Review, Vol. 21, No. 2, pp. 109-123.

McDaid, D., E. Hewlett and A. Park (2017), "Understanding Effective Approaches to Promoting Mental Health and Preventing Mental Illness", OECD Health Working Papers, No. 97, OECD Publishing, Paris.

Murtin, F. et al. (2018), "Trust and its Determinants: Evidence from the Trustlab Experiment", OECD Working Paper, forthcoming.

Murtin, F., et al. (2017), "Inequalities in Longevity by Education in OECD Countries: Insights from New OECD Estimates", OECD Statistics Working Papers, No. 2017/02, OECD Publishing, Paris.

OECD (2009), "Doing Better for Children", OECD publishing, Paris.

OECD (2012a), "Sick on the Job? Myths and Realities about Mental Health and Work, Mental Health and Work", OECD Publishing, Paris.

OECD (2012b), "Environmental Outlook to 2050: Consequences of Inaction", OECD Publishing, Paris.

OECD (2012c), "Equity and Quality in Education: Supporting Disadvantaged Students and Schools", OECD Publishing, Paris.

OECD (2014), "The Cost of Air Pollution: Health Impacts of Road Transport", OECD Publishing, Paris.

OECD (2015a), "How's life for children?", in *How's Life? 2015: Measuring Well-being"*, OECD Publishing, Paris.

OECD (2015b), "Fit Mind, Fit Job: From Evidence to Practice in Mental Health and Work", Mental Health and Work, OECD Publishing, Paris.

OECD (2015c), "Skills for Social Progress: The Power of Social and Emotional Skills", OECD Skills Studies, OECD Publishing, Paris.

OECD (2015d), "Carbon Dioxide Embodied in International Trade", OECD Structural Analysis Statistics: Input-Output.

OECD (2015e), "How's Life? 2015: Measuring Well-being", OECD Publishing, Paris.

OECD (2015f), "Education at a Glance 2015: OECD Indicators", OECD Publishing, Paris.

OECD (2015g), "Government at a Glance 2015", OECD Publishing, Paris.

OECD (2016a), "Enhancing Child Well-Being to Promote Inclusive Growth", Background Document, Meeting of the Council at Ministerial Level, 1-2 June 2016, OECD.

OECD (2016b), "PISA 2015 Results (Volume I): Excellence and Equity in Education", OECD Publishing, Paris.

OECD (2016c), "Skills Matter: Further Results from the Survey of Adult Skills", OECD Skills Studies, OECD Publishing, Paris.

OECD (2016d), "The Economic Consequences of Outdoor Air Pollution", OECD Publishing, Paris.

OECD (2016e), "Material Resources", OECD Environment Statistics (database).

OECD (2016f), "Society at a Glance", OECD Publishing, Paris.

OECD (2017a), "Educational Opportunity for All: Overcoming Inequality throughout the Life Course", OECD Publishing, Paris.

OECD (2017b), "Health at a Glance", OECD Publishing, Paris.

OECD (2017c), "Obesity Update", OECD Publishing, Paris.

OECD (2017d), "Preventing Ageing Unequally", OECD Publishing, Paris.

OECD (2017e), "Investing in Climate, Investing in Growth", OECD Publishing, Paris.

OECD (2017f), "Green Growth Indicators 2017", OECD Publishing, Paris.

OECD (2017g), "Taxation and Skills", OECD Publishing, Paris.

OECD (2017h), "OECD Affordable Housing Database", OECD, Paris.

OECD (2017i), "Child Well-Being Data Portal", http://www.oecd.org/els/family/child-well-being/data/.

OECD (2017j), "How's Life? 2017: Measuring Well-Being", OECD Publishing, Paris.

OECD (2017k), "PISA 2015 Results (Volume III): Students' Well-Being", OECD Publishing, Paris.

OECD (2017l), "Guidelines on Measuring Trust", OECD Publishing, Paris.

OECD (2016f), "Making Cities Work for All: Data and Actions for Inclusive Growth", OECD Publishing, Paris.

Offe, C. (1999). "How Can We Trust Our Fellow Citizens?", In: Warren, M.E. (Ed.), Democracy and Trust, Cambridge: Cambrigde University Press, 1999: pp. 42-87.

Oxfam (2015), "Extreme Carbon Inequality", Oxfam.

Paris, V., M. Devaux and L. Wei (2010), "Health Systems Institutional Characteristics: A Survey of 29 OECD Countries", OECD Health Working Papers, No. 50, OECD Publishing, Paris.

Principi, A., P.H. Jensen and G. Lamura (2014), "Active Ageing: Voluntary Work by Older People in Europe", University of Bristol Publishing.

Putnam, R.D. (2000), Bowling Alone: The Collapse and Revival of American Community, Simon & Schuster (eds.), New York.

Quintini, G. and S. Martin (2014), "Same Same but Different: School-to-work Transitions in Emerging and Advanced Economies", OECD Social, Employment and Migration Working Papers, No. 154, OECD Publishing, Paris.

Rajan, R. (2010), "Fault Lines: How Hidden Fractures Still Threaten the World Economy", Princeton University Press, Princeton, New Jersey

Rothstein, B. and E. Uslaner (2005), "All for All: Equality, Corruption and Social Trust", World Politics, Vol. 58, No. 3, pp. 41 72.

Rothwell, J.T. (2011), "The Effects of Racial Segregation on Trust and Volunteering in US Cities", Urban Studies, Vol. 49, No. 10, pp. 2109-2136.

Salvi Del Pero, A. et al. (2016), "Policies to Promote Access to Good-quality Affordable Housing in OECD Countries", OECD Social, Employment and Migration Working Papers, OECD Publishing, Paris.

Schochet, P., J. Burghardt and S. McConnell (2008), "Does Job Corps Work? Impact Findings from the National Job Corps Study", American Economic Review, Vol. 98, No. 5, pp. 1864-1886.

Schreiber, F., and A. Carius (2016), "The Inclusive City: Urban Planning for Diveristy and Social Cohesion" In: Worldwatch Institute (Ed): State of the World: Can a City Be Sustainable?, Washington D.C.: Worldwatch Institute, pp. 123-141.

Scrivens, K. and C. Smith (2013), "Four Interpretations of Social Capital: An Agenda for Measurement", OECD Statistics Working Papers, No. 2013/06, OECD Publishing, Paris.

Sunde, U. and T. Vischer (2011), "Human Capital and Growth: Specification Matters", IZA Discussion Paper, No. 5991, Institute of Labor Economics, Bonn.

Tabellini, G. (2008), "Institutions and Culture", Journal of the European Economic Association, Papers and Proceedings, Vol. 6 (2-3).

Uslaner, E. (2012), "Segregation and Mistrust: Diversity, Isolation and Social Cohesion", Cambridge University Press.

Van Kempen, R., and G. Bolt (2009), "Social Cohesion, Social Mix, and Urban Policies in the Netherlands", Journal of Housing and the Built Environment, Vol. 24, No. 457.

Vertier, P. (2017), "Dismantling the "Jungle": Refugee Relocation and Extreme Voting in France", Sciences Po Working Paper.

WHO (2016a), "Report of the Commission on Ending Childhood Obesity", WHO, Geneva.

WHO (2016b), "Ambient Air Quality and Health (factsheet)", World Health Organization, Geneva.

World Bank (2016), "Shockwaves Managing the Impacts of Climate Change on Poverty", World Bank Group, Washington DC.

Chapter 4. Build efficient and responsive governments

This chapter puts forward two crucial ideas: the need for a whole-of-the-government coordination and integration of inclusive growth actions, across multiple levels of government; and to inclusive policy-making, defined as the practice of identifying and incorporating citizens' views and actual needs into the design, implementation and evaluation of policies. At the national level the chapter discusses inclusive policy-making, defined as the process, including with experimentation, by which governments enable the incorporation of citizens' needs and views into the design, implementation and evaluation of policies which will help better target government programmes and increase their efficiency.

Inclusive policy making requires capacity from governments to deal with complexity in policy making, assess differentiated policy impacts from broader viewpoints while eliminating discrimination and behavioural bias, and identify complementarities and trade-offs between and within policies and policy objectives. It also requires that public policy-making is protected from undue influence, where a public decision is captured by a narrow interest group to reflect its own interest. Integrity, openness and accountability in decision-making ensure that the needs, preferences and concerns of stakeholders, including underserved populations are reflected in decision-making. These components are measured by a number of indicators, including trust in national government and satisfaction and confidence across public services. A set of best practices on inclusive growth governance in sectoral areas (e.g. innovation, skills and labour market institutions) is presented together with some governance practices that cut across several policy areas.

The Inclusive Growth Framework for Policy Action on Inclusive Growth consolidates some of the key policy recommendations to sustain and more equitably share the gains of economic growth from related OECD work, around broad principles to build efficient and responsive governments through:

(i) aligned policy packages across the government;

(ii) integration of distributional aspects upfront in the policy design; and

(iii) assessing policies for inclusiveness and growth impacts.

Inclusive policy-making

Trust in governments is weak

People's trust in public institutions has decreased, coupled with falling civic engagement und political efficacy. People's trust in institutions matters for the smooth functioning of the economy, the democratic process as well as people's well-being (Algan and Cahuc, 2013). It is essential for the success of public policies that require broader social and political consensus, and it reduces incentives for policy-makers to seek short-term gains. On average, only 38% of people across the OECD declare trusting their government, as compared to 42% ten years ago (Figure 4.1). In countries where data are available for several public institutions, the parliament is consistently reported as the least trusted entity compared to the legal system and the police (Murtin et al., 2018; OECD, 2017a; OECD, 2017b).

Figure 4.1 Lower trust in government across OECD countries

Average confidence in national government in 2014-16, and the change since 2005-07

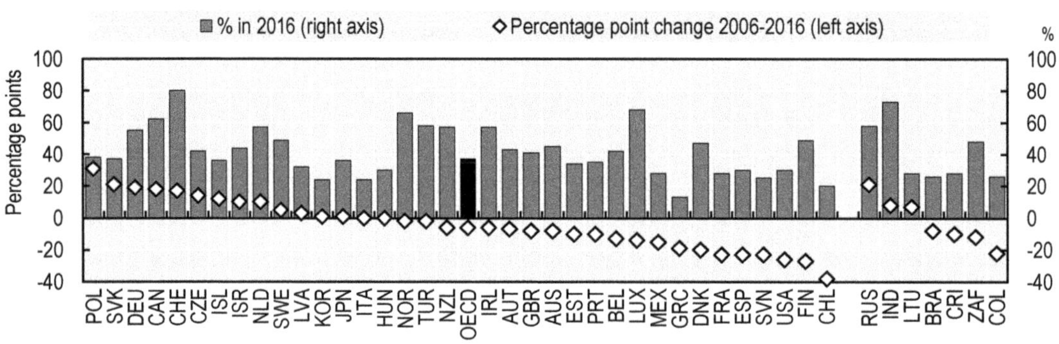

Note: Data for Iceland and Luxembourg refer to 2008 rather than 2006. The simple average covers all OECD countries.
Source: OECD calculations based on Gallup World Poll, www.gallup.com/services/170945/world-poll.aspx.

StatLink http://dx.doi.org/10.1787/888933725677

Growing distrust has been coupled with falling civic engagement. Voter turnout has steadily declined across the OECD, especially among groups who are themselves less well-represented by the political classes - the young, the less educated and those with lower incomes. Self-reported voter turnout is 14 percentage points lower for people in the bottom income quintile compared to those in the top quintile, and is around 17 percentage points lower among youth (18-24) than among older people (above 65, OECD, 2017a; OECD, 2017b). How people vote has been affected as well: in Europe, lower trust in institutions has gone in hand with higher votes for populist parties (Algan et al, 2017).

People's sense of political efficacy has only gone down. Political efficacy, or the feel of having a say in what government does, impacts on whether citizens' feel included in the political process, are motivated to engage and ultimately trust those governing them. On average, only one in three people in the OECD feel they have influence on what the government does, with this share ranging between 20% or less in Italy, Slovenia and France to 60% or more in Chile, Greece and Lithuania. Like voting, political efficacy is not distributed equally across different population groups: the less educated, less wealthy, unemployed and older people feel less empowered to influence their institutions (Murtin et al., 2018; OECD, 2017b).

Box 4.1. Measuring trust

The OECD has been developing new tools to measure people's trust and confidence, including interpersonal trust, in support of policy recommendations. As part of the OECD Better Life Initiative launched in 2011 and OECD mission to promote better policies for better lives, the OECD has initiated the OECD Trust Strategy at the 2013 OECD Ministerial Council meeting on Jobs, Equality and Trust to provide guidance, including methodological and measurement advice, to restore confidence in public institutions. These efforts are in line with the Sustainable Development Goals (SDGs), notably the Goal 16 that aims to "Promote peaceful and inclusive societies for sustainable development, provide access to justice for all and build effective, accountable, and inclusive institutions at all levels". In addition, the OECD survey of Adult Skills, PIAAC, includes questions on trust to analyse the extent to which skill acquisition and trust are related.

At the same time, several initiatives have been carried out in OECD countries to measure trust, based on comparable and statistically sound information. For example, the National Statistical Offices in New Zealand, Canada, Korea or Australia that include trust measure in their surveys. Progress has been made towards collecting and using trust indicators in line with the OECD statistical standards of validity and reliability.

Despite this progress, the measurement of trust concerns a few issues including the measurement of behavioural bias (that is, the difference between self-reported and experimental measures), interpretation limits suggesting that a distinction between trust in government and public institutions remains unclear, limited data availability in terms of timeliness and comparability across countries, and the lack of insights about what information trust measures really capture and how that can be integrated in the policy design.

Beyond the OECD sources of data used in this report, most of the data can be retrieved from unofficial sources such as the Gallup World Poll, the World Values Survey, the European Social Survey or the European Quality of Life Survey. However, the coverage varies across countries and over time as well as its representativeness (i.e. typically around 1000 persons per country). In response to these measurement challenges, the OECD launched the TrustLab, an international programme that collects information on trust relying on traditional survey-based measures, and also behavioural and experimental data. In 2017, the OECD launched in 2017 the Guidelines on Measuring Trust that support National Statistical Offices to measure trust effectively and comparably across countries. On that basis, the OECD has incorporated the measurement of trust in numerous areas such as the OECD How's Life report and the Better Life Index and the OECD Inclusive Growth Framework for Policy Action.

The decline in trust in institutions precedes and extends beyond the great recession. Trust has fallen by more than 15% points in Greece, Portugal, and Spain – some of the OECD countries that were hit hardest by the crisis. By contrast, in Germany, Poland, and Slovak Republic, which are some of the countries where trust has increased the most, the average resident is generally better off than she was in 2005 (OECD, 2017a). Nevertheless, the decline in trust extends beyond the Great Recession and sole economic drivers. In the United States, where opinion polls have collected measures of confidence in the federal government since the 1950s, trust has been continuously falling for over 50 years, from close to 8% in the early 1960s to less than 20% today (OECD, 2017g; OECD, 2017b; OECD, 2013a). Part of the declining trust may be subject to measurements issues, such as perception or cultural bias. The OECD has worked on measures of trust to help understand better the underlying concerns of citizens (Box 4.1).

Restoring trust through better services delivery

Better governance can help to enhance trust and improve citizens' perceptions of institutional and representative performance:

- High-quality public services are essential to people's lives and closely related to trust (OECD, 2017a). On average, more than two-thirds of citizens across the OECD are generally satisfied with service provision in their local area for health care, education, public transportation, and the police. Interestingly, people that have actually used a specific service over the past year report higher levels of satisfaction. However, differences in service satisfaction between countries are large, and satisfaction with certain institutions is markedly lower overall (e.g. only 49% across OECD countries trust the judicial system). Improving service quality and simplifying access could hence be a channel to improve trust.
- Improving government integrity has been found to be one of the most important determinants of trust in government and is therefore a policy priority (Murtin et al., 2018; OECD, 2017a). More than half of OECD residents consider corruption to be widespread in their government, ranging from 18% in Sweden to 89% in Italy (Figure 4.2). Since 2006, the perception of government corruption rose by 3 percentage points on average across the OECD, in line with the fall in trust in institutions. While only relying on data on the prevalence of corruption, as perceived by people, may provide an incomplete measure of the phenomenon, the sheer size (and trend) of this measure underscores that corruption is of significant concern to citizens.
- Other government characteristics that have been found to go hand in hand with high trust include government reliability, i.e. its capacity of reaction to adverse events, as well as its responsiveness and openness to citizen input (Murtin et al., 2018; OECD, 2017a; OECD, 2017b). Perceived fairness regarding treatment of minorities in public service interactions are also correlated with trust.

Restoring trust by making policy-making more responsive

Only less than half of OECD countries have developed frameworks on comprehensive citizen participation in the policy cycle. Countries have made significant progress in promoting stakeholder participation, both in the process of setting national priorities, in developing new laws and regulations, designing, implementing and evaluating public policies (Figure 4.2). Integral approaches to citizen participation in public life are seen as increasingly important for acceptability of policies and prevention of policy capture. However, only few OECD countries have developed this type of framework. Developing such a framework would favour the use of participatory practices by defining which mechanisms to use (the what), at which each stage of the policy cycle (the when), which stakeholders to involve (the who) and how citizen engagement should be encouraged to do participation right and ensure effective and efficient delivery of high quality of public policies and services, increase accountability, enhance transparency and regain people's trust in public institutions.

Figure 4.2 More than half of OECD residents perceive their governments to be corrupt

% of people considering corruption to be widespread across government, 2006 and 2016

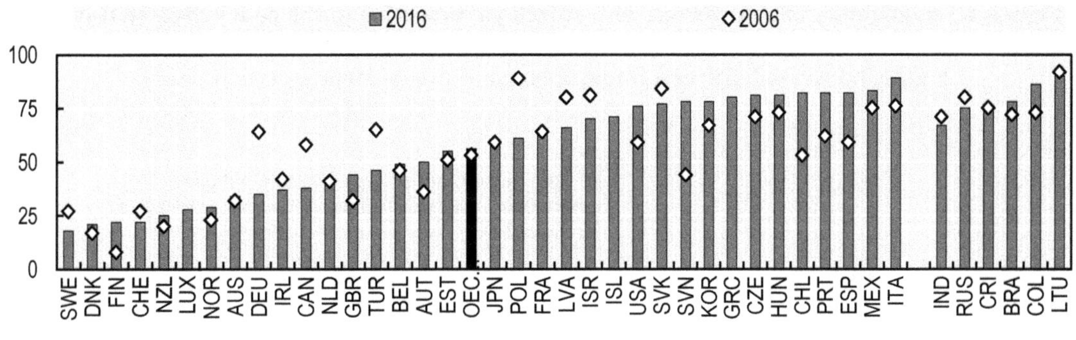

Note: The OECD average is the simple average based on the 32 countries with data for both time periods, and excludes Greece, Iceland and Luxembourg.
Source: OECD calculations based on Gallup World Poll.

StatLink http://dx.doi.org/10.1787/888933725696

Box 4.2. Types of stakeholder participation

Stakeholder participation, as defined by the OECD Recommendation of the Council on Open Government, refers to all the ways in which stakeholders can be involved in the policy cycle as well as in service design and delivery, including information, consultation and engagement. Information: an initial level of participation characterised by a one-way relationship in which the government produces and delivers information to stakeholders. It covers both on-demand provision of information and "proactive" measures by the government to disseminate information. Consultation: a more advanced level of participation that entails a two-way relationship in which stakeholders provide feedback to the government and vice-versa. It is based on the prior definition of the issue for which views are being sought and requires the provision of relevant information, in addition to feedback on the outcomes of the process. Engagement: when stakeholders are given the opportunity and the necessary resources (e.g. information, data and digital tools) to collaborate during all phases of the policy-cycle and in the service design and delivery.

Governments are increasingly carrying out open government reform agendas to ensure more responsive policy making. The OECD Recommendation on Open Government defines open government as "a culture of governance that promotes the principles of transparency, integrity, accountability and stakeholder participation in support of democracy and inclusive growth" fostering inclusive institutions that enable effective citizen participation, pluralism and a system of checks and balances contributing to inclusive growth (OECD, 2016a; OECD, 2016b). All OECD countries have established open government initiatives. While in 49% of them, there is a single open government strategy, in the other 51% open government initiatives are integrated in other strategies (Figure 4.4). 76% of the countries that stated having an open government strategy were actually referring to an Open Government Partnership (OGP) Actions Plan which are not a comprehensive national strategy. These plans serve as a crucial implementation tool for a variety of unconnected initiatives.

Figure 4.3 Availability of a document with citizen participation in the policy cycle (left panel)

Figure 4.4 Availability of a single open government strategy (right panel)

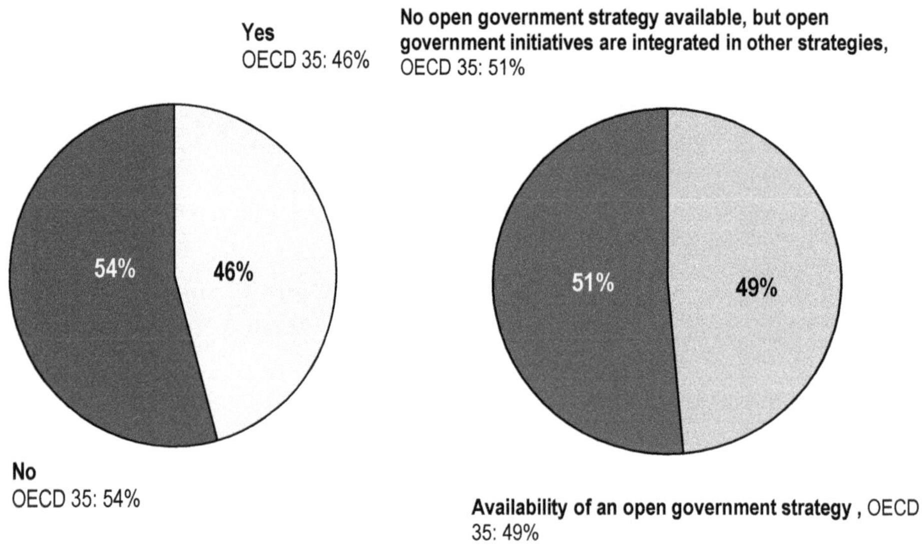

Source: OECD (2016b), Open Government: The Global Context and the Way Forward, OECD Publishing, Paris.

StatLink http://dx.doi.org/10.1787/888933725715
StatLink http://dx.doi.org/10.1787/888933725734

Digital frameworks provide opportunities - governments need to map, understand and integrate citizens' demands and needs in the design and delivery of public service strategies. In 2016, about 36% of individuals from OECD Member countries submitted filled forms via public authorities' websites. However, there are persisting differences in the use of digital government services across various population groups. When comparing the level of education of users of digital government services substantial differences can be found (Figure 4.5). On average across OECD countries in 2016, about 54% of individuals with higher education submitted filled forms via public authorities' websites, against 17% of individuals with low levels of education. This difference in the use of digital government services by education level is less important in Nordic countries (such as Denmark, Finland and Norway) while it is more important in Estonia, Greece, Hungary, Ireland, Latvia and Portugal. The level of income also seems to influence the level of digital interaction with public authorities (Figure 4.5; Figure 4.6). On average in OECD Member countries, about 49% of individuals in the top income quartile (richest) used the Internet to submit filled forms via public authorities' websites, against about 25% of individuals in the fourth income quartile (poorest).

Figure 4.5 Individuals sending filled forms via public authorities' websites in the past year

OECD countries, by education level, 2006 and 2016

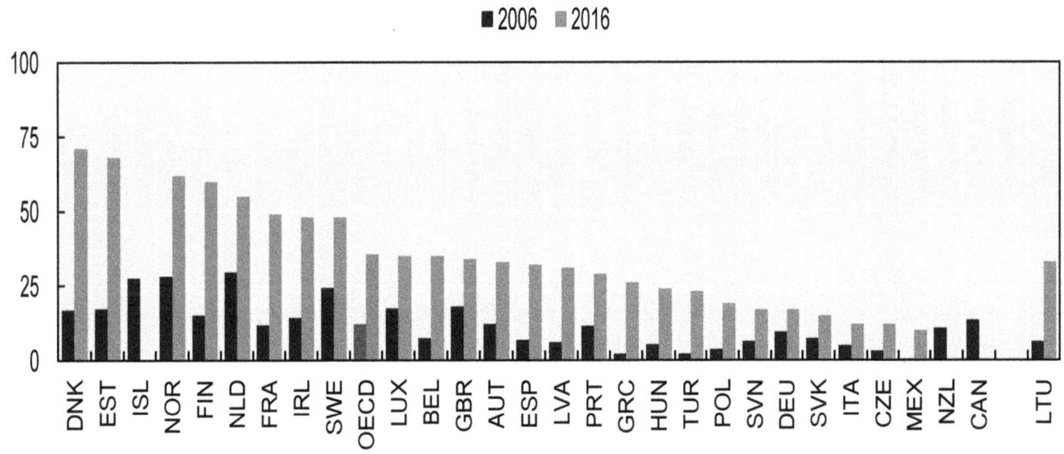

Note: Data for OECD non-European member countries are not available. Mexico: 2015 rather than 2016.
Source: OECD, ICT database; and Eurostat, Information Society database.

StatLink http://dx.doi.org/10.1787/888933725753

Figure 4.6 Individuals sending filled forms via public authorities' websites in the past 12 months

By income level, 2016

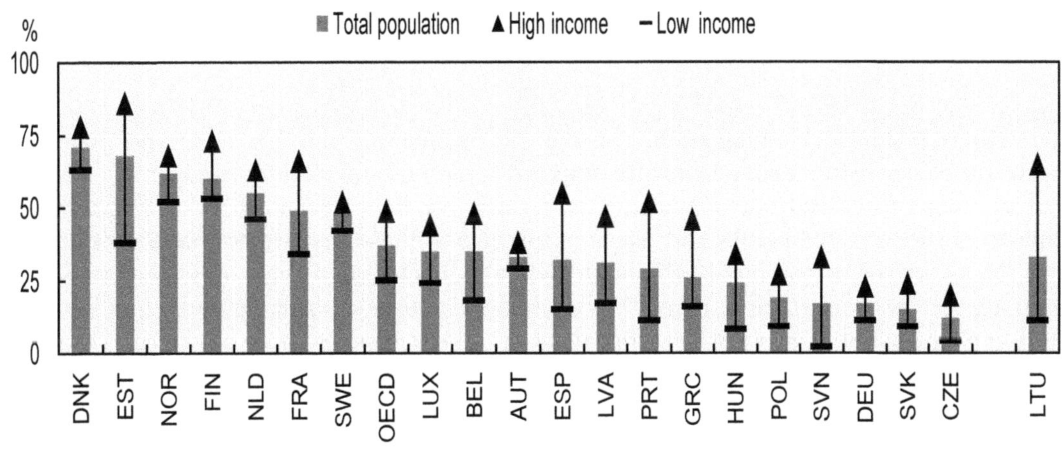

Note: Data for OECD non-European member countries are not available as well as data for Iceland, Italy, Sweden and the UK.
Source: OECD, ICT database; and Eurostat, Information Society database.

StatLink http://dx.doi.org/10.1787/888933725772

Figure 4.7 Open-Useful-Reusable Government Data Index (OURdata)

OECD countries, 2017

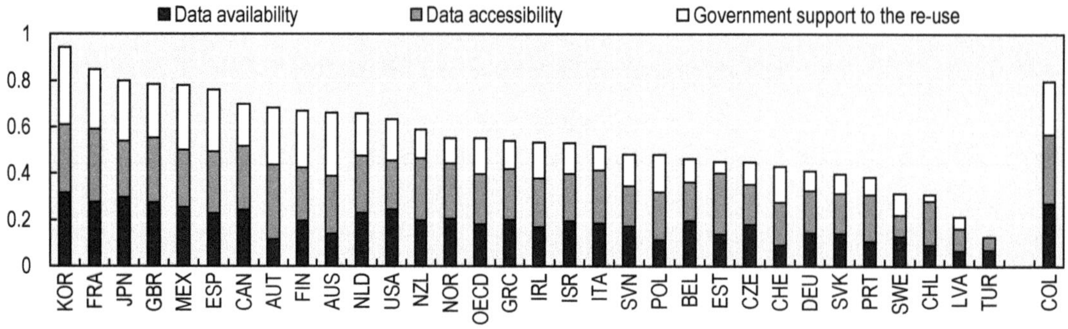

Note: Data for Hungary, Iceland and Luxembourg are not available. Denmark does not have a Central/federal data portal and are not displayed in the Index. Detailed methodology and underlying data are available in the annex online. Information on data for Israel: http://dx.doi.org/10.1787/888932315602.
Source: OECD Survey on Open Government Data.

StatLink http://dx.doi.org/10.1787/888933725791

Open Government Data policies can help to shape people-centred policies. By ensuring Open Government Data (OGD) availability, accessibility and reuse by public, private and civic actors, governments can enable the collaboration with a number of actors to improve the design of public services with a citizen-driven approach. The OECD OURdata Index (open-Useful-reusable data Index) is one of the tools (together with national OGD policy reviews and analytical work) developed by the OECD to support member and partner countries in the promotion of OGD policies to create public value, measures the efforts made by governments to foster government data availability, accessibility and re-use. According to the *2017 OURData Index* governments still need to improve their focus on using open government data to engage a comprehensive set of stakeholders from the whole OGD ecosystem to collaborate and crowdsource inputs for policy making and service delivery. The use of OGD remains therefore an untapped opportunity to empower people by letting their needs lead decisions on services and policies (Figure 4.7).

A strong stakeholder engagement can help to implement policies, tools and projects that are closer to the broader public interest. Improved stakeholder engagement allows governments to collect better evidence as a basis for their decisions. Involving a wide spectrum of interested parties and reaching out also to those that are not necessarily used to, able or willing to "get involved" should help to collect more diverse ideas and opinions, making the decisions more responsive to the society's needs at different levels and leading to a higher quality of decision-making based on a better and sounder evidence. Through engagement, stakeholders develop a sense of ownership over policy choices, reforms and projects' outcomes. In addition, stakeholders' engagement can bring voice to those that are most vulnerable to economic uncertainty and social exclusion e.g. elderly, unemployed, deprived or unserved segment of the population. Innovative forms of service delivery have targeted the need of these groups and restructure delivery around their needs lowering the social, economic and physical barriers that prevented users to access services.

Most OECD countries have implemented a requirement to engage stakeholders in developing both primary and secondary regulations. Many countries have mechanisms for involving stakeholders in regulation design, however there is quite some diversity on the actual instruments used (Figure 4.8). An increasing number of countries are using a law or even a constitutional requirement to commit civil servants to stakeholder engagement, illustrating the importance that countries give to this issue (OECD, 2015a).

Meaningful stakeholder engagement continues to face significant challenges, especially for including low-income populations. These challenges can be regrouped under the following three main categories, including (i) low administrative capacity, given lack of planning, weak mandate or incentives or a non-supportive administrative culture; (ii) hard to reach societal groups, in particular deprived segments of population (whether on the basis of social or economic backgrounds, ethnic, cultural or gender based identity or location factors); and (iii) weak incentives to participation, including issues of availability, accessibility, relevance or perceived impact of the time and effort required to engage.

Figure 4.8 Requirements to conduct stakeholder engagement - primary and subordinate regulations

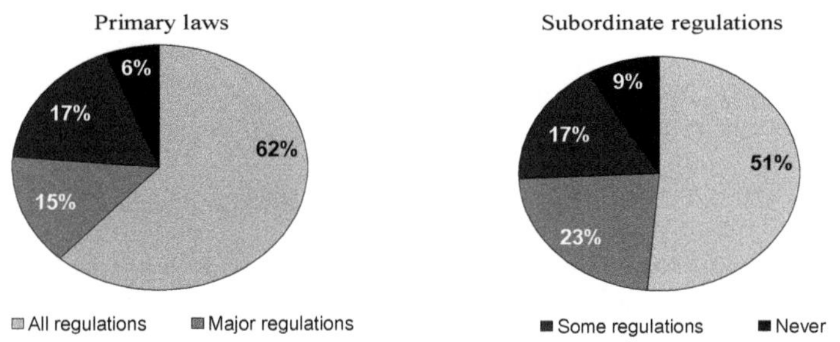

Note: Based on preliminary data from 34 countries and the European Commission.
Source: Forthcoming Regulatory Policy Outlook and 2014 Regulatory Indicators Survey results.

StatLink http://dx.doi.org/10.1787/888933725810

Figure 4.9 Types of consultation

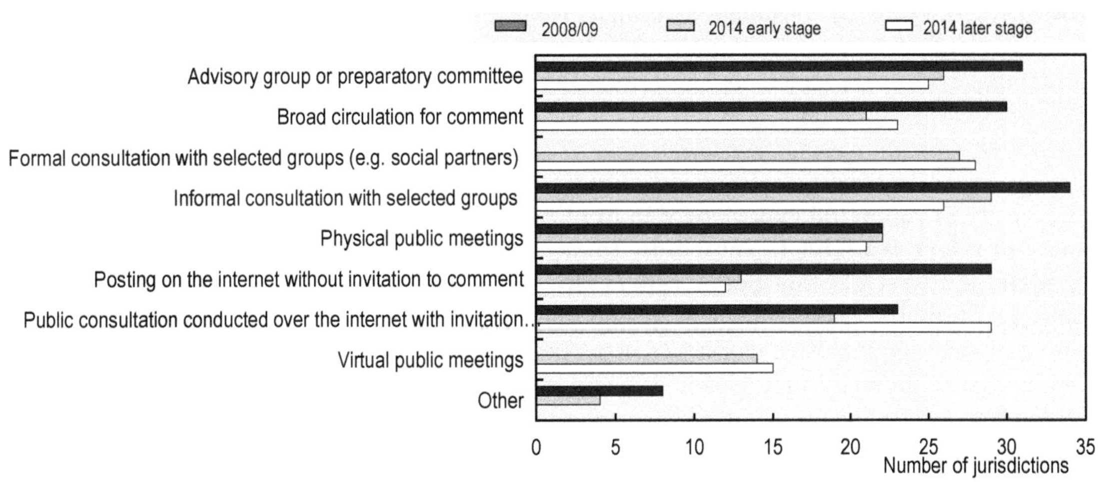

Note: Early stage refers to stakeholder engagement that occurs at an early stage, to inform officials about the nature of the problem and to inform discussions on possible solutions. Later stage consultation refers to stakeholder engagement where the preferred solution has been identified and/or a draft version of the regulation has been issued. Based on data from 34 countries and the European Commission.
Source: OECD (2015b), OECD Regulatory Policy Outlook 2015.

StatLink http://dx.doi.org/10.1787/888933262760

Figure 4.10 Obligation to provide feedback on comments

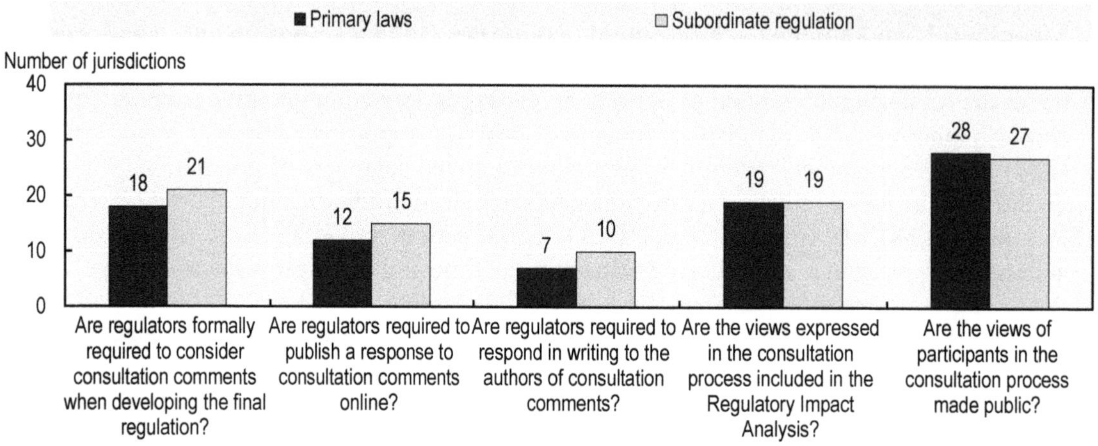

Note: Based on data from 34 countries and the European Commission.
Source: OECD (2015b), OECD Regulatory Policy Outlook 2015.

StatLink http://dx.doi.org/10.1787/888933262835

Despite a formal requirement to engage stakeholders, it has yet to become part of the day-to-day work of policy makers and citizens. For that to happen, stakeholders need to be engaged before the final regulatory development phase to ensure meaningful inputs into the rule-making process. Currently few countries systematically consult with stakeholders before they made a decision to regulate in order to explore possible options to address possible problems, for example through the use of green papers. Furthermore, all affected parties should be considered in order to guarantee inclusiveness and a level playing field. Countries use various types of consultation processes involving different types of stakeholders (StatLink 2http://dx.doi.org/10.1787/888933725810

Figure 4.9). Limiting consultations to the "usual suspects" through targeted consultations (i.e., over-relying on meetings with special groups) might discriminate against SMEs, new entrants, and foreign traders and investors (Figure 4.10; OECD, 2015a; OECD, 2015b).

Mainstreaming gender equality and diversity in public life

Diversity of views and experiences in public sector organisations can help expand the pool of talent available to contribute to organisational performance, and can lead to policies and services that better reflect citizens' needs. Equal representation of women and men in public employment is an important indicator of progress towards building a more diverse and inclusive workforce in the public sector. In 2015, gender balance was the main goal of diversity strategies in 15 European Union countries of which 11 are OECD countries. Across the OECD, the representation of women in public employment is larger (58%) than in total employment (45%). This picture is consistent with the representation of women in central government, where they account on average for 53% of employees (2015). Greece, Italy, Denmark, Belgium and Spain have a relative gender balance (51% to 52% of women). Hungary has the highest share of women in central government (72%), followed by Poland (69%) and the Slovak Republic (68%). On the other side of the spectrum are Japan (18%), Korea (29%) and Switzerland (31%).

There is no gender parity across institutions and sectors. In fact, one of the reasons contributing to an almost gender equal share of public employment is that some key public sector occupations, such as teachers or nurses, are heavily female dominated differently from other occupations. This highlights a persisting gender-based occupational segregation. Higher the positions, the fewer women work in them. Although gender balance at the most senior levels is an important indicator of the role that women play in decision-making and policy making, with a greater chance of inclusive outcomes, the leaky pipeline at management level appears consistent across the public sector and very little progress have been reported in recent years. In the 28 European Union countries for which data are available, women held 35.3% of the highest administrative positions in national government in 2016 – a minimal increase of 5.1% over 2013. As for the second most senior level, women accounted for 41.1% of posts, a tiny increase of 2.5% over 2013. Behind these average figures, there are variations from country to country, particularly at the highest levels of the civil service (OECD, 2016d; OECD, 2017e). Looking at individual country trends, very few countries achieved gender parity. In Poland, Greece, Iceland and Latvia the share of women in senior positions is the highest (between 50% and 54%). The smallest shares are found in Japan (3%), Korea (6%) and Turkey (8%). Iceland and Norway are the countries where the share of women in senior positions has increased the most since 2010 (by 12 and 11% points). In Denmark, Portugal and Spain, the share of women in senior positions has decreased by about 3-4% points. In central government, the extent to which women hold senior positions varies considerably.

Steering policies towards gender parity in the most senior levels of administration can help to attract more women into these positions. Hiring targets for women are in place in 10 OECD countries and 6 OECD countries have promotion targets for women. In many countries the public sector also offers more flexible working conditions compared to the private sector. For example, in 16 OECD countries the public sector offers more child or family care arrangements than the private sector.

New forms of open governance are emerging with significant potential for more inclusive policy-making. The role of government is constantly evolving as citizens and other stakeholders are better informed with digitalisation and demand that policies and decisions reflect their preferences, needs and views. This has contributed to a new form of governance that goes beyond traditional participatory approaches and to transform accountability lines, emphasising the sharing of power and decision-making, information and mutual respect between governments and stakeholders. The OECD Recommendation of the Council on Open Government defines it as any interested and/or affected party, including: individuals, regardless of their age, gender, sexual orientation, religious and political affiliations; and institutions and organisations, whether governmental or non-governmental, from civil society, academia, the media or the private sector.

Preventing and tackling policy capture for policies to benefit the worst-off

Policy capture can strongly challenge responsive policy-making. Policy capture is by definition the opposite of inclusive policy-making, but it also perpetuates or even exacerbates social and economic inequalities and thereby endangers inclusive growth (OECD, 2016c). Public policies determine to a large extent the distribution of costs and benefits in an economy. Tax exceptions, subsidies, private sector participation in government services, emission standards, public health policies and education grant programmes, to name but a few, directly influence who gets what. Public decisions over such policies are therefore at risk of being unduly influenced away from the public interest towards the interests of specific groups or individuals. Whenever policies are captured, the obtained undue benefits can be reinvested in further influence-seeking, thereby maintaining or exacerbating inequalities of all types.

Policy capture fuels a vicious cycle of inequality, and undermines the capacity to reform and weakens the economic growth potential of economies. Indeed, where a weak integrity system is making the capture of policies a viable option, obtaining "legal" protection against competitive pressure through undue influence may be the most efficient way of obtaining rents for companies (OECD, 2016c; OECD, 2017e). Recent data from the Eurobarometer shows that there is a widespread perception that the only way to succeed in business is to have political connections, that favouritism hampers business competition and that too close links between business and politics lead to corruption (Figure 4.11; OECD, 2016c; OECD, 2016e). In turn, the same survey shows that most respondents say that the financing of political parties is not sufficiently transparent and supervised. Political finance, however, is one of the ways private interests can influence policy-making (OECD, 2017d; OECD, 2017e).

Figure 4.11 The value of connections to government

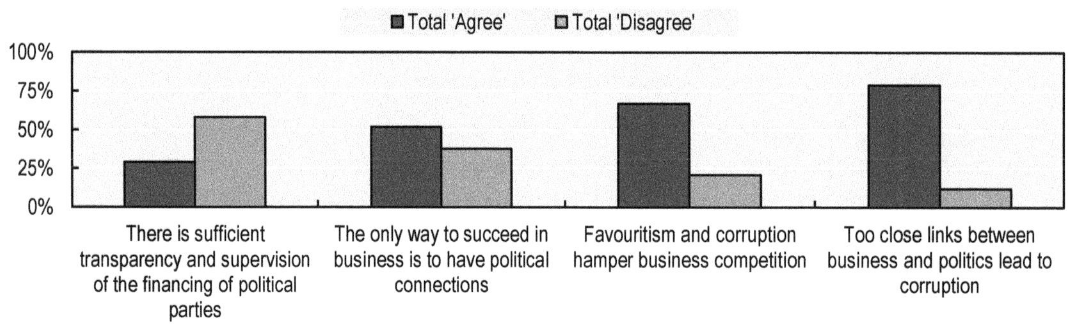

Source: European Commission (2017), Standard Eurobarometer 87.

StatLink http://dx.doi.org/10.1787/888933725829

Addressing the vicious cycle of policy capture is key to recover trust of citizens. Reports from investigative journalism (such as the Panama or the Paradise Papers) that are increasingly unveiling (often legal but morally) questionable benefits accruing to elite suggest that citizens increasingly perceive policy-making as exclusive and serving only vested interests where well-connected elites benefit at the cost of the public interest. A survey conducted by the World Economic Forum amongst youth around the world, shows that 48.6% of respondents see corruption and lack of transparency as the most important factor contributing to inequality in their countries (Figure 4.12; Figure 4.13).

Strategies against policy capture need to go beyond anti-corruption. The complexity and sometimes legal nature of policy capture strategies require measures that go beyond narrow anti-corruption policies and underscore the value of improving inclusiveness and accountability, and of promoting values as a guide beyond formal rules (OECD, 2017d; OECD, 2017e). A strategy against capture therefore requires actions by policy makers that complement and reinforce each other in four key areas:

- **Levelling the playing field:** Engaging the participation of stakeholders with different interests ensures an inclusive decision-making process that is more resilient to capture, as it becomes more difficult for one interest group to influence the decisions without triggering resistance by the other groups. Levelling the playing field requires for instance guaranteeing equal access to lobbying opportunities, fair rules on political financing of elections and campaigns, but also including users of public services in an easy manner, like setting water tariffs, into their regulatory process. The Water Industry Commission for Scotland for instance has established a Customer Forum to illicit and input preferences, evidence and feedback into its Strategic Price Review of Water Charges from 2021 to 2027.

- **Enforcing the right to know:** To enable an effective participation and stakeholder engagement, and to facilitate social control over decision-making processes, external actors need to have access to relevant and reliable information in an easy and accessible way; for instance information about who has been involved in a public decision-making process, or whether public officials have ties to private firms, e.g. a politician who has worked or has been invited to conferences of the pharmaceutical industry while being involved in decisions related to the health sector.
- **Promoting accountability through competition authorities, regulatory agencies and Supreme Audit Institutions (SAI):** External control, as well as competition policies and regulation of markets with market failures are essential for an environment conducive to accountability in both the public and private sector. For instance, ensuring competition can prevent the risk that established firms lobby for market entry barriers to protect their businesses, and independent regulators can prevent firms who are delivering public services from abusing from the monopoly power. It is important to ensure a "culture of independence" in nurtured to drive the appropriate behaviour as explained in the OECD guidance on the broader governance of regulators (OECD, 2017). Also, SAI can externally audit the policies related to SDG 10 and their results, and thereby contribute to hold the government to account. Shielding the responsible agencies themselves from undue influence is crucial, of course, as they are particularly likely to become targets of capture;
- **Applying organisational integrity policies:** Decisions that could be captured are taken by individuals acting in an organisational environment; therefore, defining clear standards of conduct, promoting organisational cultures of integrity, and ensuring a sound control and risk management framework provide guidance on how to design organisational resilience to capture. For instance, a clear gift and conflict-of-interest policy can avoid that public officials become trapped in a relationship of reciprocity, where it becomes increasingly difficult to say "no" to those who in the past have invited them to conferences, dinners or sent them bottles of wines.

Figure 4.12 A cycle between inequality and policy capture

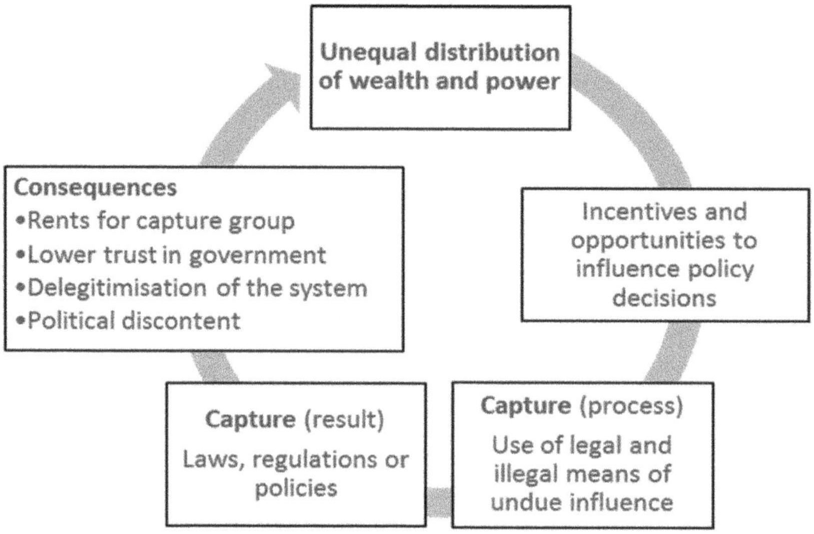

Source: OECD Secretariat.

Figure 4.13 Youth see corruption and lack of transparency as key factors of inequality

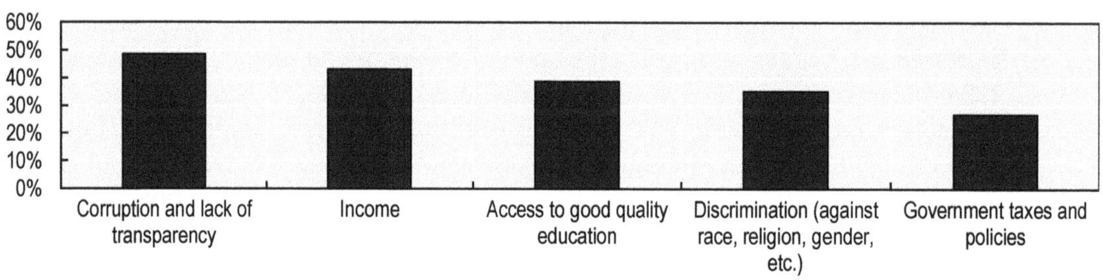

Note: In response to the question: What are the most important factors contributing to inequality in your country?
Source: World Economic Forum (2017), Global Shapers Survey 2017.

StatLink http://dx.doi.org/10.1787/888933725848

Effective governance of inclusive growth agendas

Creating mechanisms to coordinate policy-decisions across the board

In today's global interconnectedness, challenges have grown in complexity for national and subnational levels of governments. Governments' challenges have become multidimensional in their nature and, sometimes, global in their impact. Governments are facing these challenges in an unprecedented context of fiscal stabilisation and in an environment in which trust in government is still below pre-crisis levels (OECD, 2017a). Consequently, traditional sector-based approaches to policy-making are increasingly less effective in improving results including on inclusive growth as they do not reflect strategic considerations from other policy sectors, nor do they incorporate practices and tools to implement integrated responses. As a response, integrated diagnostic tools offer the best support to reform efforts that can respond successfully to today's multidimensional policy challenges facing governments.

Underpinning these integrated approaches are key enablers including:

- **Political vision**, democratic commitment and leadership to define and support the development of long term priorities and policy decisions and to clarify institutional responsibilities across the public sector in support of inclusive growth.
- **Evidence-informed policy-making**: to root governance and policy initiatives in practices that worked in similar contexts, though ensuring appropriate set up for evidence take up, and tools such as monitoring and evaluation and strategic foresight, while ensuring that the public agenda and policy priorities are set in an open an inclusive way and following integrity standards.
- **Whole-of-Government co-ordination**: to ensure that governments' departments and agencies are working together across silos to achieve a shared goal.
- **Innovation and change management**: to incentivize the generation and implementation of new ideas while ensuring that the human and cultural administrative dimensions are being taking into account to guarantee the success and sustainability of reforms.

Screening policies for their inclusiveness impacts: the role of evaluation

Looking at the government process through a gender lens leads to better informed policy-making and more equal outcomes for society. A countries' ability to promote gender equality relies on their capacity to design policies that can effectively respond to the gender needs of society. A clear example is provided in the case of Iceland, where gender analysis has helped ensure policy outcomes that align with government goals in relation to gender equality. Many tools exist for gender differentiated impact of policies, facilitated through the use of tools such as gender impact assessments, gender budgeting and the collection of gender-disaggregated and gender-sensitive data. The example of Sweden, a country that adopted strategic gender equality and mainstreaming policies tailored to each branch of power – executive, legislative and judicial – is an inspiring example of how gender mainstreaming can become a concrete, whole-of-government commitment and framework of action.

Despite the growing interest and commitment of OECD Member and partner countries, challenges continue to affect the inclusive design, implementation and evaluation of policies and programmes across the board. To be most effective, a gender lens should be applied to each strategic phase of the policy and budget cycles. Most countries which currently engage in gender budgeting report that they do not necessarily apply gender budgeting tools at all the stages of the budgeting process.

High level political commitment, the application of a gender lens to each stage of the spolicy and budgeting cycle mechanisms can help ensure that governments design and deliver policies that lead to more equal outcomes for men and women. Weak systems for accountability and scrutiny in relation to policies and their gender outcomes is still a challenge for effective gendered evaluation of policies. Legislatures have an important role to play both as champions of gender equality and in ensuring effective oversight of government. In 2016, 22 OECD countries had formed parliamentary committees focused on gender equality. However, their existence alone is not sufficient to guarantee more gender sensitive policies and budgets. In Mexico, out of 1523 initiatives discussed in the

Congress in the years 2015-2016, only 42 (2.75%) came before the Gender Equality Committee and almost all of them were focused on amendments to the General Law on Women's Access to Life Free from Violence and the General Law for Equality between Women and Men (OECD, 2017a; OECD, 2016f). This example demonstrates the common pitfall of gender equality committees focussing largely on women-specific policies. To be most effective, these committees should look at how broader policies impact men and women differently (Box 4.3).

Box 4.3. A case study: The use of gender impact assessments to improve policy design in Iceland

In 2015, the budget committee of the Icelandic Parliament proposed a significant modification to a legislative proposal regarding income tax. The proposal aimed to simplify the income tax system through removing the right of higher-income partners to benefit from unused tax credits of lower-income partners. While the committee was initially in favour of preserving the entitlement, the Ministry of Finance and Economic Affairs applied a gender lens to its analysis of the proposal and brought to light that this measure predominantly benefitted men who are the higher-income partner in 75 out of 100 marriages in Iceland. Specifically, the proposal would increase men's disposable income, increasing the gender income gap, contrary to the goal of economic equality between men and women pursued by Iceland. Thanks to the information from the gender impact assessment of the policy, the initial proposal of the budget committee was amended.

Source: OECD (2016f).

Inclusiveness of all population groups, not just women as homogenous groups, is now at the core of policy-making. A telling illustration is given by the 2030 Agenda, whose overarching objective is "no one left behind". Its Goals and targets are intended to be universal – applying to all countries, and to all population groups within countries. The 2030 Agenda encourages focusing on the poorest (target 1.1 calls for policies to "eradicate extreme poverty for all people everywhere") and those in the most vulnerable situations, including children and young people, ethnic minorities, migrants, disabled and other disadvantaged groups based on other relevant characteristics. Some specific goals and targets are explicitly directed towards certain groups, such as target SDG 8.8 on labour rights for migrant workers, or target SDG 11.2 on access to public transport for women, children, persons with disabilities and older persons. In 2015, when world leaders adopted the United Nations Resolution 70/1, "Transforming our world: the 2030 Agenda for Sustainable Development" they therefore emphasised the importance of accessible, timely and disaggregated data.

Box 4.4. Behavioural insights and inclusive growth

Behavioural insights use an evidence-driven, inductive approach to incorporate lessons derived from behavioural and social sciences to improve the design and delivery of public policies. By focusing on how people make decisions in real-world contexts, policies can be shaped to remove biases that restrict good decision making in order to improve well-being and promote equitable, balanced and inclusive growth.

Behavioural insights have been applied to fighting unemployment, facilitating inclusion, and reducing poverty. OECD (2017) notes a strong focus on promoting outcomes for end-users through "nudges" that help overcome cognitive and behavioural biases and through more complex interventions such as "boosting" individual's skills and knowledge.

For example, the Singapore Workforce Development Agency (WDA), a statutory board of the Ministry of Manpower (MoM) conducted a behavioural experiment to increase the job placement rate for job-seekers in Singapore. The result was a 17% increase in the number of workers finding placements, compared to the control group, which could result in 4 000 more job seekers finding jobs per year if implemented across all WDA career centres in Singapore.

Employment and Social Development Canada (ESDC), the government department responsible for social programmes and the labour market at the federal level, introduced behavioural insights principles into the on-line Job Posting pages to facilitate greater use of on-line platform facilitating better matching between jobs and job-seekers. The different "nudges" that were tested created more uptake and use of the platforms, ranging from 67% to 122% increase in clicks compared to the control group.

The UK Department for Business, Energy, and Industrial Strategy (BEIS) and Behavioural Insights Team (BIT) found that low adult literacy and math skills contribute to ill-health and social exclusion. In a 10-week trial, text message nudges were used to increase attendance by adult learners in school by 7% and decrease drop-out rates by 36%. The Consultative Group to Assist the Poor (CGAP) supported the World Food Programme (WFP) Kenya to assess and provide behavioural remedies to counteract problems with digital cash transfers for food aid. The result was an increase in the number of payments completed using the new debt card-based digital cash transfer scheme one year after the intervention, including 32% using the card more than once a month and 16% more than three times a month.

The Western Cape Government (WCG) Department of Community Safety worked with ideas42 and researchers from the University of Cape Town to identify other, behaviourally-informed solutions to improving safety in South Africa's low-income communities. A prototype "Safety Tool" app was designed and tested to help young people choose safe weekend and evening activity options, and make plans around those options. The results of the experiment showed that the app had a powerful effect: at the end of the intervention, the treatment population was found to be half as likely to participate in unsafe activities as the control population.

Source: OECD (2017f), Behavioural Insights and Public Policy: Lessons from Around the World, OECD Publishing, Paris.

Leaving no one behind requires the use of disaggregated data in the design, implementation and evaluation of policies. Data based on national averages miss most of the opportunities to identify inclusion challenges. While in most cases survey data can be disaggregated by age, gender and some measure of socio-economic background (e.g. education, occupation or, more rarely, income), comparative evidence on other social markers (e.g. disability, ethnicity, sexual orientation) is sparser. Responding to the demand for better information on inequalities in well-being will require taking steps for improving the breadth and comparability of the available micro-data; and for integrating different data sources to provide a portfolio of statistics joined up via a set of core variables.

New approaches to inclusive growth policies and tools should include behavioural insights. The application of behavioural science in policy making is growing globally with over 130 public bodies institutionalising this approach in policy making (Box 4.4). Behavioural approaches can be instrumental in merging different policy disciplines, open government initiatives and integrity policies for a more "user-centric: approach for inclusive policy making in a number of ways. Firstly, behavioural approaches can be used to identify the needs and perceptions of citizens that reduce or eliminate bias in common stakeholder engagement tools and attract greater citizen participation. For instance, a behaviourally informed chatbot has been used by the Government of Jersey to engage citizens in key policies such as on the environment and tax. The traditional government surveys usually have a response rate of 4%, while the behaviourally informed chatbot has a response rate of over 50%, with repeated participation. Secondly behavioural insights techniques can trial and test interventions before they are implemented to ensure they achieve the policy objective with the actual and not assumed behaviours of the target population. Evaluations that determine the true drivers of behaviour (especially in "hard to reach" target groups) can provide real data and evidence on the problems seeking to be addressed. They can inform decision-makers on the appropriate course of action which may be legislative, regulatory or alternatives, such as making information more salient or structuring national programmes to illicit behavioural incentives for change.

Strengthening accountability

Social accountability plays a key role as it ensures that the voices of people are heard. It is also acknowledged that the role of citizens in policymaking has transformed the relationship between the government and the citizenry and that it is key for governments to enhance citizens' trust. For instance, the existence of mechanisms such as free, fair and transparent elections, a functioning party system, access to public information as well as the inclusion of a wide range of stakeholders (CSOs, youth, elderly, minorities, people with disabilities) in policy design, and service delivery and more importantly, policy evaluation are key to hold governments accountable. Furthermore, access to justice and legal empowerment are also fundamental to give people the awareness and tools to more effectively participate in open government and consultation initiatives but also shed light on corrupt practices and push for legal and regulatory protection Finally, the role of media and journalism, by acting as watchdogs and as a means to provide information can also be described as being key for accountability in order to ensure that a wide range of individuals irrespective of their race, colour, sex, language, religion, political or other opinion, origin, disability, or sexual orientation can have access to timely and accurate information without discrimination or bias.

Effective scrutiny of government policies and performance by a wide range of stakeholders, including citizens, lies at the heart of democratic accountability. As the budget is the central policy document of government, parliaments need to engineer processes which allow for effective budgetary scrutiny while fostering accountability and fiscal discipline. The legislature must be empowered to independently review the budget and related documents, to debate and influence budget policy, and to hold the government to account. Evidence of the legislature reasserting its budgetary role can be found across the OECD, with legislatures among other things setting up new oversight committees and committee procedures, enlarging budget staff, and demanding improved and more complete budgetary information from government. One particularly striking trend has been the rise of specialised budget research units within parliaments and independent parliamentary budget offices. Legislatures are also taking on new roles which promote increased fiscal responsibility such as approving ex ante fiscal frameworks.

The OECD Recommendation of the Council on Budgetary Governance [C(2015)1] **highlights the role of parliament.** Forthcoming OECD Best Practices for Parliamentary Budgeting seek to underpin these broad principles and to provide guidance on how legislatures can most effectively engage across the budget cycle, promoting legislatures that are both empowered and fiscally responsible. The Recommendation states that the "national parliament has a fundamental role in authorising budget decisions and in holding government to account" and that countries should: "provide for and inclusive, participative and realistic debate on budgetary choices by offering opportunities for the parliament and its committees to engage with the budget process at all key stages of the budget cycle, both ex ante and ex post as appropriate." The Recommendation also highlights the role of parliaments in ensuring that performance, evaluation and value for money are taken into account in the budget process (8.a). OECD legislatures have moved from a mainly financial focus in budget scrutiny to increasingly integrating performance information in budgetary discussions (OECD, 2015c).

As a representative and deliberative body, the legislature provides a forum to debate different viewpoints from across society. Committee hearings are among the traditional processes that allow for the legislature to hear from a range of stakeholders. Legislatures are also seeking more modern methods to encourage public participation and collect evidence from more diverse audiences, such as, crowdsourcing platforms, video interviews, web-chats and surveys, focus groups and other events.

Independent fiscal institutions (IFIs) or other structured, institutional processes support the credibility of budgeting. The credibility of national budgeting – including the professional objectivity of economic forecasting, adherence to fiscal rules, longer-term sustainability and handling of fiscal risks – can be supported by independent fiscal institutions (IFIs) or other structured, institutional processes for allowing impartial scrutiny of, and input to, government budgeting. Diverse examples of IFIs have existed for decades (e.g. Belgium, 1936, the Netherlands, 1945, Denmark, 1962, Austria, 1970 and the United States, 1974). The Recommendation of the Council on Principles for Independent Fiscal Institutions aims to assist countries to design an enabling environment conducive to the good performance of an IFI and to ensuring its long-run viability. The experience of countries with more long-standing institutions shows that – even if government's do not always agree with IFIs' analysis – these institutions are important partners for finance ministries and legislative budget committees in promoting credible fiscal policies (OECD, 2014).

Improving transparency and integrity of the policy-making process is important, recognising its importance for informed decision-making but curbing the risk of undue influence and unfair competition. Remedies to secure unbiased and inclusive policy-making include increasing transparency and integrity in lobbying and better managing conflict of interest. Regulation can be used to address concerns that lobbying has been high on many governments' agendas including lobbying registry, code of conduct and public employment regulation. *The Recommendation of the Council on Transparency and Integrity in Lobbying* [C(2010)16]called on countries to introduce regulations to increase transparency in the interaction between public officials and lobbyists thus reducing policy capture. In addition, institutional measures such as external audit and verification are critical in this regard alongside asset and private interest disclosure by public officials. Options are also available for regulating political finance on a context specific basis, including by promoting the use of online technologies for greater transparency and scrutiny, allocating sufficient human and financial resources to the electoral monitoring bodies and mapping potential integrity and compliance risks.

Governments are increasingly implementing open government initiatives that promote inclusiveness - such as digital government, access to information, budget transparency, openness and accessibility as well as citizen participation in service delivery including youth and disadvantaged groups in policy making, inclusive and participatory budgeting or initiatives on gender equality. These initiatives not only allow for governments to have a clear understanding of a wide range of citizens' needs and demands, allowing better targeted and defined public policies and, thus reducing inequalities in society, but also, provide the tools and avenues from citizens to hold government accountable. An open government approach can increase the interaction between governments and their citizenry and ensure accountability. Improving the accountability of the public sector was the second main objective of all countries when implementing open government strategies and initiatives and the most important for countries such as France, Iceland and Israel (Figure 4.14Figure 4.14).

Figure 4.14 Initiatives on open government being or been implemented

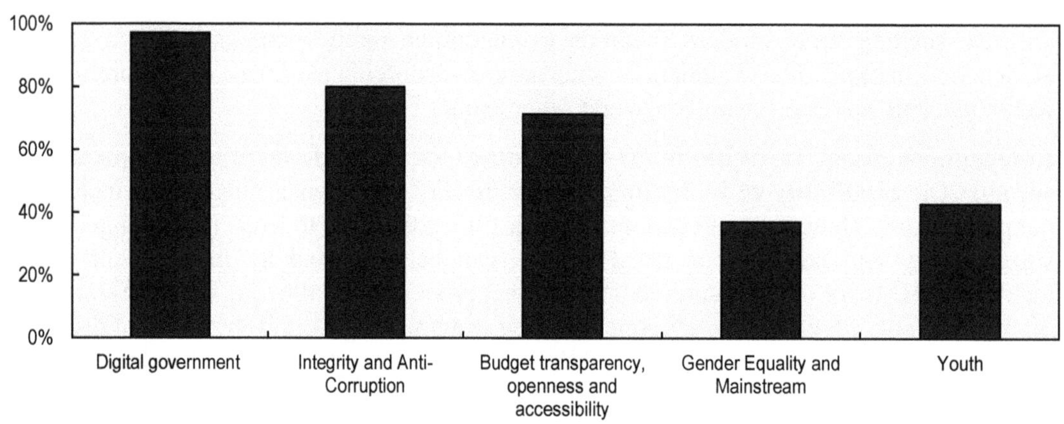

Source: OECD (2016b), *Open Government: The Global Context and the Way Forward.*

StatLink http://dx.doi.org/10.1787/888933725867

government initiatives and implementing them at sector level. For instance, a lack of incentive among government institutions to co-ordinate and insufficient financial and human resources are among the most frequently cited challenges for institutions responsible for horizontal co-ordination of open government strategies and initiatives (Figure 4.15).

At the sectoral level, similar concerns have been raised. In OECD countries, 63% of the Ministries of Health and 41% of the Ministries of Finance claimed that lack of or insufficient financial resources as one of the five main challenges in successfully implementing initiatives on open government at the sector level (Figure 4.16). The lack of financial resources negatively impacts the proper implementation of these initiatives at the national and sector level and might jeopardise the success of the overall open government strategy. Not fully implemented, they can be negatively perceived by citizens leading them to trust less on government actions.

Figure 4.15 Main challenges indicated by countries to co-ordinate open government initiatives

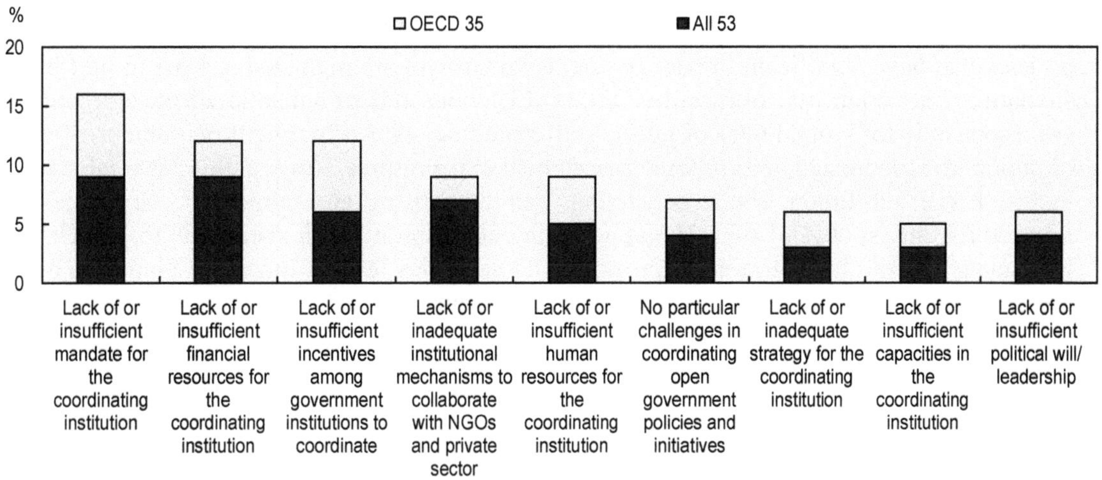

Note: Countries were asked to name their main three challenges in co-ordinating open government initiatives. This figure shows only the number one challenge that countries listed.
Source: OECD (2016b), Open Government: The Global Context and the Way Forward.

StatLink http://dx.doi.org/10.1787/888933725886

Figure 4.16 Challenges to implement open government at the sector level

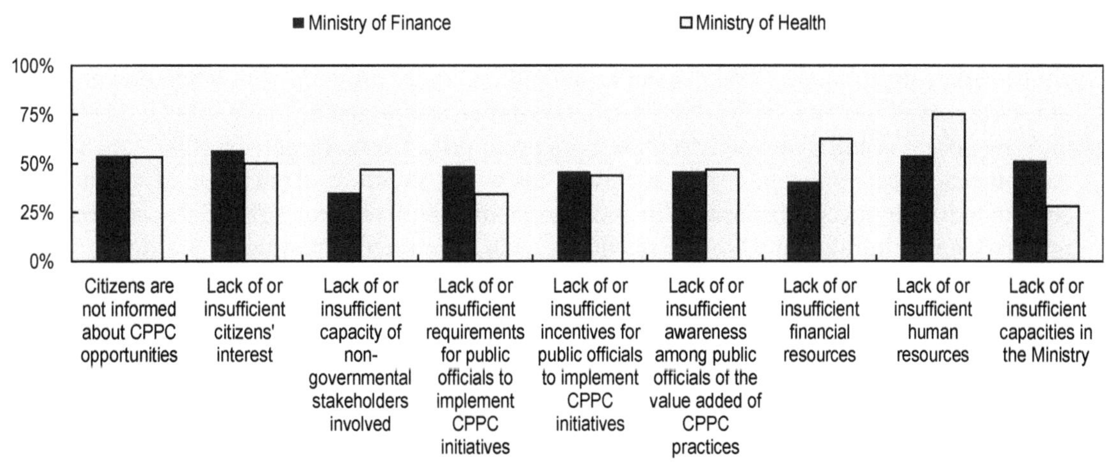

Note: Ministry of Finance n=37 countries (30 OECD countries), Ministry of Health n=32 countries (25 OECD countries). Japan's Ministry of Finance did not provide an answer to this question.
Source: OECD (2016), Open Government: The Global Context and the Way Forward, OECD Publishing, Paris. http://dx.doi.org/10.1787/9789264268104-en.

StatLink http://dx.doi.org/10.1787/888933725905

Open government initiatives need to be implemented to allow countries to fully reap the benefits of the open government towards effective public governance and to achieve increased accountability and inclusive growth. One way to ensure a proper implementation is to acknowledge the challenges faced when co-ordinating open Managing multi-level governance and decentralisation

A whole-of-government approach at the central government level will have greater potential impact on inclusion if all levels of government are on board. Many of the policies that have significant impact on Inclusive Growth are managed at least in part by subnational governments. Across the OECD, 137 thousands of subnational governments are responsible for around 63% of public staff spending, 49% of public procurement, 59% of public investment and 40% of total government expenditures. Responsibilities related to inclusion (i.e. education, social protection, health, housing and community amenities) account for almost 60% of subnational government expenditure on average in the OECD. Increasing decentralisation trends across OECD countries lead to increased emphasis on the need for sound multi-level governance arrangements.

For the last two decades, many OECD countries have experienced growing decentralisation trends strengthening the decision power of regions and local governments, the tiers closer to citizens. The Regional Authority Index (RAI), which is the most comprehensive measure of the real degree of power of subnational governments, shows that 52 out of 81 countries around the world have experienced a net increase in decentralisation (Hooghe et al., 2016). Decentralisation has increased through two main channels: the reinforcement of local autonomy as well as the strengthening of existing or new regions. This trend has touched all unitary and federal countries which no longer have substantive differences in terms of their degree of decentralised spending or tax autonomy (OECD, 2017g; OECD, 2013a).

There is no single model of decentralisation that is most conducive to Inclusive Growth. The OECD works extensively on the pre-conditions needed to make decentralisation work, notably the need to adapt institutions to places (OECD, 2015). This may imply a need for “asymmetric decentralisation”. Asymmetric structures can arouse controversy –uniformity is often easier to defend on equity grounds– but when power and other resources are unevenly distributed, asymmetric approaches may result in more inclusive politics and give voice to those who previously felt marginalised (OECD, 2015). Asymmetric decentralisation has received growing attention from several countries confronted with severe disparities in local capacities and various territorial, political or international cultural contexts. The results of such asymmetric treatments are difficult to assess since they can improve or worsen the efficiency and effectiveness of the public sector as a whole. Asymmetric responsibilities may strengthen or weaken the allegiance of differentially treated communities to the nation state as a whole (OECD, 2017g; OECD, 2013a). However, the results of this process are context-dependent. Countries need to assess carefully the challenges and the potential gains and costs that such a process can drive; which responsibilities and how can they be devolved are crucial questions that need to be addressed to improve the efficiency and effectiveness of the public sector as a whole (OECD, 2018).

OECD countries are increasingly experiencing asymmetric decentralisation arrangements. Subnational governments have differentiated responsibilities that can vary by capacities, population or characteristics like ethnicity, identity or geographic characteristics. Asymmetric arrangements have been particularly used to address urban challenges; around two-thirds of metropolitan areas in the OECD now have a metropolitan governance body (OECD Metropolitan Governance Survey, 2014). With these, countries are responding to metropolitan challenges that have a direct impact on local well-being by, for instance, improving the governance of transport or environmental policies.

Decentralisation reforms can be beneficial to productivity growth and inclusion but their ultimate effect depends on the broader policy environment. Decentralisation reforms have been implemented for a wide variety of reasons, among them, the need to improve the efficiency and quality of public services and to enhance regional and local productivity and growth. Some evidence suggests indeed that decentralisation and growth are positively correlated (OECD/UCLG, 2016). For example, a 10 percentage point increase in the subnational tax revenue share is associated with approximately 2% higher GDP per capita in the long run. At the same time, decentralisation is associated with somewhat higher inequality (OECD Decentralisation and Inclusive Growth, 2018). Overall, the effect of decentralisation on growth depends on the broader policy environment and the quality of the institutional framework within which subnational governments operate. The OECD has developed a list of guidelines that help make decentralisation work, based on practical experience from countries OECD Decentralisation and Inclusive Growth, 2018.

Multi-level governance mechanisms that reshape and improve interaction between public authorities can ensure coherent and effective policy decisions. Appropriate multi-level governance arrangements can make decentralisation sustainable by strengthening the institutional capacity of subnational bodies and enhancing policy dialogue and co-ordination between levels of governments (Allain-Dupré, 2018). Platforms for vertical co-ordination have been established in several OECD Member states, in particular federal countries: 28 countries in the OECD have put in place some structures of co-ordination. Often these structures are related to environment, infrastructure, transport, technology, and development. Despite their expense and the time needed to establish them, standing commissions and intergovernmental consultation boards that create a permanent conduit for co-operation and communication across parties and levels of government can facilitate reform when the time comes. Creating a culture of co-operation and regular communication is crucial to effective multi-level governance and long-term reform success.

References

Algan, Y. and P. Cahuc (2013), "Trust, Growth and Well-being: New Evidence and Policy Implications", IZA Discussion Paper, No. 7464.

Murtin, F. et al. (2018), "Trust and its Determinants: Evidence from the Trustlab Experiment", OECD Working Paper, forthcoming.

OECD (2010), "OECD Recommendation on Transparency and Integrity in Lobbying", OECD Publishing, Paris.

OECD (2013a), "Fiscal Federalism 2014: Making Decentralisation Work", OECD, Paris.

OECD (2013b), "Government at a Glance 2013", OECD Publishing, Paris.

OECD (2014), "OECD Recommendation on Principles for Independent Fiscal Institutions", OECD Publishing, Paris.

OECD (2015a), "Government at a Glance 2015", OECD Publishing, Paris.

OECD (2015c), "OECD Recommendation on Budgetary Governance", OECD Publishing, Paris.

OECD (2016a), "Fair and Inclusive Education Systems: Lessons from PISA 2015 for the United States", PISA, OECD Publishing, Paris.

OECD (2016b), "Open Government: The Global Context and the Way Forward", OECD Publishing, Paris.

OECD (2016c), "The Governance of Inclusive Growth", OECD Publishing, Paris.

OECD (2016d), "Financing Democracy: Funding of Political Parties and Election Campaigns and the Risk of Policy Capture", In OECD Public Governance Reviews, OECD Publishing, Paris.

OECD (2016e), "Investing in Integrity for Productivity", In Working Party of Senior Public Integrity Officials, GOV/PGC/INT(2016)6.

OECD (2016f), "OECD recommendation of the council on gender equality in public life", OECD Publishing, Paris.

OECD (2017a), "Trust and Public Policy: How Better Governance Can Help Rebuild Public Trust", OECD Publishing, Paris.

OECD (2017b), "Guidelines on Measuring Trust", OECD Publishing, Paris.

OECD (2017c), "OECD 2017 Survey on National Gender Equality Frameworks & Public Policies", OECD Publishing, Paris.

OECD (2017d), "Preventing Policy Capture: Integrity in Public Decision Making", In OECD Public Governance Reviews, OECD Publishing, Paris.

OECD (2017e), "OECD Recommendation of the Council on Public Integrity", OECD Publishing, Paris.

OECD (2017f), "Behavioural Insights and Public Policy: Lessons from Around the World", OECD Publishing, Paris.

OECD (2017g), "Multi-level Governance Reforms: Overview of OECD Country Experiences", OECD Multi-level Governance Studies, OECD Publishing, Paris.

OECD (2018), "Making Decentralisation Work: a Handbook for Policy-Makers", OECD Publishing, Paris.

OECD (2015b), "OECD Regulatory Policy Outlook 2015", OECD Publishing, Paris.

ORGANISATION FOR ECONOMIC CO-OPERATION AND DEVELOPMENT

The OECD is a unique forum where governments work together to address the economic, social and environmental challenges of globalisation. The OECD is also at the forefront of efforts to understand and to help governments respond to new developments and concerns, such as corporate governance, the information economy and the challenges of an ageing population. The Organisation provides a setting where governments can compare policy experiences, seek answers to common problems, identify good practice and work to co-ordinate domestic and international policies.

The OECD member countries are: Australia, Austria, Belgium, Canada, Chile, the Czech Republic, Denmark, Estonia, Finland, France, Germany, Greece, Hungary, Iceland, Ireland, Israel, Italy, Japan, Korea, Latvia, Luxembourg, Mexico, the Netherlands, New Zealand, Norway, Poland, Portugal, the Slovak Republic, Slovenia, Spain, Sweden, Switzerland, Turkey, the United Kingdom and the United States. The European Union takes part in the work of the OECD.

OECD Publishing disseminates widely the results of the Organisation's statistics gathering and research on economic, social and environmental issues, as well as the conventions, guidelines and standards agreed by its members.

OECD PUBLISHING, 2, rue André-Pascal, 75775 PARIS CEDEX 16
(03 2018 20 1 P) ISBN 978-92-64-30165-8 – 2018

www.ingramcontent.com/pod-product-compliance
Ingram Content Group UK Ltd.
Pitfield, Milton Keynes, MK11 3LW, UK
UKHW051501290926
15471UKWH00008B/1342

9 789264 301658